KARA ELIZABETH LEWIS

ASCENSION

If the Light is in you, the Light within these pages will respond.

To my beautiful daughter, Tatiana.

She is an heiress. Royalty is her birthright.
Remind her of the crown that she wears, a gift that was already given to her.
Lift her up. Honor her. The entire Universe resides in her DNA.
Her Spirit, her Nature, her Purpose is already written in the stars.
She is an Oracle. Her very essence is a gift to the world.

Keep following the paths that lead you to Light (that's where the magic is)!

FOREWORD

When I first met Kara in the halls of the school she worked in, I immediately knew she was "my people." She was telling me about the art programs she organizes for her elementary school students, which included meditation and different types of expressing themselves through art. Later, we reconnected when Kara invited myself and six other diverse women into her home to test out a curriculum she was building. We met weekly and took turns bringing snacks. Kara had a chakra focus, explanation, discussion, and art project to help us dive deep.

This space was safe, healing, transforming. The seven of us were mostly strangers, some of us friends from prior, but over those 7 weeks, we bonded, we cried together, laughed together, and explored a deep need within each of us. We began to be kinder to ourselves, more self aware, more compassionate, and more conscious. Whether we were artists or not, we each felt free around a small table in Kara's living room with glue, beads, and paint, magazine cutouts and photos. We shared about our belief systems and where they stemmed from, how we were changing them and how we wanted to be a light to the world, to our families, to ourselves.

When I learned that Kara was taking that curriculum and putting it into a workbook, I was thrilled. I was even more humbled when she asked me to help lay out the pages and represent her and her brand throughout the book. Her passion, talent, creativity and journey is inspiring. I am better for knowing Kara. She signifies what we all want to do. She let go of everything that wasn't true to herself, and she pursued this work. Watching her walk away from other jobs to dive deeper into this dream has been a gift to me and many others.

Ascension speaks to me. It speaks to the phoenix inside me, rising from the ashes. It reminds me to spread my wings, to get a new perspective. It grounds me and lifts me up at the same time. Revisiting this curriculum through the design and layout of this book has taken me on a journey of my own, doing more of what I love and less of what I don't.

Thank you, Kara, for gifting the world with *Ascension*.

Jordan Lacenski
J.L. Consulting Group, Owner
SheWolf Collaborative, Co-Founder

The first time Kara's energy crossed my path was months before I met her. I was living in Barcelona and consulting remotely with Natalie Mangrum in Baltimore, MD on her Own Your Story pilot program. Natalie excitedly told me that an amazing artist from Greensboro, NC had applied to join the pilot cohort. She was floored that someone would drive 12 hours round trip to attend the 90 minute in-person meetings every month.

"This artist has an amazing story to share and would be the perfect addition to the cohort, but do you think it's crazy that she wants to spend so much extra time and energy traveling to our meetings?" Natalie asked me.

"It's her energy, let her put it where she wants!" was my response.

Six months later, this energy came full circle when Kara blindly reached out to a designer referral to help her with the cover design for *Ascension*—that designer was me.

First we began with the cover design, which was simply just fun to work on! Later, Kara asked if I would be able to help with completing the manuscript design her talented layout designer Jordan established. Little did I know the transformative journey I would take as I read through the content I was designing.

It has been a joy and an honor to help Kara bring *Ascension* to life on the page. Her story is different from mine, but the emotions and learnings (and unlearnings!) she shares could be my own. The way in which Kara has organized years of research, practice, and personal experience in this book has helped me make peace with my own past. But, just as importantly, it has created a deep well of empathy in me for the unhealed pasts of some of the people I love most. This empathy has been the greatest gift in helping me raise my own vibration.

As you make your own journey through *Ascension*, may you feel the energy of grace and compassion flowing from these pages into your own heart.

Megan McCarthy
Megan McCarthy Global Creative

TO THE READER

"I had been running on the hamster wheel of life for ten years strong, but I had never really stopped to consider whether or not I actually wanted to be there. As I began to look around at my life, I found that I was bored with fake people, fake institutions, fake conversations. I was uninspired by my reality and craving 'the sacred' in a way that is hard to describe in words. I needed substance, meaning, depth, purpose. There was so much darkness in the world and my spirit was thirsty for light."

Over the course of a year, while creating this project, I could not shake the voice in my head—pointing out the fact that I'm not a formally trained writer, or reminding me that 'real writers' and critics would soon read my work and call me out for all of the imperfections. A friend left me with a little wisdom. She said, "it's impossible to be an impostor when you operate from your heart and soul—which you do!!" And she was right. I have poured my heart and soul into this book. It is raw, vulnerable, authentic and honest—illuminating the fact that we are all expansive spiritual beings, learning lessons through a lifetime of human experiences. None of it is supposed to be perfect. It's supposed to be beautiful.

I am grateful for the opportunity to share my journey of healing, wholeness, and peace. I have come to learn, through many evolutions, that the most important thing we will ever create is our own life. In order to paint a picture of reality that is profoundly beautiful, we must commit ourselves to the sacred work of growth and expansion. *Ascension* is an instructed journey to holistic healing and wellness for the mind, body, and spirit including living meditations, journal prompts, artistic expression, and peaceful practice.

If you are a seeker, I invite you to follow the path.

Awaken your Sacred Self, raise your energetic vibration, heal your wounds, find your peace, and tune yourself to the frequency of the Divine Matrix. If the Light is in you, the Light within these pages will respond.

Sending light and love to all of you,
Kara Elizabeth

If you are interested in a deeper experience, visit ***artistkaraelizabeth.com/ascension*** for playlists, art kits, tutorials, and more!

CONTENTS

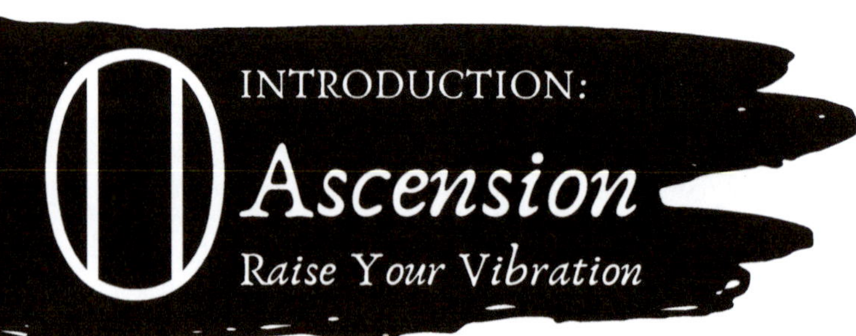

"Out of the darkness, shall ye rise upward, one with
the light, and one with the stars."
—Emerald Tablets

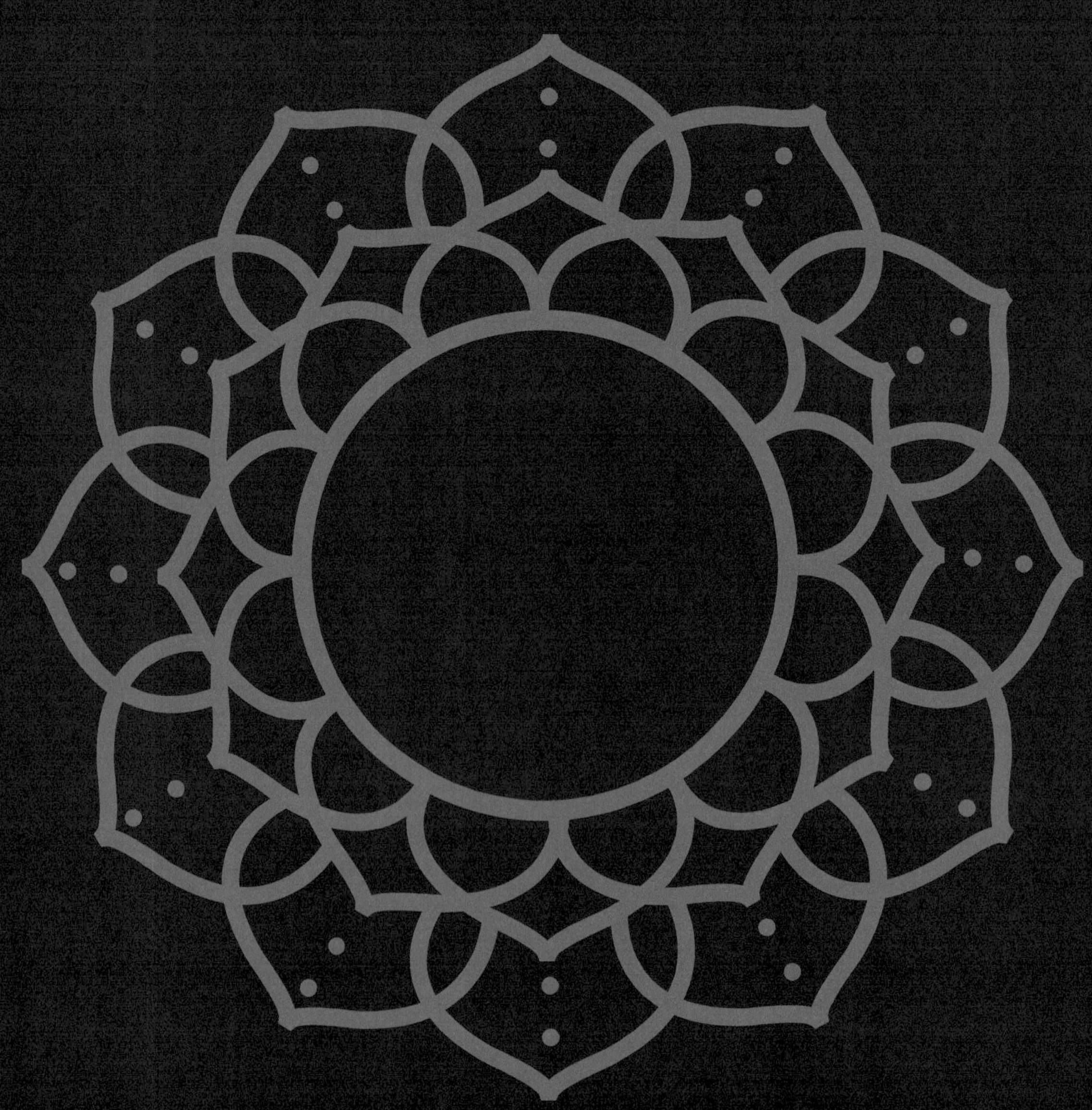

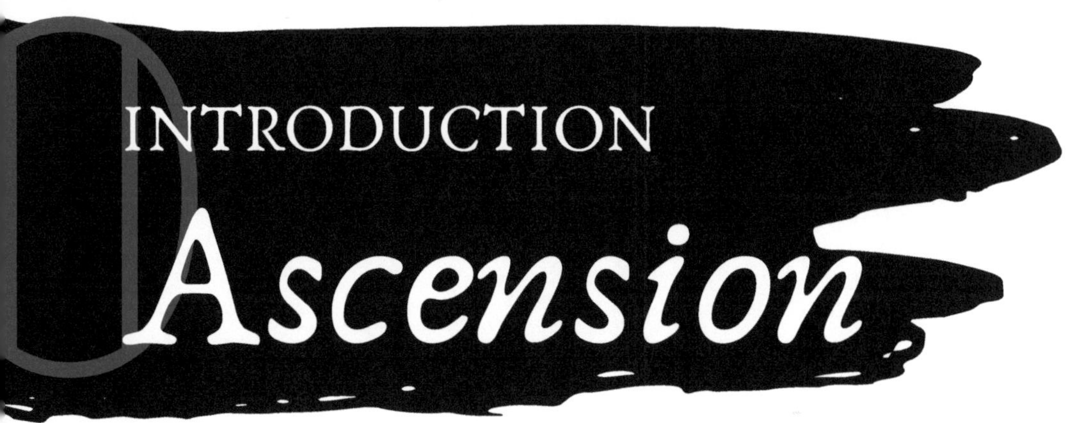

INTRODUCTION
Ascension

Quantum Physics is the magical science of spirituality, proving that we are energetic Light beings whose thoughts and emotions carry vibrational frequencies, influencing both our inner and outer realities.

Low-vibrational frequencies (shame 20, guilt 30, apathy 50, grief 75, fear 100, desire 150, pride 175) cause disease within the physical, mental, emotional, and spiritual body. High-vibrational frequencies (courage 200, neutrality 250, willingness 310, acceptance 350, reason 400, love 500, joy 540, peace 600, enlightenment 700+) restore on a cellular level and upgrade human biology.

To elevate your vibrational frequency, it is a matter of healing, cleansing, and restoring the seven major energy centers within the body, known as chakras. You must learn to quiet the shadow so the voice of your Higher self can lead you to the Light.

How fulfilling is your everyday life?

"You yourself are your own obstacle. Rise above yourself." —Hafiz

Intention: Honor your Higher Self
Human experience: Shadow
Spiritual practice: Light

CHAKRA SYSTEM:

Processing centers for spiritual and emotional energy, aligned with the spine, nervous system, endocrine system.

THE MEMORY OF TRAUMA IS STORED WITHIN THE CHAKRA SYSTEM AS A NEGATIVE ELECTRICAL CHARGE, UNTIL IT IS HEALED.

"Learn to differentiate between the sound of your spirit guiding you and your traumas misleading you."

—Unknown

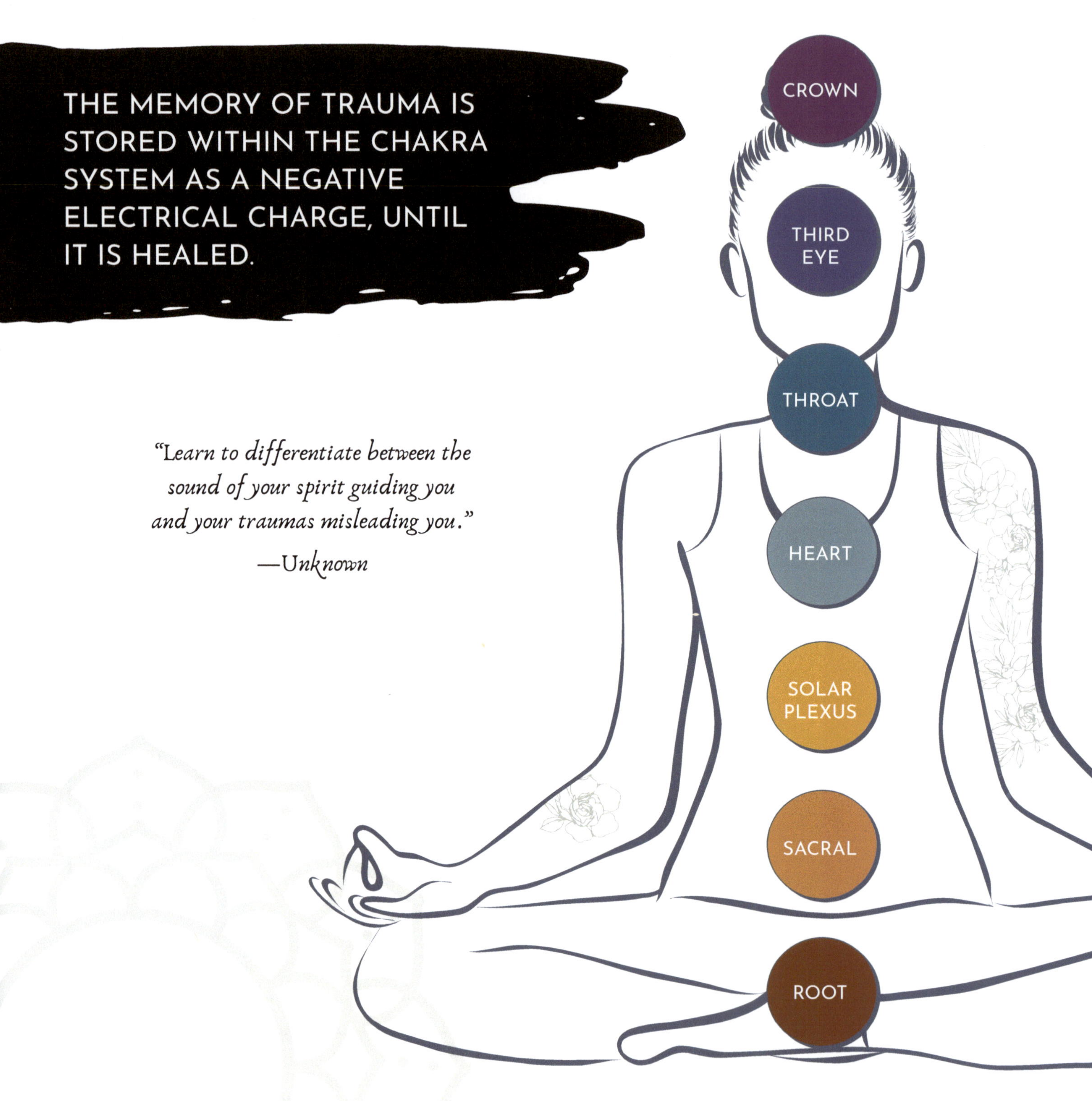

ASCENSION:
Raise your vibration

The unconscious self is impulsive, reactive, and self-serving.

It is motivated by a need for attention, validation, and approval.

This is your Shadow.

The Higher self is patient, peaceful, and connected.

It is motivated by creation, authentic expression, and love.

This is your Light.

SHADOW MISLEADING YOU

- FEAR
- ANXIETY
- GUILT
- BLAME
- DISAPPOINTMENT
- SHAME
- GRIEF
- SADNESS
- LIES
- GOSSIP
- SEPARATION
- PRIVILEGE
- ATTACHMENT
- MATERIALISM

SPIRIT GUIDING YOU

- SAFE
- SECURE
- CREATIVE
- HAPPY
- COURAGE
- CONFIDENCE
- LOVE
- ACCEPTANCE
- TRUTH
- PEACE
- JUSTICE
- INCLUSIVITY
- BALANCED ENERGY
- SPIRITUALITY

Intention: Honor your Higher Self
Human experience: Shadow
Spiritual practice: Light

EMOTIONAL VIBRATION CHART

According to David R. Hawkins, M.D., Ph.D., every thought and emotion has its own vibrational frequency, ranging from 1-1,000.

Anything below 200 is considered unhealthy, destructive energy.

Anything above 200 is considered healthy, healing energy.

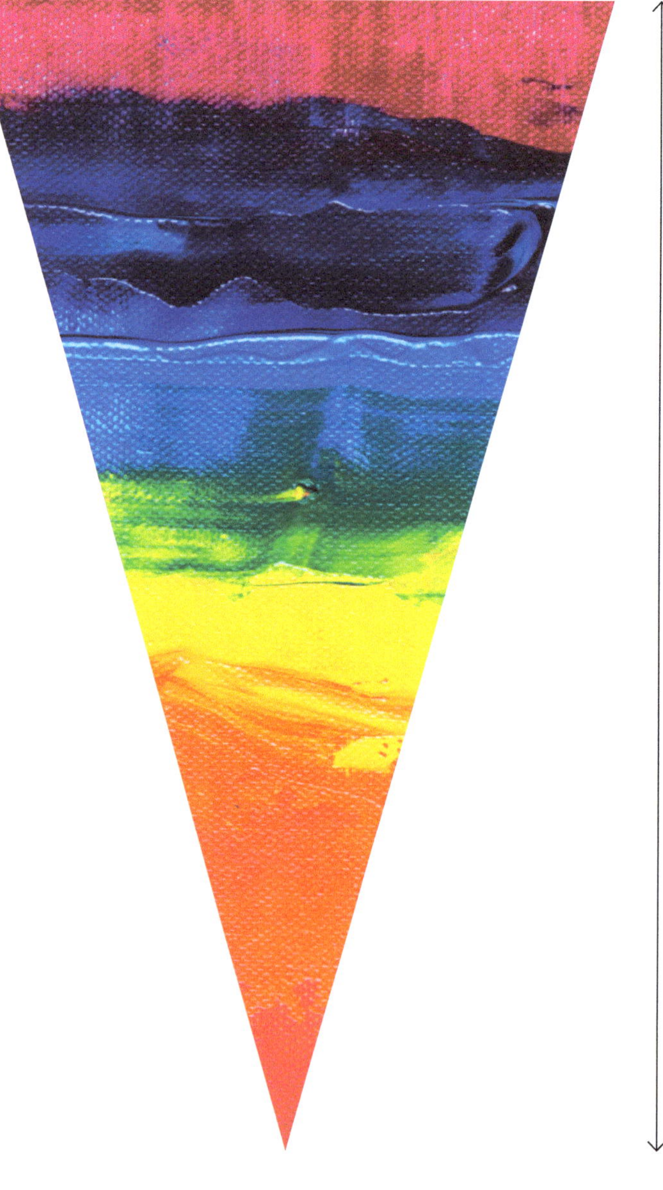

Who immediately comes to mind when you think of high-vibe people?
How do you know when you are in the presence of healthy, healing energy?

Who immediately comes to mind when you think of low-vibe people?
How do you know when you are in the presence of destructive, unhealthy energy?

Intention: Honor your Higher Self
Human experience: Shadow
Spiritual practice: Light

In what areas of your life are you guided by your Highest self?

In what areas of your life does your shadow lead?

Energy is transferable. Are you a conduit of positive or negative energy? Is your energy healing or harmful to others?

Does the energy of other people (at home, school, work, community) affect your energy in a positive or negative way?

Intention: Honor your Higher Self
Human experience: Shadow
Spiritual practice: Light

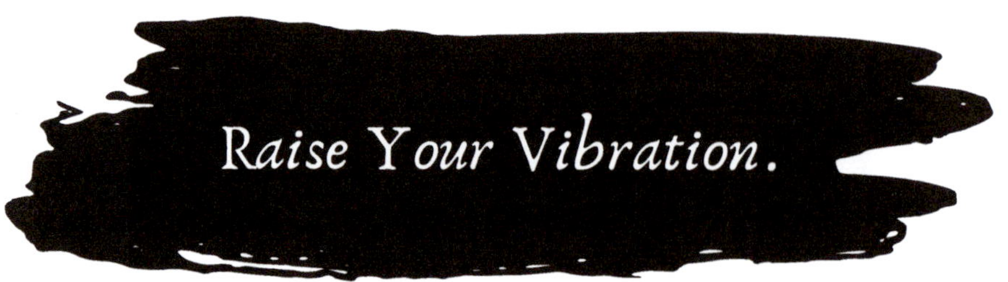

Sit up straight to align your chakras from the top of your head to the base of your spine. This posture allows energy to flow organically through your core. Close your eyes and practice moving your awareness to different locations on your body— elbow, knee, heel, earlobe, hip—pausing at each location before moving to the next. Now, practice this technique with memories—move your awareness from one memory to another—stopping briefly to observe each one.

You are in control of your awareness. When you notice your shadow leading, practice moving your awareness to Light. In every moment, you are being confronted with two choices: Repeat the same old low-vibrational patterns of thoughts, emotions, and behaviors, or honor your Higher self by choosing to evolve.

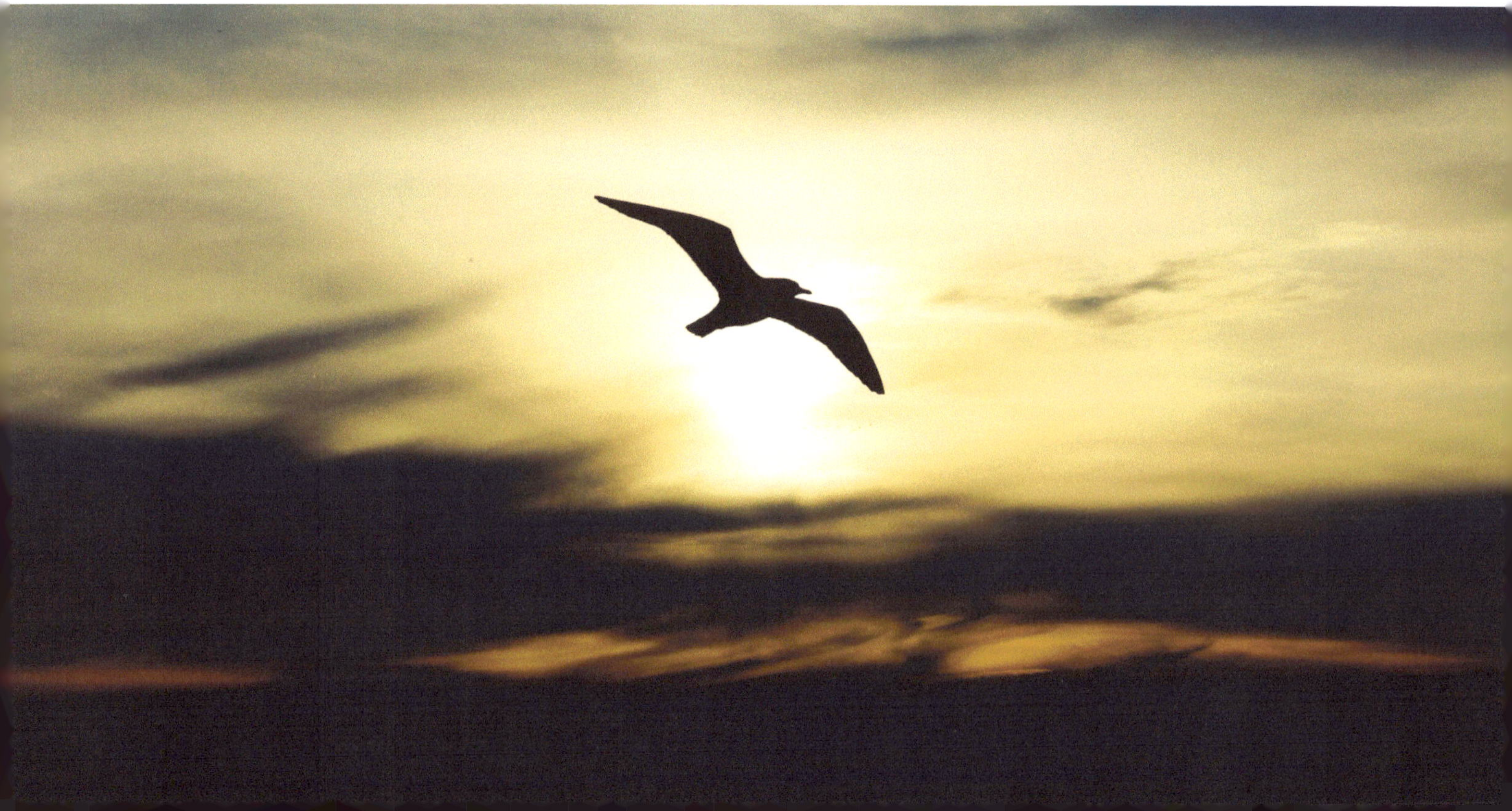

HOLISTIC WELLNESS
Practice Honoring Your Higher Self: Raise Your Vibration

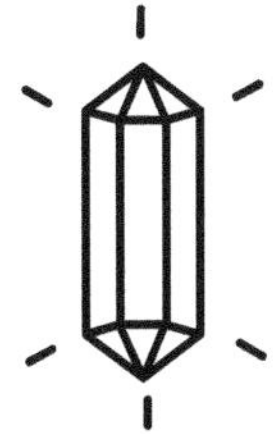

CRYSTALS

Crystals emit positive, uplifting, energizing, and calming vibrations.

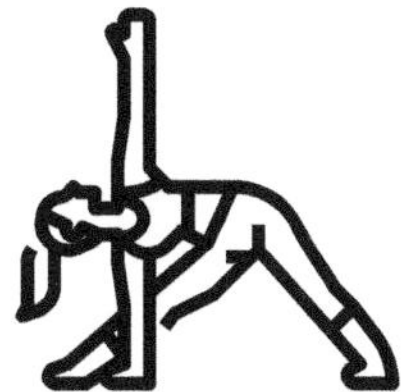

YOGA

Yoga grounds the body, builds strength, improves sense of balance, body awareness, and concentration.

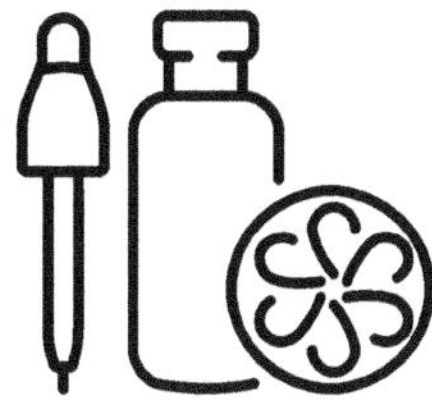

ESSENTIAL OILS

Natural plant extracts promote health and well-being for the body, mind, and spirit.

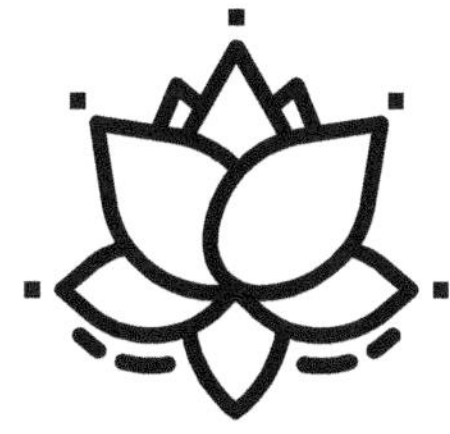

WELLNESS

Your diet is not only what you eat. It is what you watch, listen to, read, and the people you hang around.

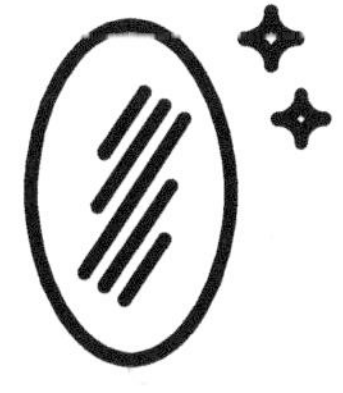

AFFIRMATION

Positive statements can help you challenge and overcome self-sabotaging and negative thoughts.

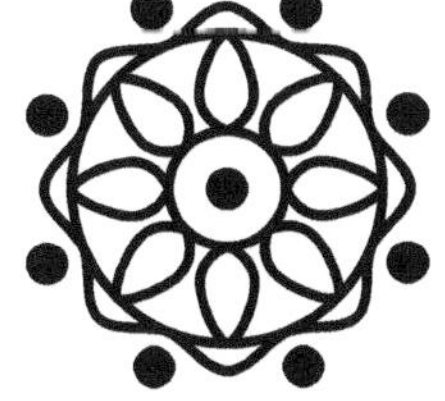

MEDITATION

A practice to train attention and awareness, and achieve a mentally clear and emotionally calm and stable state.

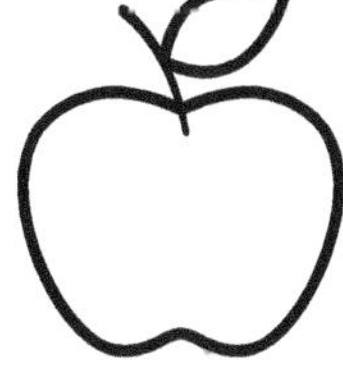

FOOD

The vitamins and minerals, phytochemicals and antioxidants in plants help keep your cells healthy so that your immune system can function at its best.

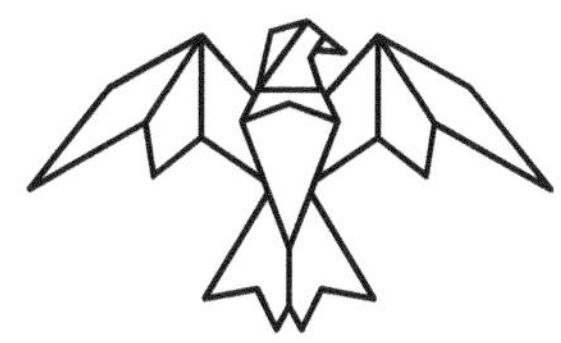

ASCENSION

Rising up to a higher state of Being.

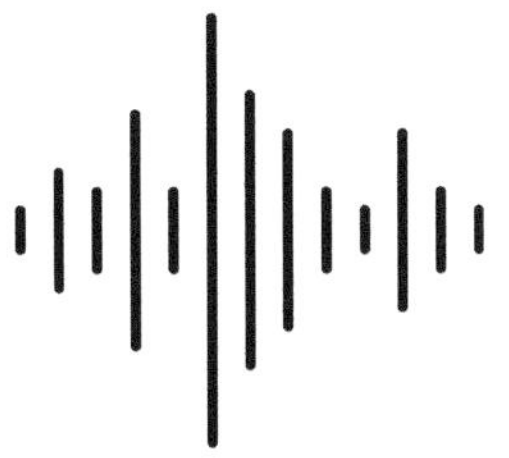

SOUND

Certain rhythms, sounds, and vibrations can help you resist and recover from a wide variety of ailments.

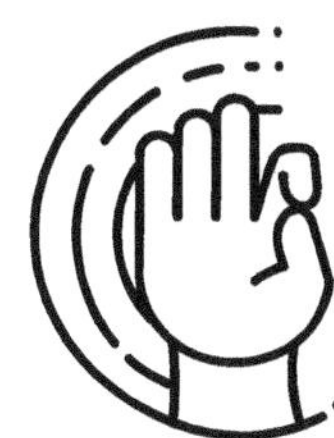

MUDRA

Gestures of the hands to balance the energy of the body and purify the body's biomagnetic field.

COLOR

Known to create peace, serenity, and quiet the mind best.

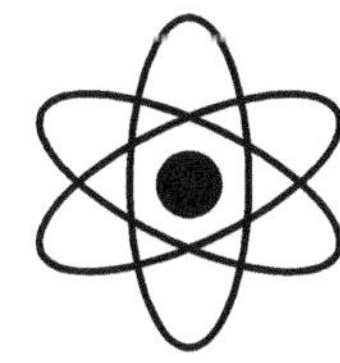

KARMA

Everything is energy. Energy vibrates. Vibrations attract. The energy that you send out into the world is exactly what comes back to you.

CREATIVE FLOW
Artistic Expression

Mandalas

A Mandala is a sacred healing circle that represents the Universe and all that is contained within it. Mandalas are used to increase our spiritual awareness and guide us back home to ourselves.

Materials Needed

Paper

Pencil

Eraser

Plate / Round template

Scissors

Sharpie

Intention: Honor your Higher self
Human experience: Shadow
Spiritual practice: Light

MANDALAS
Instructions

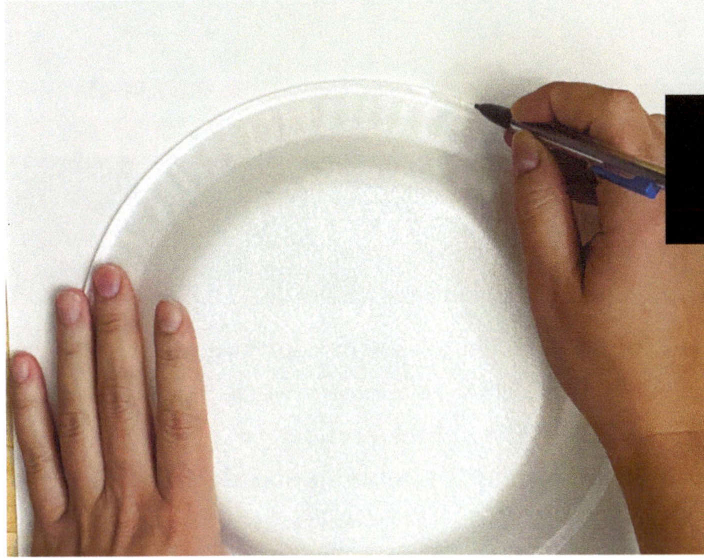

Trace a big circle on a piece of paper. Cut it out.

Fold the circle in half.

Fold it in half again. And fold it in half again.

Using a pencil, draw a design of lines and shapes on one of the pie sections (make sure some of your lines touch the edges).

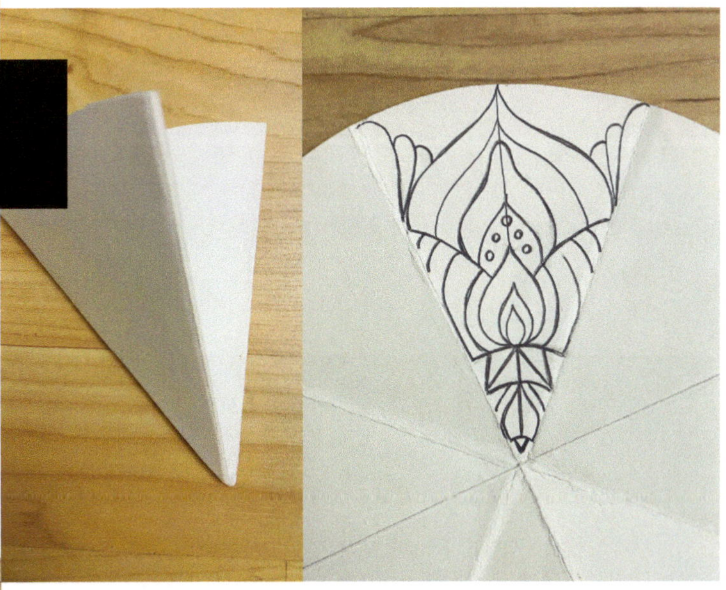

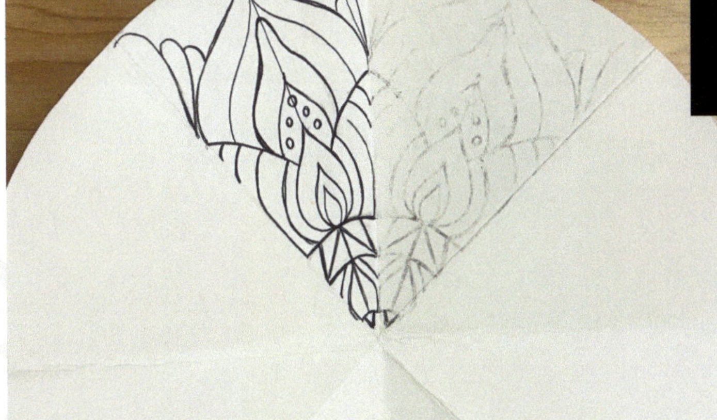

Using the existing crease, fold the drawn piece over onto the piece next to it and rub using the plastic handle of scissors (or other hard plastic). You will have to press pretty hard! If you can't get a good transfer, darken your lines with the pencil and try again.

MANDALAS
Instructions

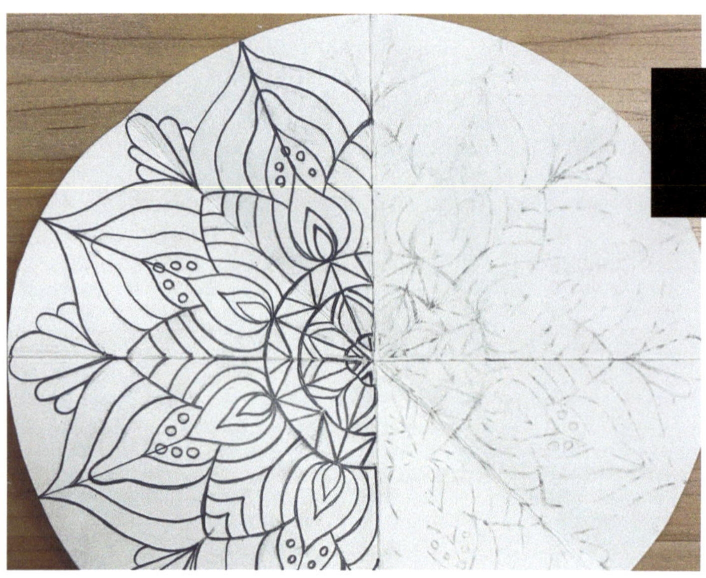

Step 4

Trace the transfer lines with your pencil to darken them. Now, fold those two sections over onto the two blank sections next to those and repeat the rubbing and darkening process. Now fold those 4 sections onto the blank 4 sections and repeat.

Step 5

Trace the pencil lines with a fine-point Sharpie marker (ultra-fine does not work well for this step).

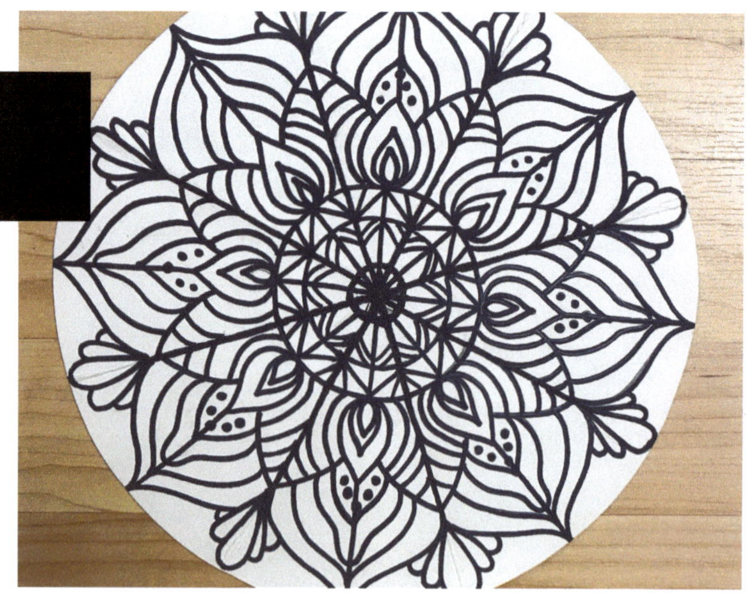

"Maybe the journey isn't so much about becoming anything. Maybe it's about unbecoming everything that isn't really you, so you can be who you were meant to be in the first place."

—Paulo Coelho

Intention: Honor your Higher Self
Human experience: Shadow
Spiritual practice: Light

"The goal of life is to make your heartbeat match the beat of the universe, to match your nature with Nature."
—Joseph Campbell

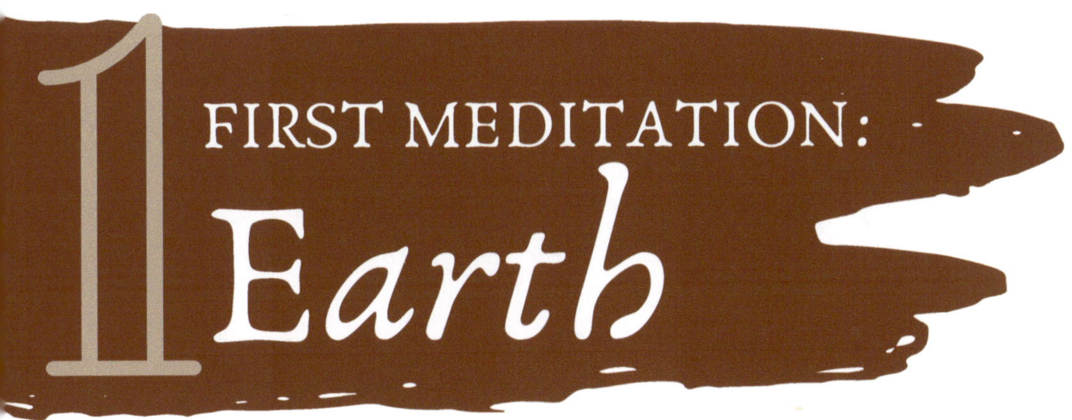

The Root Chakra represents the Earth; our physical bodies; as well as our presence in, and connection to, the physical world.

It is important to remember that the physical body is a biological organism, an extension of the Natural World. In order to thrive and function at optimal health, the body needs to be nourished and restored daily with Sunlight, Earth, Rest, Water, Plants, Nutrients, Oxygen, and High Vibrational Energy. The body needs nature because the body is nature.

Sink your roots deep into the Earth.
She is an abundant source of Life and Healing Energy.

List 3 things that you can do to nourish your physical body:

"Your body is your temple. Keep it clean for the soul to reside in." —B.K. Iyengar

Intention: One with Nature
Human experience: Self-preservation (fear and anxiety)
Spiritual practice: Self-awareness (security and vitality)

ROOT CHAKRA:

Survival, instinct, basic trust, safety, security

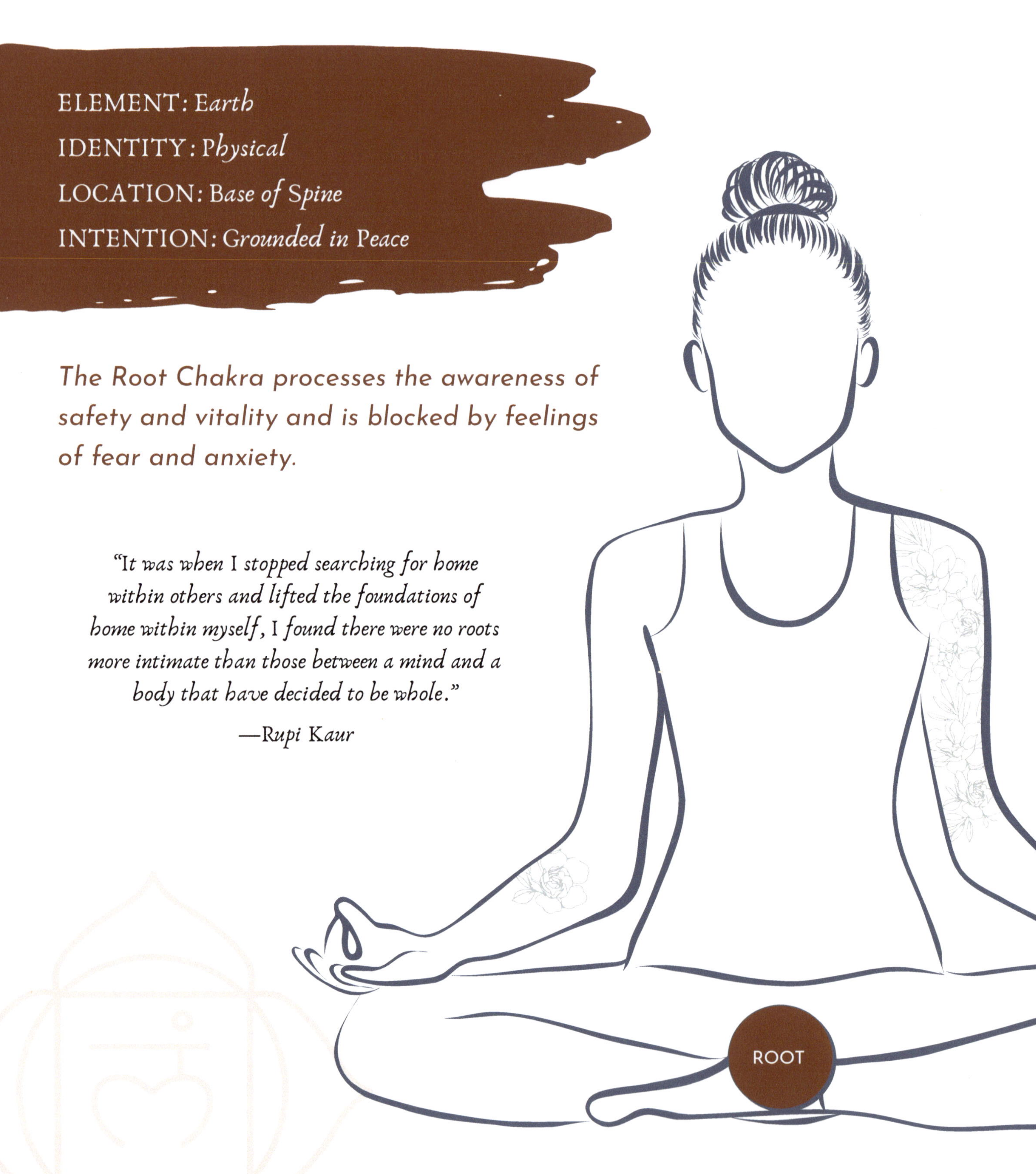

ELEMENT: *Earth*
IDENTITY: *Physical*
LOCATION: *Base of Spine*
INTENTION: *Grounded in Peace*

The Root Chakra processes the awareness of safety and vitality and is blocked by feelings of fear and anxiety.

"It was when I stopped searching for home within others and lifted the foundations of home within myself, I found there were no roots more intimate than those between a mind and a body that have decided to be whole."

—Rupi Kaur

ROOT CHAKRA:

Grounded in peace

The following deficient and excessive energies carry low-vibrational frequencies. They are collected and stored in the root chakra, blocking the flow of spiritual energy. If your thoughts, feelings, or behaviors fall into one of these two categories, the healing in this energy center has not yet begun.

Balanced energy in the Root Chakra is connected in many ways to your health and physical state of being. Meat, dairy, sugar, and processed foods create an acidic environment within the body, causing mucus and feeding disease. Density inside the physical body lowers your vibrational frequency, making it difficult to hear and access your Higher self. An Alkaline diet (nature) eliminates mucus and disease from the body. When the body is less dense it is easier to tune-in to the Divine Matrix. Honor your Higher self by nourishing your body with nature, creating a physical environment that is conducive to healing and vitality.

Raise Your Vibration

DEFICIENT ENERGY	BALANCED ENERGY	EXCESSIVE ENERGY
• FEARFUL	• SAFE	• GREEDY
• ANXIOUS	• SECURE	• LUST FOR POWER
• UNSURE	• CENTERED	• AGGRESSIVE
• UNSTABLE	• GROUNDED	• MATERIALISTIC
• UNGROUNDED	• FULL OF LIFE	• CYNICAL
• FLIGHTY	• FULL OF ENERGY	• OVERLY PRACTICAL
• NO BELONGING	• DYNAMIC PRESENCE	• HABITUAL
• LACK OF IDENTITY	• CONFIDENCE	• TIED DOWN
• POOR HEALTH	• VITALITY	• DIFFICULTY LETTING GO
• LOW ENERGY	• PHYSICALLY HEALTHY	• STUBBORN
• EXHAUSTION		• OVERLY STRUCTURED
• LOW SELF ESTEEM		

Intention: One with Nature
Human experience: Self-preservation (fear and anxiety)
Spiritual practice: Self-awareness (security and vitality)

Who/What makes you feel safe and secure? Centered? Balanced?
How often do you participate in peaceful practices? How do you ground yourself?

How do you deal with stressful situations?
Do your choices harm or heal your physical body? Do you worry a lot?

What are your biggest fears? What makes you feel anxious or uncomfortable? Think through your life story.
Who/What created these fears?

What triggers you to feel angry, aggressive, or controlling?
How do you behave?

Intention: One with Nature
Human experience: Self-preservation (fear and anxiety)
Spiritual practice: Self-awareness (security and vitality)

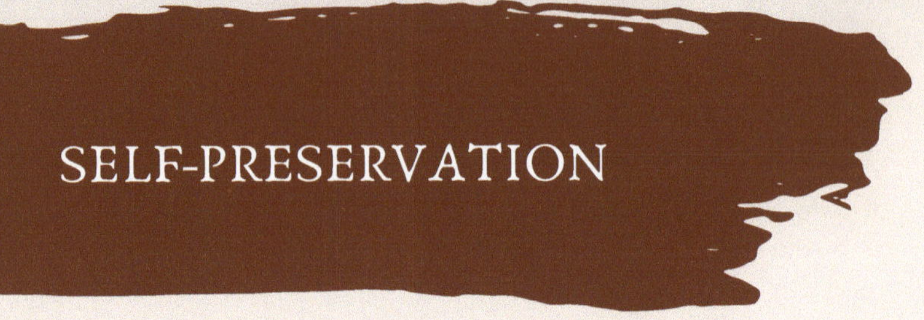

My Experience with Fear and Anxiety

"Often it's the deepest pain which empowers you to grow into your highest self."
—Karen Salmansohn

I was four years old when my father violently beat my three-year-old sister. I was the only other person in the house, on the other side of a locked door. Her screams were piercing. I threw my tiny body against that door as hard as I could, pleading with him to stop. I could feel her pain deep down in my bones. Terrified and helpless, I cried myself to sleep right there on the floor, in front of her door. She was still bruised and swollen two days later when my mom returned home from her weekend assignment at the hospital. She made an excuse to get us out the door and to the hospital. We ended up driving many hours through the night to safety. I didn't see him again for years.

I was seven when my brother's father came into our lives. His touch was rough and aggressive. It hurt when he grabbed me. It hurt when he tickled me. His hands left bruises on my little body. He used to hold me down with all his weight on top of my chest, pin my arms over my head with one hand, and secure my face with the other. He positioned his mouth around my mouth and nose like a suction and blew as hard as he could. I was terrified every time, fighting to get away, gasping for air, tears burning my eyes. He did that to me often and without warning. The day he left was just as traumatic. We pulled into the driveway after being out for the day. As soon as we stepped out of the car we were surrounded by police, guns drawn, pointed directly at us. The officers were all screaming over one another, "Get on the ground! Get down on the ground!!" The sound of so many gunshots so close to my head was deafening. I sobbed on the ground, face in the dirt, hands over my ears. I was nine years old.

I was twelve when my cousin and I were chased barefoot through the woods at church camp by an angry mob of boys throwing sticks at us, calling us niggers. On my fourteenth birthday, my friends and I were assaulted by the police in the middle of the afternoon because he said we "fit the description." I was thrown up against a cold brick wall and full body searched, aggressively, by a grown man in broad daylight.

"The habits you created to survive will no longer serve you when it's time to thrive. Get out of survival mode."
—Ebonee Davis

I became a mama at the age of twenty-four. By the time my daughter was eight, she was full of playful energy, just like her father. When she was with him, they would wrestle and horseplay all day together. My daughter pressed for my participation in the games that she loved so much, but I had a strong aversion to chaotic movements and aggressive touch. Unable to elicit positive interaction, she began to feed off the negative. She thought it was funny to run full speed in my direction to get a reaction. One day she jumped on top of me, laughing hysterically, to engage in a tickle fight. I exploded in a burst of anger, consumed with the fear and anxiety from my childhood. My heart was racing inside my chest, adrenaline raging through my body. I glared at her and pushed her off of me. She looked at me through innocent eyes, caught off guard by my response. She was a little girl trying to connect with her mama. But in that moment, I was a little girl trying to protect myself from a danger that was no longer there.

"People raised on love see the world differently from people raised on survival."
—*Tupac Shakur*

Self-preservation is our natural instinct to survive within the environment that we are born into. It is our original navigation system, programmed by the fears and anxieties we experience as children. Yes, this system has helped you survive, but it will not help you thrive. In fact, this system is part of the unconscious mind and is an impulsive reaction to danger: fight, freeze, hide, or run. It is the conscious mind that must be accessed in order to be greater than your suffering. My childhood fears taught me to quietly tuck myself into the background. I was terrified of loud noises, violence, anger, and aggression. I flinched every time someone touched me. I learned to observe my surroundings like a hawk, trust no one, and be ready to protect myself against threat at all times.

"Until we have met the monsters in ourselves, we will keep
trying to slay them in the outer world."
—*Marianne Williamson*

Presence is key to healing and restoring this energy center. The secret is to be right here, right now, fully engaged in the present moment, rather than replacing the present moment with a memory from your past. The memory of trauma will continue to dominate your thoughts and behavior patterns until you decide to consciously change the narrative. We are powerful creators. The magical practice of alchemy is our superpower. Who are you without your suffering? Who would you be if you were the creator of your story, rather than the product of it? When I feel myself recycling old fears or feeding into anxiety, I close my eyes and ground myself in peace. I bring my awareness back to the present moment and remind myself that I am safe.

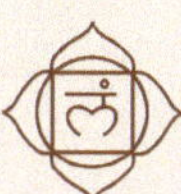

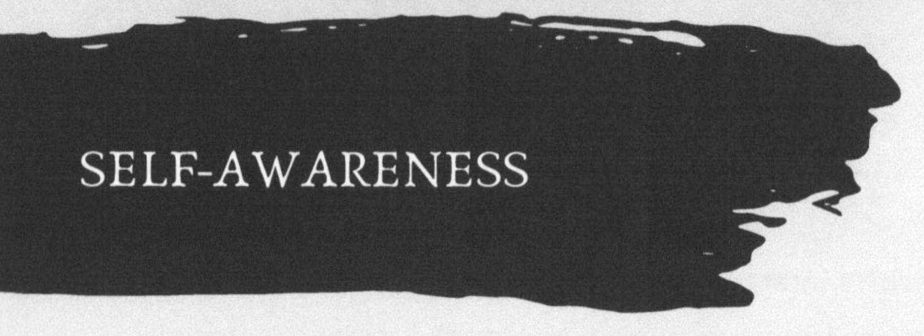

My Experience with Identity, Safety, and Vitality

"Birthplace: Earth Race: Human Politics: Freedom Religion: Love"

I was confronted about my identity so much as a child, I developed a deep insecurity about my own reflection. Growing up in a mixed-race family (black and white), I saw myself equally of both, but not particularly one or the other. Being biracial in a world divided by race is the biggest cosmic joke of all time. Questions about my identity were often confrontational or smothered in emotion. I was bored by the conversation, mostly because I was tired of explaining my existence to people. From my perspective, we were all one race, born on one planet. My family members ranged from the palest white skin to the darkest black skin, and I loved them all equally. It was ridiculous to think that one was better or worse than the other. I decided early to unbind myself from the confines of labels. I would not attach my identity to anything that would keep me separate from, or in opposition to, another. I saw people for who they were—and frankly, thought that most humans, regardless of race, were exhausting.

> *"Without dignity, identity is erased. In its absence, men are defined not by themselves, but by their captors and the circumstances in which they are forced to live."*
> —Laura Hillenbrand

As I got older, I learned to be a chameleon. What was acceptable and appropriate within one reality was inappropriate and unacceptable within the other, and vice-versa. There wasn't a safe space to just exist. It was a game of shapeshifting depending on who I was going to be around that day. If I wasn't careful, I would be called out for talking too "ghetto" in one neighborhood or too "bougie" in the other. I might be reminded that I was "too light-skinned to act black" or "too brown-skinned" to act white. "Mulatto," "mixed breed," and "mutt" were often hurled at my face, "all in good fun," of course. I was constantly bombarded by the insecurities of other people. I was an outsider on the inside of both worlds. Being an observer of two worlds, rather than a participant of one, created a unique perspective, from a wider point of view. I could see very clearly that cultural conditioning and belief systems were a construct of the matrix, a delusional facade to keep us divided.

I was 38 years old when I finally took a DNA test to learn more about my ethnicity. Here were the results

35%   England & Northwestern Europe

20%   Scotland

18%   Nigeria

8%   Cameroon, Congo, & Western Bantu Peoples

8%   Wales

7%   Benin & Togo

2%   Mali

1%   Germanic Europe

1%   Northern Africa

I had been sitting on the edge of my seat for weeks, waiting for the confirmation that read, "You are an alien from a different dimension." What a relief it was to learn that I am, in fact, a human. I am incredibly honored to come from such an abundance of culture and history. My ancestors have given me the gift of their strength and wisdom, written into the very code of my DNA.

"I wonder if things would be different if we all watched the sunrise, walked barefoot on the earth and slept out under the stars more often. Maybe it wouldn't fix all the hurt and anger in the world, but it would damn sure fix some of it."

—Brooke Hampton

As a child, I found more peace with Nature than I did with people. Growing up in West Virginia provided endless opportunities for grounding and connection. I spent my early childhood years catching crawdads and salamanders in the creek, swimming at the waterhole, climbing trees, running through open fields, hiking up mountains, exploring the woods, riding horses, and laying under the stars. I grew up as a country girl, a wild spirit—a barefoot-in-the-dirt, sun-on-my-face, fresh mountain air kinda-girl. Birds and bees, crickets, and frogs—was my kinda music kinda-girl. I was in tune with it; pulled to it; in awe of it. Nature offered expansion, freedom, and a powerful knowing that soothed my soul. Nature was where I could be vibrant and alive. It was where my spirit was most directly fed and energized by Source. I did not know what to call the powerful energy that pulsated throughout the natural world, but I knew it was worthy of praise.

Self-awareness offers a deeper understanding of who we are and how to thrive within our environment. As a society, we are far removed from who we are and where we come from. The matrix teaches that the body is a machine, medical doctors are the healers, and pharmaceuticals are the medicine. The truth is, the body is nature, we are magical beings with the capacity to heal ourselves, and all of the medicine that we could ever need is given in abundance by the Earth. The physical body is an avatar, used to navigate the planet. You must care for it and keep it healthy because whatever you choose to put into it, is exactly what it will become.

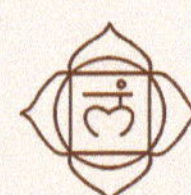

PEACEFUL ✣ PRACTICE
Root Chakra

> *Go outside among the trees*

Go outside often to be among the trees. Feel the cold Earth under your bare feet. Feel the warmth of the sun on your face. Cultivate a deep curiosity and childlike wonder for the beautiful variety of life. Be astonished and inspired by creation. Fall in love with being alive. Listen to the songs of the birds. Watch the squirrels play. Nature will teach you that it is a great miracle to be alive.

When your world is spinning out of control, come out of the head and into the body. Regulate your energy by slowing your breath. Unclench your jaw; relax your shoulders; drop your tongue from the roof of your mouth. Inhale fresh air deep into your lungs. Tune in to the Life Force Energy vibrating through your Being. Feel it. Melt into it. Surrender to it. Become it. Ground yourself in peace and stillness. This practice is a communion with your Higher Self, and a sacred offering to the Divine Matrix.

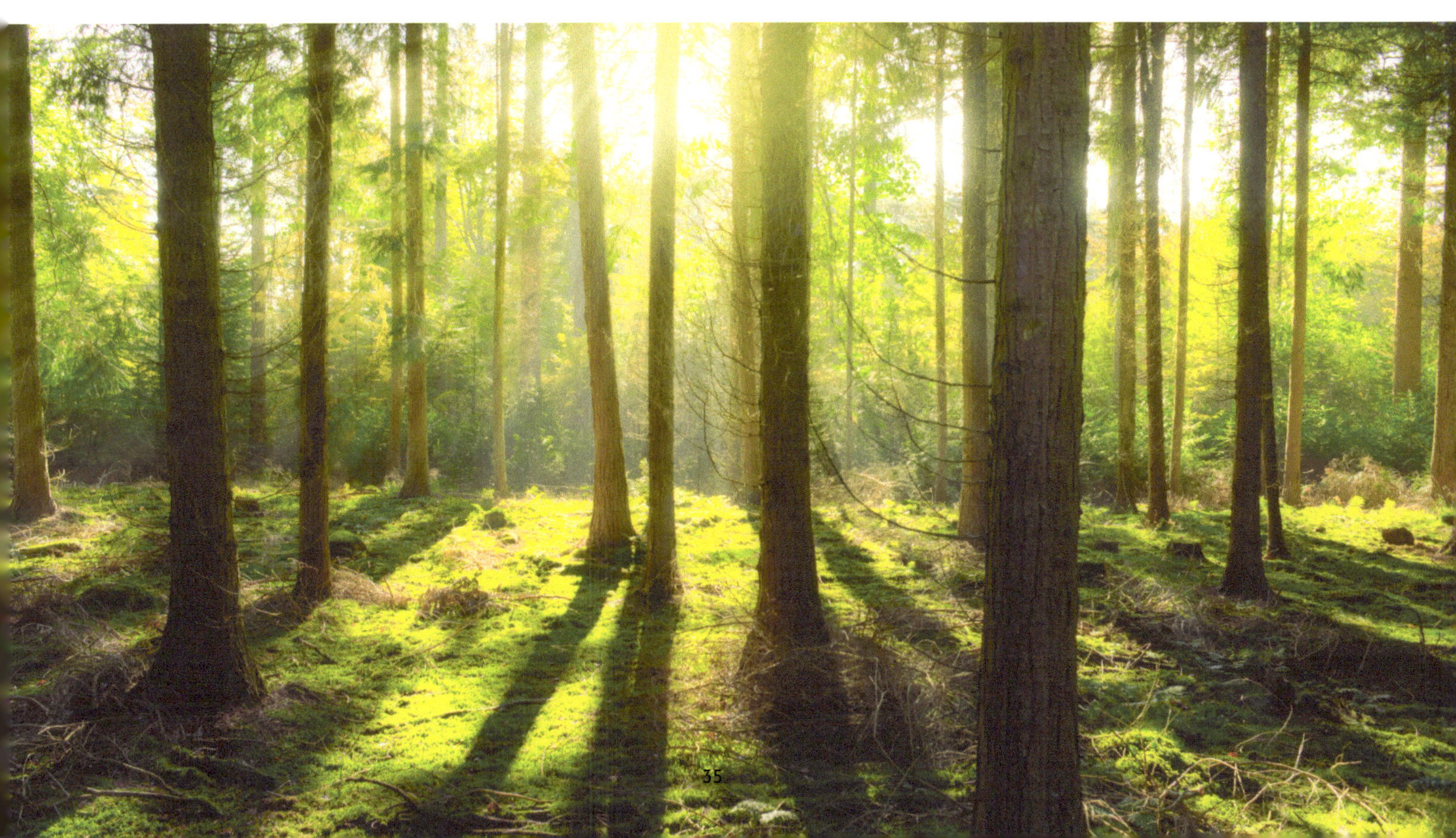

HOLISTIC WELLNESS

Practice Becoming One with Nature: Grounded in Peace

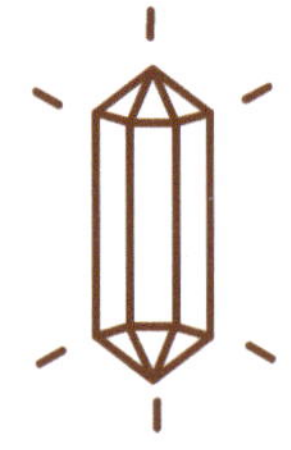

CRYSTALS

Red Jasper, Garnet, Red Tigers Eye, Black Tourmaline

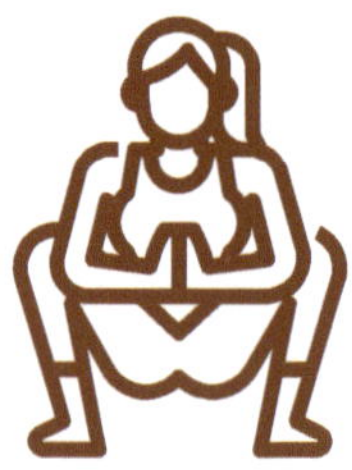

YOGA

Garland Pose

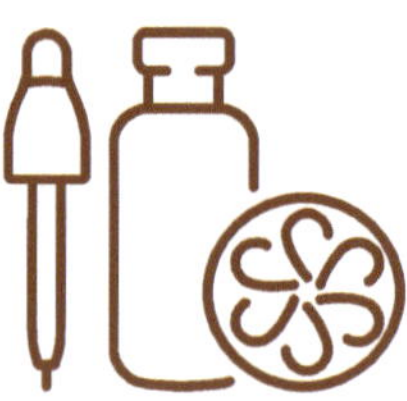

ESSENTIAL OILS

Vetiver, Ylang Ylang, Patchouli, Cinnamon, Cedar Wood

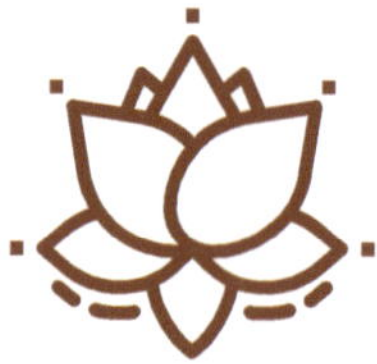

PHYSICAL WELLNESS

Incorporate healthy and nourishing foods, physical activity, and sleep on a regular basis.

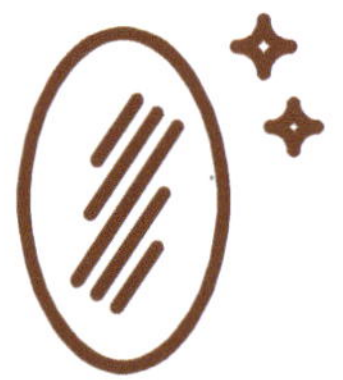

AFFIRMATION

I am grounded and protected at all times. I am connected to the present moment. I am peaceful. I am one with nature.

MEDITATION

Inhale fresh air deep into your lungs. Unclench your jaw; relax your shoulders; drop your tongue down from the roof of your mouth. Release the tension in your body.

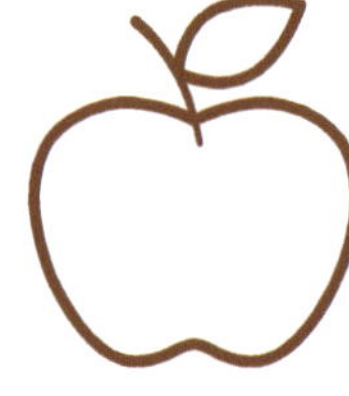

FOOD

Red Apples, Beets, Tomatoes, Pomegranates, Strawberries, Raspberries, Sweet Potatoes, Ginger, Turmeric

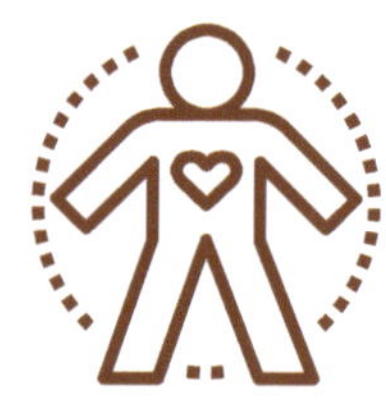

PHYSICAL AWARENESS

The ability to connect the body, a biological organism, to the Natural World. The body's greatest healing is found in nature.

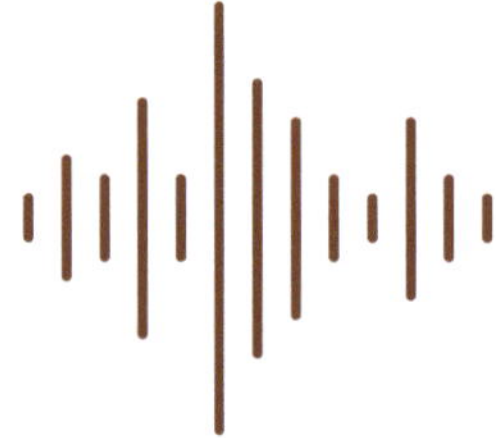

SOUND

Liberating guilt and fear.

396 Hz

MUDRA

"Survival": Thumb and index fingers touch. Arms straight, hands on knees.
Long L-A-A-A-A-M

COLOR

Red Increases: Physical Energy, Stamina, Grounding, Spontaneity, Stability, Passion

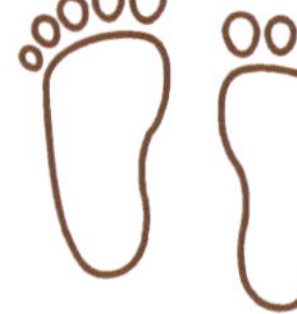

GROUNDING

Put your body in direct, uninterrupted contact with the Earth (soil, sand, or water).

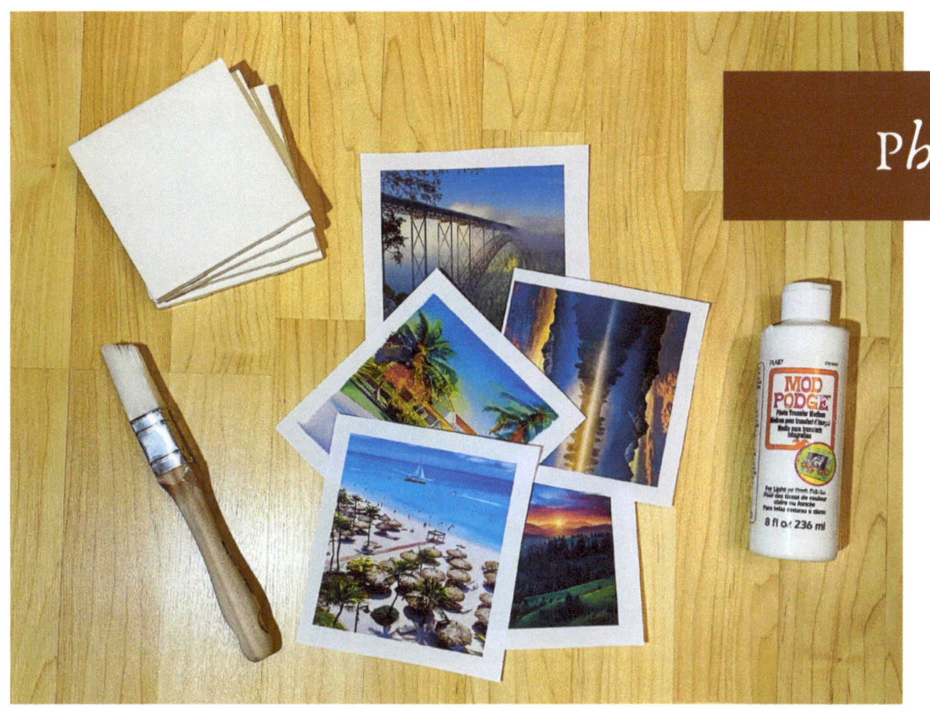

Photo Transfer Tiles

These tiles will serve as reminders to balance your energy by connecting with nature. The matrix is not designed to nourish the Spirit. Make the experience of peace and stillness a priority in your life.

Materials Needed

Ceramic Tiles

Images, printed with ink

Mod Podge, photo transfer medium

Scissors

Paint Brush

Sealant

Sand Paper (optional)

"Those who dwell among the beauties and mysteries of the Earth are never alone or weary of life."

—*Rachel Carson*

Intention: One with Nature
Human experience: Self-preservation (fear and anxiety)
Spiritual practice: Self-awareness (security and vitality)

PHOTO TRANSFER TILES
Instructions

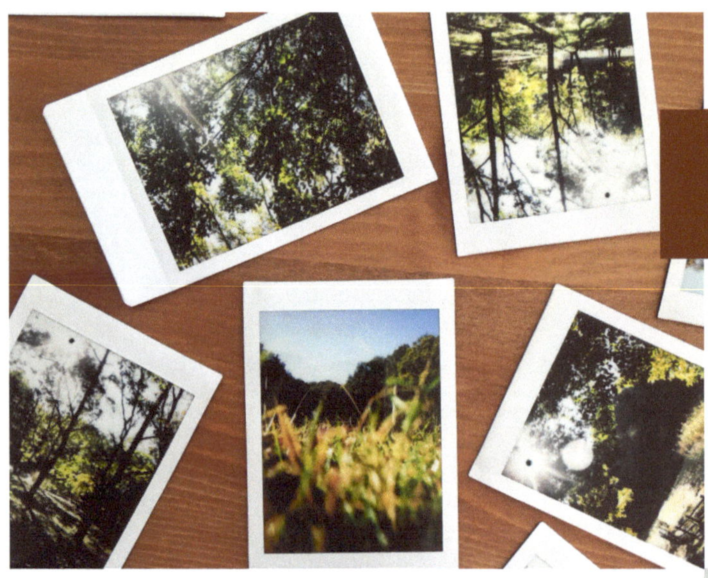

Step 1

Choose images that represent spaces within the Natural World that have brought you the most peace. Size and cut your images to fit the surface area of your tiles.

Step 2

Remove dust from the surface of each tile using a damp towel. Allow to dry. Apply a thin layer of mod podge to the surface of the tile and the front surface of the image.

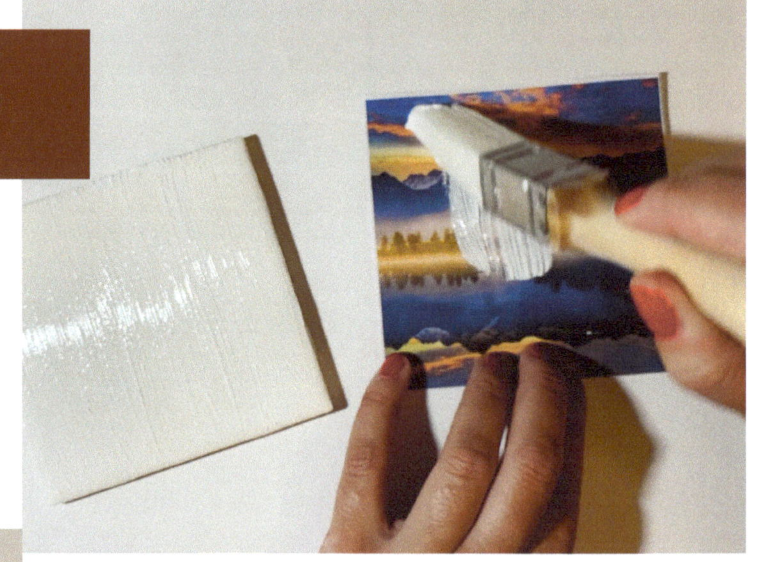

Step 3

Lay the image facedown on top of the tile. Use your finger to gently rub the image from the center, out towards the edges. Remove excess glue with a paper towel. Allow to dry overnight.

PHOTO TRANSFER TILES
Instructions

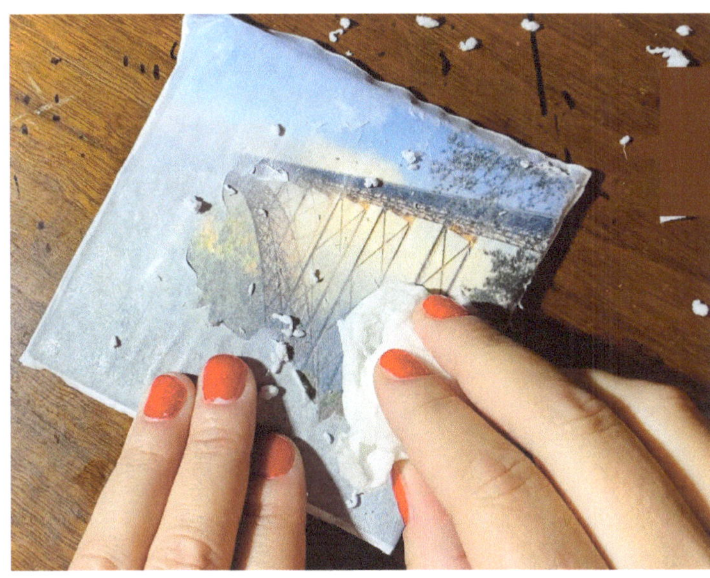

Step 4

After drying, gently rub the top layer of paper away using a wet paper towel in a circular motion. This process will slowly reveal the image, in reverse. You may have to do this more than once, if after it dries a white film remains. It is very easy to rub right through the image so take your time and work gently. After the white film is completely removed, allow tiles to dry.

Step 5

Use the sand paper to distress the edges then coat the surface with a sealant. Display your tiles as a daily reminder to spend more time in nature and to dedicate time to the things that bring peace to the body, mind, and spirit.

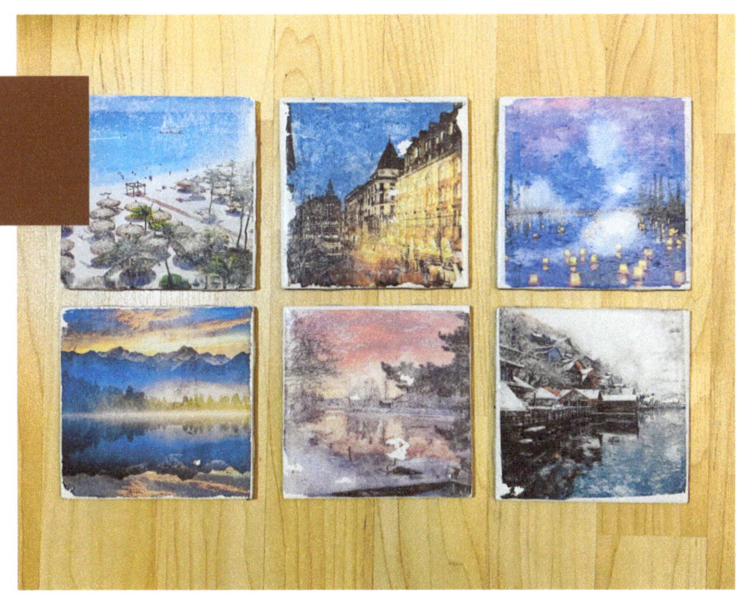

"Whatever brings you the most peace, should get the most time." —*Unknown*

TIME TO REFLECT

"We often forget that we are nature. Nature is not something separate from us. So when we say that we have lost our connection to nature, it means that we have lost our connection to ourselves."
—Andy Goldsworthy

Intention: One with nature
Human experience: Self-preservation (Fear and Anxiety)
Spiritual practice: Self-awareness (Security and Vitality)

CONSCIOUS CONNECTIONS

Connect with your Roots

Sleep Well

Create Peace in your Home

Ground Yourself

Eat Plants

Practice Self-Discipline

Drink Naturally Alkaline Spring Water

Clear Toxins from the Body

Be present, Mindful, Aware

Exercise

Listen to your Body

Sit in Nature

DID YOU KNOW?

"The moment your foot touches the Earth, your physiology changes, an immediate normalization begins. And an anti-inflammatory switch is turned on. People stay inflamed because they never connect with the Earth, the source of free electrons, which can neutralize the free radicals in the body that cause disease and cellular destruction." —Dr. James Oschman

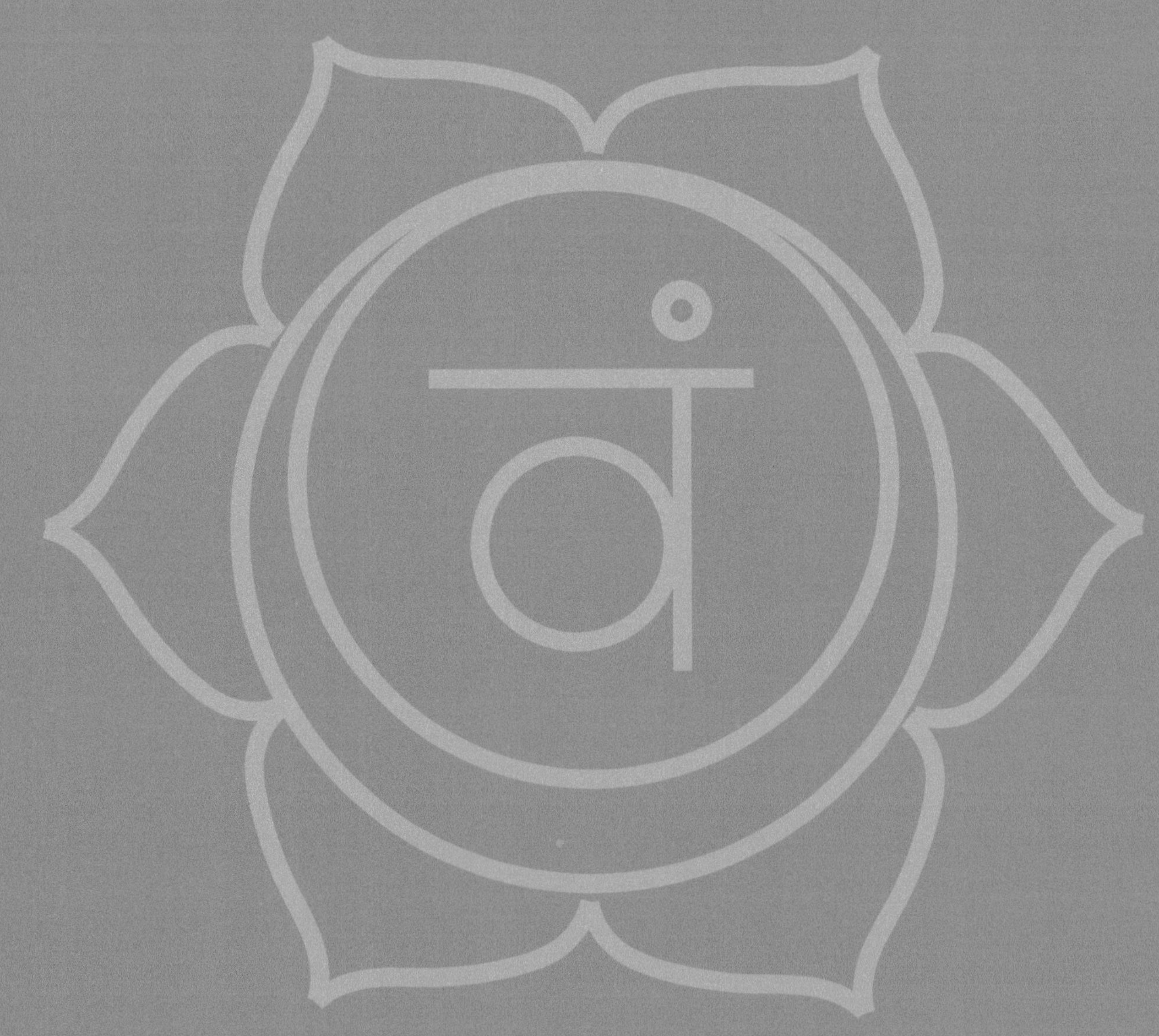

"Let the mind flow like water. Face life with a calm and quiet mind and everything in life will be calm and quiet."
—Thich Thien-An

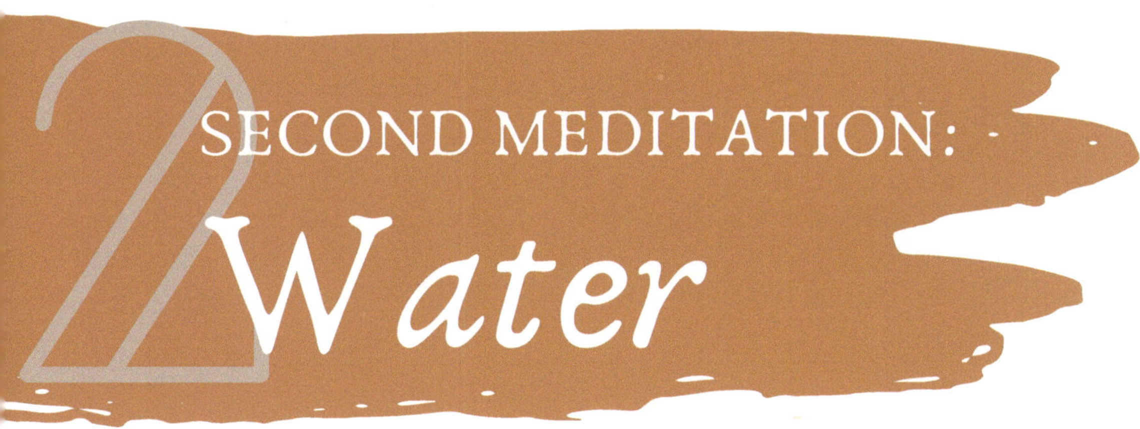

The Sacral Chakra represents Water, the world of emotions, and the natural flow of Life.

When we allow our emotions to move gracefully like a river rather than sitting stagnant like a reservoir, we free ourselves from unnecessary suffering. Trauma lingers within the body and brain, causing patterns of negative thoughts and behaviors. You have the power to override old patterns and create new ones by consciously replacing impulsive and reactive emotions with emotions that serve your Ascension. Clear out negative energy to make space for Light. Allow your Higher self to guide you on a journey of healing. Embrace the waves of transformation.

Surrender and Flow.

Which experiences in your life have caused you great suffering? What trauma do you feel and relive? What is the lesson?

"Life will give you whatever experience is most helpful for the evolution of your consciousness." —Eckhart Tolle

Intention: Choose to be Happy
Human experience: Self-gratification (guilt and blame)
Spiritual practice: Self-exploration (gratitude and joy)

SACRAL CHAKRA:

Movement, emotions, relationships, sexuality

ELEMENT: *Water*
IDENTITY: *Emotional*
LOCATION: *Below navel*
INTENTION: *Create happy*

The Sacral Chakra processes the awareness of gratitude and joy and is blocked by feelings of guilt and blame.

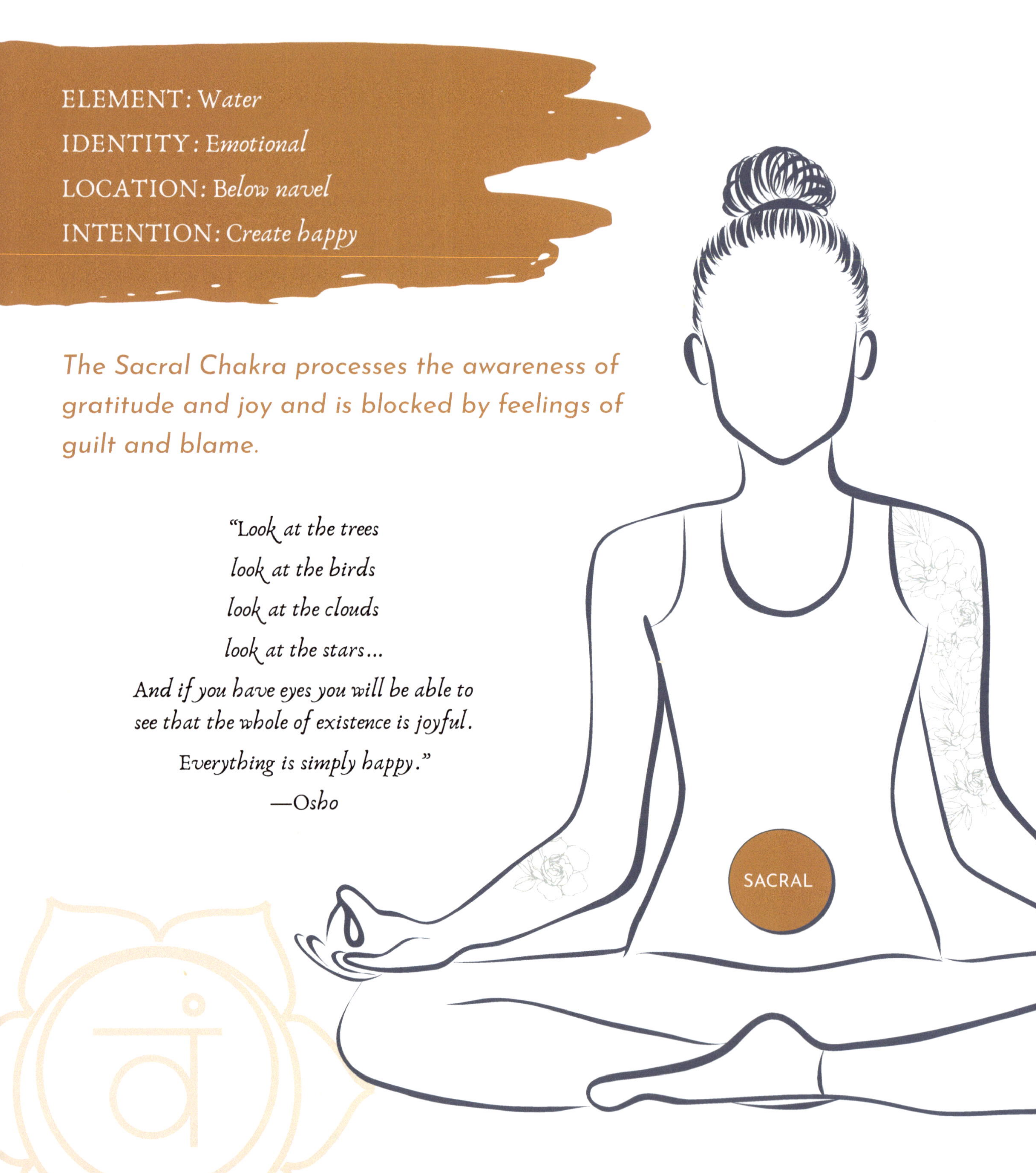

> *"Look at the trees*
> *look at the birds*
> *look at the clouds*
> *look at the stars…*
> *And if you have eyes you will be able to see that the whole of existence is joyful.*
> *Everything is simply happy."*
> —Osho

SACRAL CHAKRA:
Surrender & flow

The following deficient and excessive energies carry low-vibrational frequencies. They are collected and stored in the sacral chakra, blocking the flow of spiritual energy. If your thoughts, feelings, or behaviors fall into one of these two categories, the healing in this energy center has not yet begun.

Balanced energy in the Sacral Chakra is connected to our ability to transcend our own suffering. The ability to raise your own vibration is your super-power. Honor your Higher self by being intentional with your emotional energy. Create an electromagnetic field that attracts universal flow and abundance.

Raise Your Vibration

DEFICIENT ENERGY	BALANCED ENERGY	EXCESSIVE ENERGY
• RIGID BELIEFS	• HEALTHY BOUNDARIES	• OBSESSIVE ATTACHMENT
• ISOLATION	• CREATIVE NEW IDEAS	• OVERLY SENSITIVE
• NO CREATIVITY	• OPEN	• LOOSE BODY AND PELVIS
• LACK OF SPONTANEITY	• OPTIMISTIC	• ADDICTIVE PERSONALITY
• FEAR OF INTIMACY	• EMBRACE CHANGE	• HIGHLY SEXUAL
• GUILT	• PASSIONATE	• HEDONISTIC
• DESPAIR	• EMOTIONALLY CONNECTED	• SEDUCTIVE
• LOW LIBIDO	• FLUIDITY AND GRACE	• OVERLY STRICT
• EMPTINESS	• SEXUAL FULFILLMENT	• PUNISHING
• RIGID BODY	• GRACEFUL MOVEMENT	• MANIPULATIVE
• NO SOLUTIONS TO PROBLEMS	• CAPACITY FOR DEEP PLEASURE	• SELF-INDULGENT
• PRUDISH	• DEPTH OF FEELING	• OVERLY EMOTIONAL
• NUMB	• CREATE THE LIFE YOU WANT	• FIXATED ON SEX
• LACKS DESIRE/PASSION/EXCITEMENT	• NURTURING TO SELF AND OTHERS	
• OUT OF TOUCH WITH EMOTIONS	• HEALTHY LIBIDO	
• AVOIDS PLEASURE AND RELAXATION		

Intention: Choose to be Happy
Human experience: Self-gratification (guilt and blame)
Spiritual practice: Self-exploration (gratitude and joy)

Who/What makes you feel happy? Full of Joy? Creative? Passionate? Free?
Do you prioritize your passions? How do you recharge and replenish your energy?

How do you deal with feelings of emotional isolation?
When in your life did you feel alone or excluded?

Think through your life story.

What do you feel guilty about? What do you blame yourself for?

In what areas of your life do you overindulge in pleasure and/or gratification?

My Experience with Guilt and Blame

"Your story isn't calm. The road has been chaotic at times, filled with detours and rain and loss so sudden, and soon. Sometimes the bliss was so elevated your heart could hardly hold it. Sometimes it was maddening to have, and then to lose. You learn soon enough that it hardly ever goes as planned – gentle, easy, and smooth. But that my friend, is what makes you fascinating. You have something to tell. Something you've walked through. Something wild. Something courageous. Something true. You're made of stories within stories within even more stories. Those quiet depths of you."

—Victoria Erickson

I was married at twenty-two, pregnant at twenty-three, and a mama at twenty-four. It all happened so fast. I went from party-girl college student to wife and mother in the blink of an eye. I didn't think twice about this new life that I was walking into. I was in love with who I thought was the most perfect man. He was gentle and kind, patient and generous, a dreamer and a visionary. His identity was not conditioned by popular culture and I found that to be such a breath of fresh air. He grew up in the South, a musician and a preacher's kid, dedicated to his faith and to his practice. I was in awe of the light that radiated from his Being because it was literally the most beautiful thing that I had ever seen. I met him when I was 16 and I knew as soon as I laid eyes on him, that one day I would be his wife. Who would have known that the house we were getting ready to build would be in ruins by the time we were thirty years old?

We graduated from college the year after our daughter was born and moved back to North Carolina shortly after. Because she was young, we decided that I would stay home the first couple of years to care for her and he would begin his career. He accepted a position that required an hour of travel, both ways. He left early every morning and didn't return home until late in the evening. Almost every weekend we packed our car with a suitcase, instruments, a baby, all her bags, and drove an hour to Greensboro. Saturday was dedicated to rehearsal and Sunday to service. I sat in the pews both days, entertaining a toddler, before packing up and driving back home Sunday night.

"What is the greatest lesson a woman should learn? That since day one, she's already had everything she needs within herself. It's the world that convinced her she did not."

—Rupi Kaur

I was twenty-six years old, miles away from family and friends, alone with a small child on most days, and slowly but surely losing my mind. I didn't know who I was in this new role. I didn't know what to do with myself or how to exist as something other than a feeding, cooking, cleaning machine. I felt undereducated on the subject of being a mom, overwhelmed by the uncertainty of my performance, completely exhausted by the load of work that came with the job, and an incredible amount of mom guilt because I didn't think I was doing any of it right. I was impatient because I was stressed and stressed because I was impatient. I wonder where it comes from—the idea that the essence of who we are isn't enough? As if we aren't magical spiritual beings, with stardust in our veins, galaxies in our eyes, and the entire Universe in our soul.

> *"When I look in his eyes, I don't see perfection. I don't see a love story that would necessarily be something people would watch on a big screen and dream about – I see someone who would fight for me and protect me and love me, in spite of all the ways I am still a wreck. I see home."*
> —Melanie Shankle

The new me was anxious and worried but my husband's presence was peaceful and reassuring. He offered emotional strength and stability; he was my calm in the storm. He saw me, he paid attention, he reminded me to breathe. He was faithful and committed to me. He never made me doubt for one moment that he would spend the rest of his life loving me the very best way he knew how. Our family tradition was to take long walks around the neighborhood and share about the day. On days we were both at home, we played badminton or horseshoes, filled the kiddie pool for water fights, worked in the yard, or cooked on the grill. We enjoyed hosting parties and entertaining guests. My husband always made a point to laugh and play with everyone, including the children. Their little eyes would light up, excited to be acknowledged and validated. He was fun, happy, and willingly gave away copious amounts of light and love. Everyone was drawn to his warm disposition, and I admired that about him. Sometimes, when he was playing too hard, he would stop to catch his breath. In a wide stance, hands on his hips, breathing heavy, smiling from ear to ear, he would scan the room to find his next mischievous point of entry. Sometimes we would catch eyes and telepathically high-five each other. We were proud of the life that we created together. Those were our best days.

On our worst days, there was distance and incredible loneliness.

When our daughter turned three, I decided that it was time to take off the apron and get back to work. We weren't comfortable sending her to daycare, so he and I traded places. He would be a stay-at-home dad, and I would get started on my career. A year later, I was teaching full time, attending graduate school part-time, and trying—with what energy I had left—to keep the house clean, the child reared, and the husband fed. Like most women, I was overworked and underpaid. Bills were piling up and arguments were common. Exhausted most days and lonely most nights, he and I were slowly drifting apart. While I spent hours worried and stressed about life, he spent hours playing games on the Xbox. I loved my husband and my daughter more than anything in the world, but I couldn't see myself anywhere in our equation. I was a mom and I was a wife, but I had no idea who I was. On the outside, I was frantically treading water. On the inside, I was drowning. I felt like the only option I had was to save myself.

"It's so important to heal your own wounds, investigate your own pain, and resolve your own turmoil, because those closest to you, will always bear the deepest scars when your world detonates."
—Wes Ceekuno Whitsett

My daughter was four years old when the bomb exploded. The tension in our house was so thick, you could have cut it with a knife. Emptiness and isolation turned a once-happy home into a war zone. My daughter was confused by the sudden lack of love and affection that usually filled the house and held everything together. Our suffering was boiling over, and she was caught in the crossfire. On one evening in particular, her little four-year-old shaky voice filled the room. "Why are you so mean, mommy?" Those words hit like a ton of bricks. My eyes were burning long before I had time to process that my heart had been ripped from my chest. When I turned to look at her, I saw my younger self, shrinking into a corner, scared and uneasy. She was my mirror— and I was horrified by my reflection. I saw my father. I saw an unhealed child raising a child. I saw the passing down of wounds, one generation after the other.

"Guilt is to the spirit, what pain is to the body."
—Elder David A. Bednar

Divorce followed soon after. Leaving was by far the hardest thing I have ever experienced in this lifetime. I watched my husband drown in his own tears, too many times to count, pleading with me to keep our family together. I held my daughter in my arms every night for a year while she cried herself to sleep. "Why do I have to miss you when I'm with daddy, and miss daddy when I'm with you?" Over the next two years, she continued to confront me. Giant words from such a tiny body, slicing me wide open every time. I still carry this guilt around deep in the pit of my stomach. I blame myself for causing so much suffering. "Dear God. I am so very sorry for what I have done." I blame myself for all of our broken pieces.

Self-gratification is our natural instinct to satisfy our own impulses; to seek out pleasure and indulge in desire. When I was a kid, my mother's desires were framed as the next new adventure. I learned to embrace change because it was the only thing consistent in my life. My reality was fluid. Homes, schools, friends, family, and experiences were here one day, gone the next. I learned to be indifferent to loss. I wasn't taught to consider the domino effect of selfish decisions. "The grass is greener on the other side," is a pretty common conversation, when you grow up in poverty. "The other side" meant a mattress to lay on at night instead of the floor, central heat in the house instead of a space heater in one room, a car to drive instead of long walks and bus rides, enough food for mom to eat too instead of pretending like she wasn't hungry. The very foundation of a poverty mindset is comparison, not appreciation. I have come to learn that the grass is actually green where you water it. There will always be weeds that need to be pulled, but that does not necessarily mean that the garden should be abandoned.

Gratitude is key to healing and restoring this energy center. When I notice that I am complaining, blaming, or playing victim, I close my eyes and give thanks for all of the blessings in my life. I bring my awareness to the things that bring joy to my heart. I transcend the negative emotion, immediately shifting my vibrational frequency to one that I will prosper from. Take a moment to think about people and situations that trigger an impulsive or reactive emotion. What do you complain about? Who do you blame when things aren't going your way? Your triggers point to where you are not free—those are the areas that need healing. Freedom can only be obtained through total acceptance of every moment, good and bad. Stop complaining about life. Learn how to surrender and flow.

My Experience with Gratitude and Joy

"The ego says, 'I shouldn't have to suffer,' and that thought makes you suffer so much more. It is a distortion of the truth, which is always paradoxical. The truth is that you need to say yes to suffering before you can transcend it."

—Eckhart Tolle

Trauma changes us...

I was fourteen years old when my mom stopped coming home. Days would pass before we would see her again. When she did come home, she would sleep, almost unconscious, for days. Once awake, she was back out the door again. This continued for months, though at the time it felt like an eternity. I was the oldest of four, so it fell on me to care for my two youngest siblings, ages six and two. (My third sibling had already been sentenced by a Federal Grand Jury to live full-time, until the age of eighteen, in a juvenile detention center). There were many days that I had to beg the owner of the local corner store for food because the cabinets and fridge were empty. I would load the kids up in the stroller, walk to find food, then head back home to feed them, bathe them, and put them to bed. There were moments when I laughed and played with them; moments when I was mean and hateful towards them; moments when I sobbed, loud, on my knees in front of them. I was scared. I was given a responsibility that was too heavy to carry.

Up until the age of fourteen, I thought my mom was superwoman. Isn't it a funny thing? When we are young, we think our parent's story begins and ends with us. Like they didn't experience an entire lifetime of stories and traumas before we showed up. I didn't understand that she was fragile. I had no idea that she was suffering. I learned later that during her childhood, she suffered many years of trauma and sexual abuse at the hands of various men in her family. The generational curse of trauma will continue to recycle itself over and over again, until someone in the family line transcends it.

"When it hurts, observe. Life is trying to teach you something."

—Anita Krizzan

When she finally healed herself and came home for good, I ran. I was devastated because she wasn't who I thought she was. I was angry at her for abandoning us. I felt unloved and unworthy. My sadness was hollow, and I wanted to avoid that feeling at all costs. Drugs became my healer, my comfort, my escape from the real world. Depression was like a heavy chain around my neck. As long as I was high, I didn't have to acknowledge the weight of sadness or carry it around with me. Drugs helped me stuff down the pain of feeling alone and afraid and offered a feeling of happiness that my reality didn't provide. I was consumed by them, well-hidden for years behind layers of numb. Drugs weren't hard to find in a college town. Every person I knew either had them, sold them, or knew someone who did. Plant medicine was my daily drug of choice, but harder drugs followed.

> *"A wise woman once said, 'fuck this shit' and she lived happily ever after."*
> *—Unknown*

In ninth grade, before my world fell apart, I was a 4.0 student, second chair flute, head majorette, cheer captain, and an up-and-coming track star. By the end of my 10th grade year, I was a 0.8 student, skipping school regularly, and eating LSD like it was candy. Each morning I was presented with the same dilemma: would I go commune with nature, connect to a deeper level of consciousness, and learn from the spirits in the trees? Or would I go conform to the matrix, be indoctrinated by dogma, and learn from the lies in our textbooks? I chose the friends-nature-drugs option the majority of the time.

The abundance of shitty parenting in Morgantown provided endless opportunities for kids to fall through the cracks. One day, a bunch of us were tripping on LSD in the attic of a friend's house. About four hours in, I remember sitting straight up, looking around the room at every one of my drugged-induced friends, and right in that moment a wave of awareness washed over me. I wasn't looking at "them," I was looking at myself. They were my reflection. I felt incredibly seen, exposed, convicted by a knowing greater than myself. Once upon a time, I had envisioned so much more for my life. Who was this person that pain has turned me into? Panicked, I jumped up without saying a word, walked down the stairs, and out the front door. I continued through south park and downtown, then across the Westover bridge. My walk turned into a run, down the long back road that ran parallel to the Monongahela River. I did not stop until I reached my mom. She was sitting on the front porch, smoking a cigarette. I felt an urgency to get to her, as if my life depended on it. "You have to get me out of here mom, I'm going to die here. You have to save me." Two weeks later, with a couple hundred dollars in her pocket, she prayed over our old rundown van, and drove me to North Carolina.

Self-exploration offers a deeper understanding of why we think, feel, and behave the way that we do. It is the practice of acknowledging who we are, compared to who we want to be. As a teenager, I was lost in a sea of dark emotional turmoil. I did everything I could to stuff it down, brush it under the rug, pretend it wasn't there, but ultimately it influenced everything else in my reality. Emotional intelligence teaches us to acknowledge negative feelings as they come and go, without becoming the low-vibrational emotion that is attached to them. Life will always be messy and imperfect. Our daily experiences are proof of that fact. How do you behave when you become frustrated or annoyed about the phenomena happening around you? Driving behind a slow car when you're running late? Talking to a rude customer service rep who isn't resolving your problem? Responding to a waiter who got your order wrong? Engaging in a conversation with someone who has different political or religious views? Dealing with a fussy child after a long day at work? You can acknowledge that you are feeling frustrated without allowing yourself to become angry or mean. Give yourself permission to rise above the bullshit. Give yourself an opportunity to respond to life through your spiritual practice rather than your emotional conditioning.

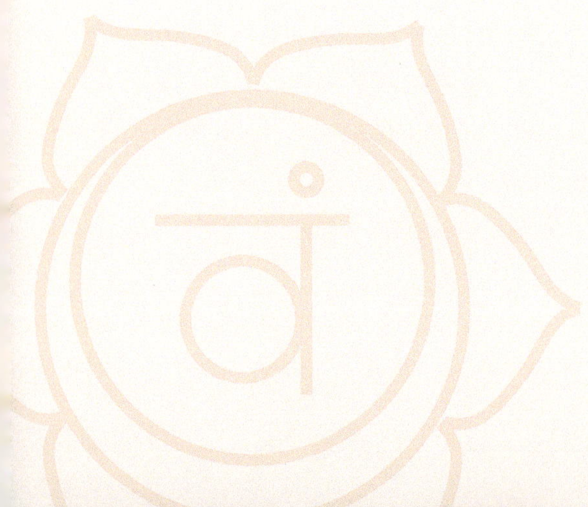

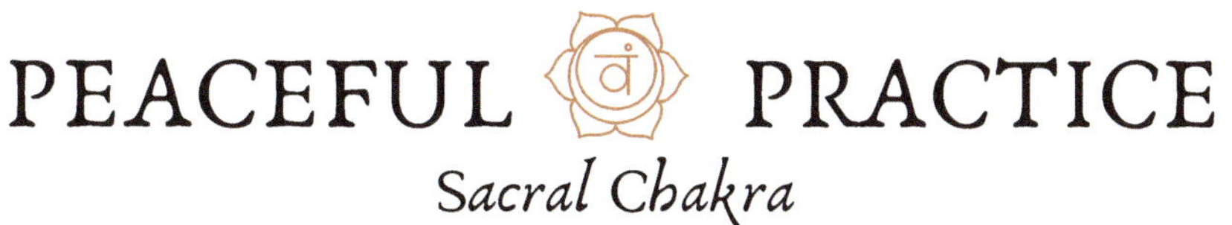

PEACEFUL PRACTICE
Sacral Chakra

Make space for your authentic self by connecting to the foundation of human expression: sing, dance, paint, play, make, laugh, explore, discover. Create beautiful things. Smile at every person you see. Choose to be happy.

Bring into your awareness all of the things that bring you the most joy, the most laughter, and the most love: the things you are grateful for. Experience those feelings within your body. Let it wash over you until you become it. This vibration is sacred; Gratitude is the language of the Universe. The more you shift your vibration to the frequency of gratitude, the more magical life becomes, and the more will show up in your life to be grateful for.

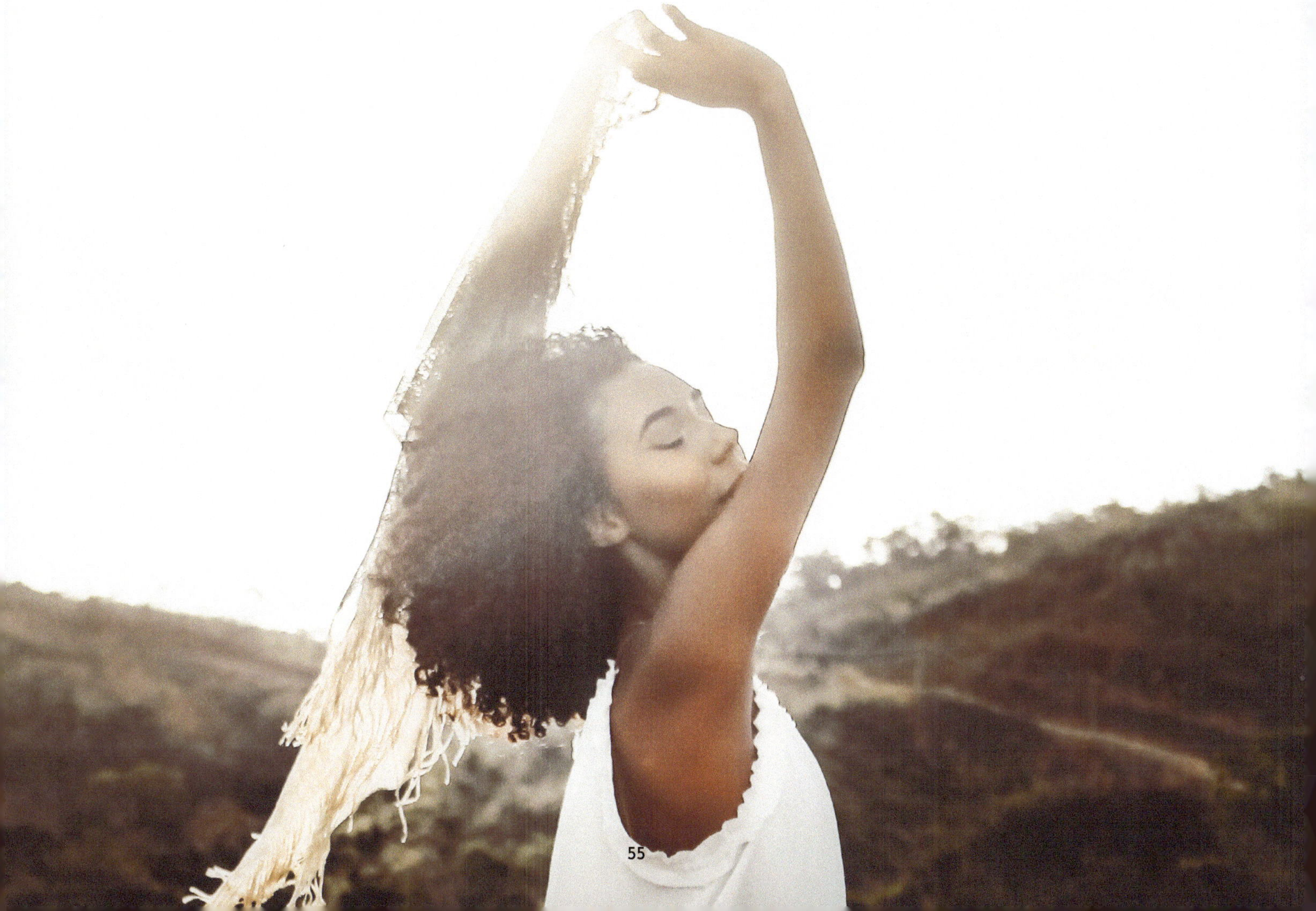

HOLISTIC WELLNESS

Practice Choosing to be Happy: Surrender and Flow

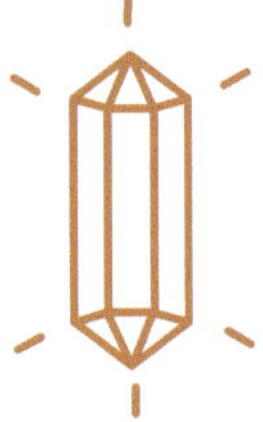

CRYSTALS

Moonstone, Peach Aventurine, Orange Calcite, Carnelian

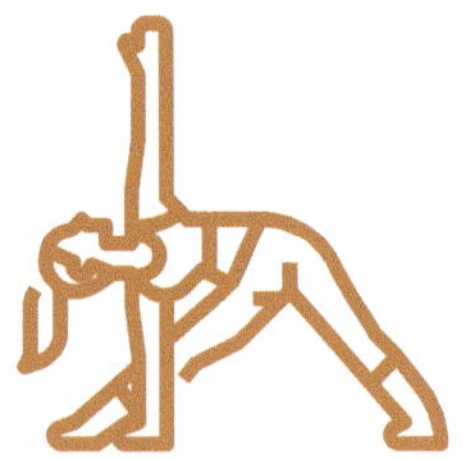

YOGA

Triangle Pose

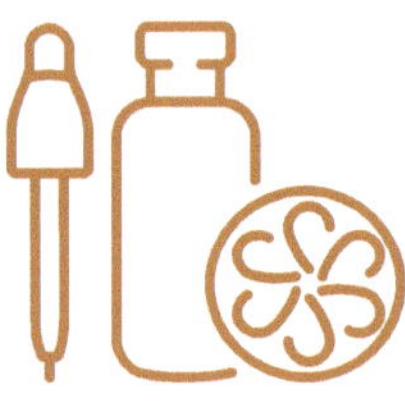

ESSENTIAL OILS

Lemongrass, Orange, Neroli, Jasmine, Geranium, Ginger

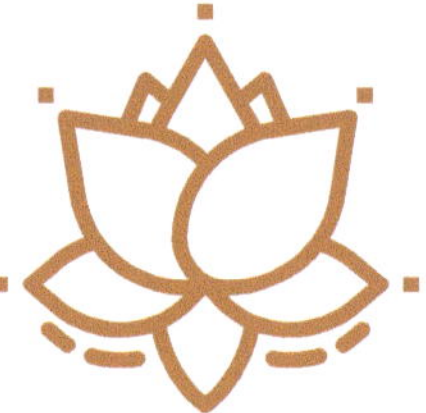

EMOTIONAL WELLNESS

Work through life's challenges, build resiliency, know that setbacks can be overcome.

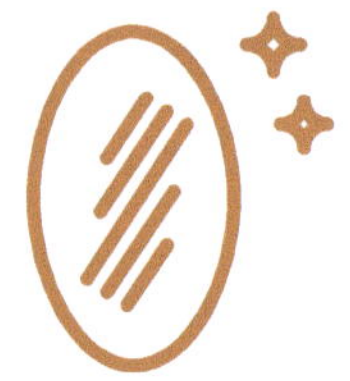

AFFIRMATION

I allow my emotions to flow through me in a healthy way. My body is sacred and I am living with creativity and passion.

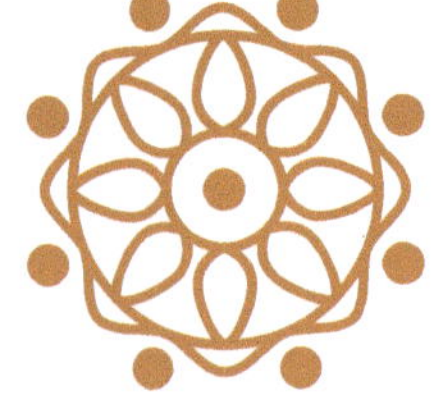

MEDITATION

Bring to mind what you are grateful for. Feel the emotion of joy and gratitude in every inch of your body. Smile & breathe into it.

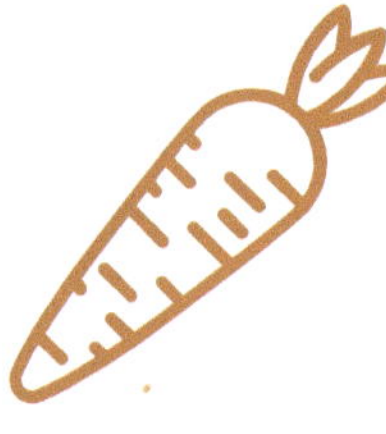

FOOD

Carrots, Mango, Pumpkin, Oranges, Orange Peppers, Peaches, Apricots, Sweet Potatoes, Almonds, Walnuts, Sesame, Cinnamon

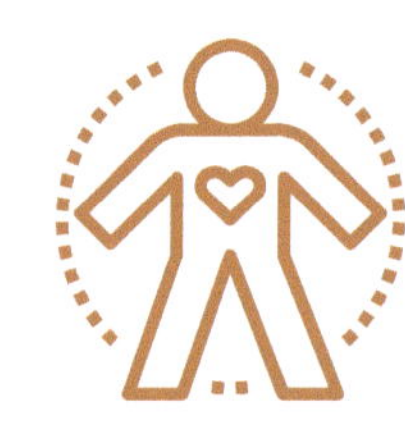

EMOTIONAL INTELLIGENCE

The ability to acknowledge the feeling without becoming the emotion. Witness it. Allow it. Let it go.

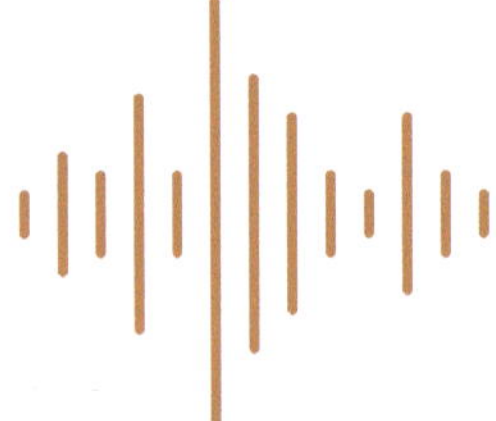

SOUND

Undoing situations and facilitating change.

417 Hz

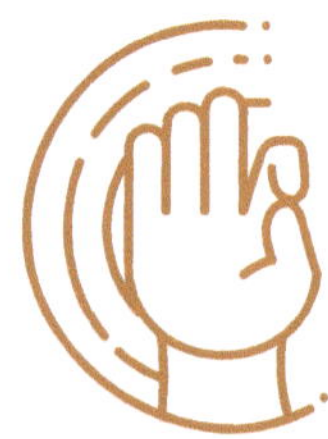

MUDRA

"Creativity"

Place hands in your lap with palms facing upward. Right palm resting on top of left.

Long V-A-A-A-A-M

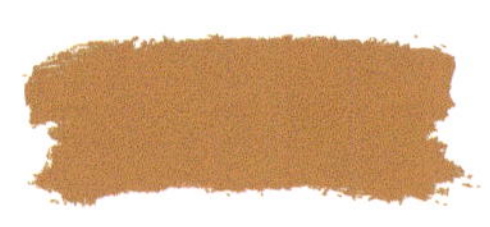

COLOR

Orange Stimulates:

Creativity, Productivity, Pleasure, Optimism, Enthusiasm, Emotional Expression

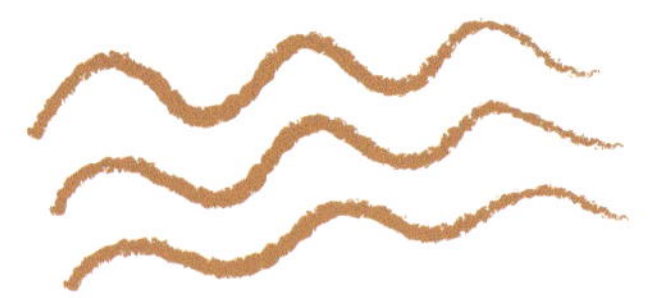

FLOW

Emotional Vibration is the language of the Universe. High Vibration is your prayer, unlocking magic and connecting you to the Divine Flow of Life.

CREATIVE FLOW
Artistic Expression

"It's hard to see the picture, when you're standing inside the frame." —Unknown

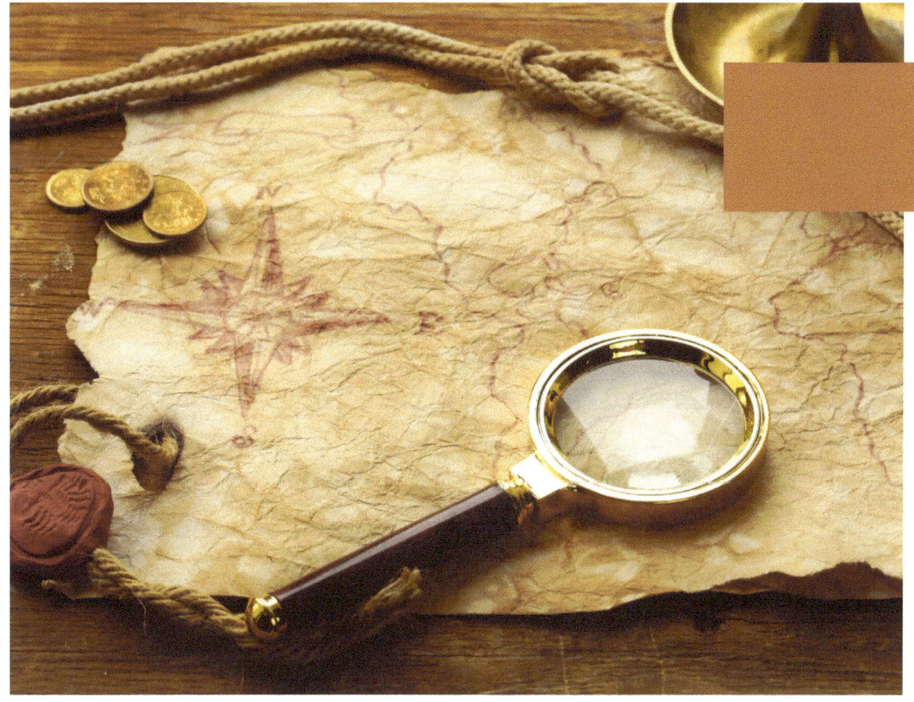

Found Objects

"Healing from pain is a choice.
You have to consciously decide
that you deserve to be free, that
you deserve to let go of the weight
that has been holding you down
for too long."

–S. Mcnutt

Collect *"found objects"* that represent the following 7 categories:

1. Fear: What causes nervousness/anxiety?

2. Guilt: What do you blame yourself for?

3. Disappointment: What are you ashamed of?

4. Grief: What did you lose that caused great sadness?

5. Lies: When did a negative perception that someone had about you, become
    your negative perception about yourself?

6. Separation: Where has your privilege intersected with another's oppression?

7. Attachment: What material thing do you feel you cannot live without?

Intention: Choose to be Happy
Human experience: Self-gratification (guilt and blame)
Spiritual practice: Self-exploration (gratitude and joy)

FOUND OBJECTS
Instructions

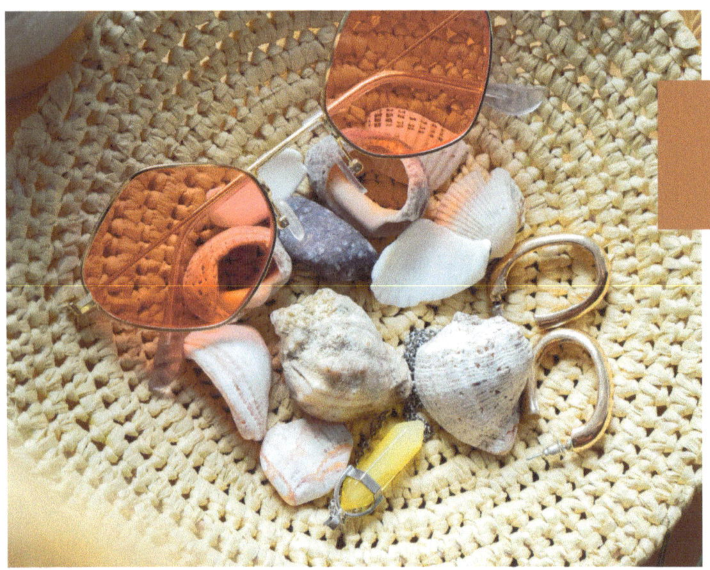

Step 1

These "found objects" are small symbolic representations of the stories attached to each category. Think through your timeline, childhood to adulthood. You are looking for GIANT moments in your story, the moments that have forever changed you.

Step 2

By pulling the energy of these stories out of the body and assigning a small, tangible symbol to them, it helps you to see the picture more clearly. Every time you bring your awareness to these traumatic events in your timeline, you have the opportunity to change the narrative. You can observe the pain that it caused you, but you can also practice observing the lesson and considering the healing that is available to you. It is not the specific event that is hurting you; the event is over. It is your thoughts and emotions surrounding those events that continue to hurt you. How can you change your thoughts, rewire your brain, change your lenses? How do you soothe and heal these monsters so they do not carry on impulsively, subconsciously caging you? Talk about it. Write about it. Sing about it. Dance about it. Create about it. You must get it out of your body, again and again and again and again, until what was once big and traumatic begins to lose its power over you. Display your found objects as a collection of art. Look at them everyday, hold them, experience them. Your younger self is still waiting to be healed. Go to her, acknowledge her, soothe her, then walk her to the Light. There are lessons to be learned and stories to be told. It is time to rewrite your narrative. Dr. Joe Dispenza said, "a memory minus the emotional charge is called wisdom."

"All emotions, even those that are suppressed, have physical effects. Unexpressed emotions tend to stay in the body like small ticking time bombs—they are illnesses in incubation."
—Marilyn Van Derber

SACRAL CHAKRA

SURRENDER AND FLOW
CHOOSE TO BE HAPPY

"Find out what makes you kinder, what opens you up and brings out the most loving, generous, and unafraid version of you—and go after those things as if nothing else matters… Because, actually, nothing does."

—*George Saunders*

CONSCIOUS CONNECTIONS

Acknowledge emotions, positive and negative

Seek out the lesson in every experience

Feel gratitude

Focus on the positive

Smile often

Practice random acts of kindness

Manage stress in a positive way

Uphold the qualities of an authentic friendship

Learn to handle conflict in a healthy way

DID YOU KNOW?

Emotion = energy in motion. When you give emotions momentum, they grow and create very powerful vibrations. Those vibrations are not only contagious, they are also magnetic. If you allow negative emotions to go unchecked, you will suffer, those around you will suffer, and you will pull more suffering into your reality. Be creative with your emotional energy. Otherwise, it will work against you.

Intention: Choose to be Happy
Human experience: Self-gratification (guilt and blame)
Spiritual practice: Self-exploration (gratitude and joy)

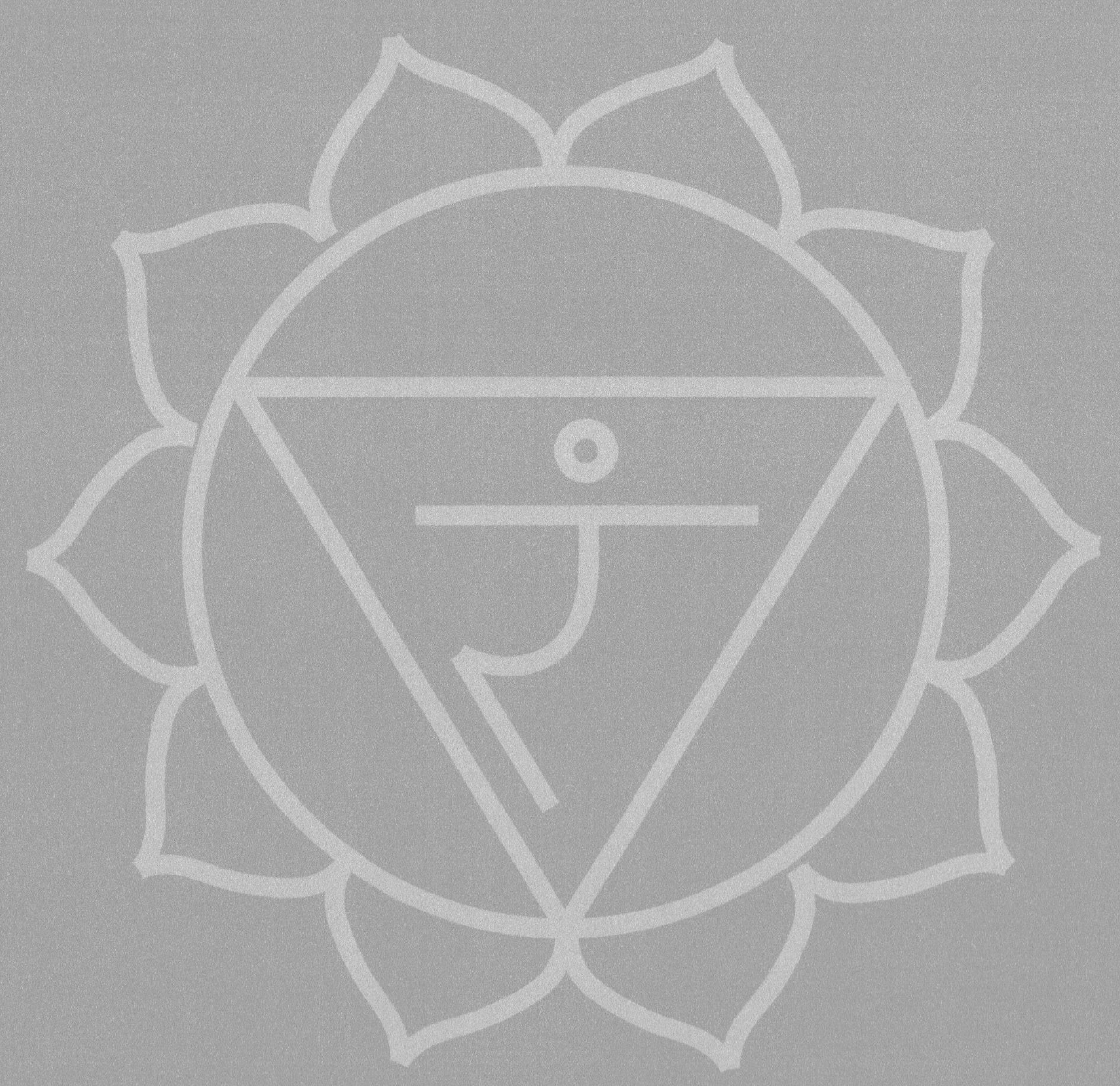

"Be fearless in the pursuit of what sets your soul on fire."
—Jennifer Lee

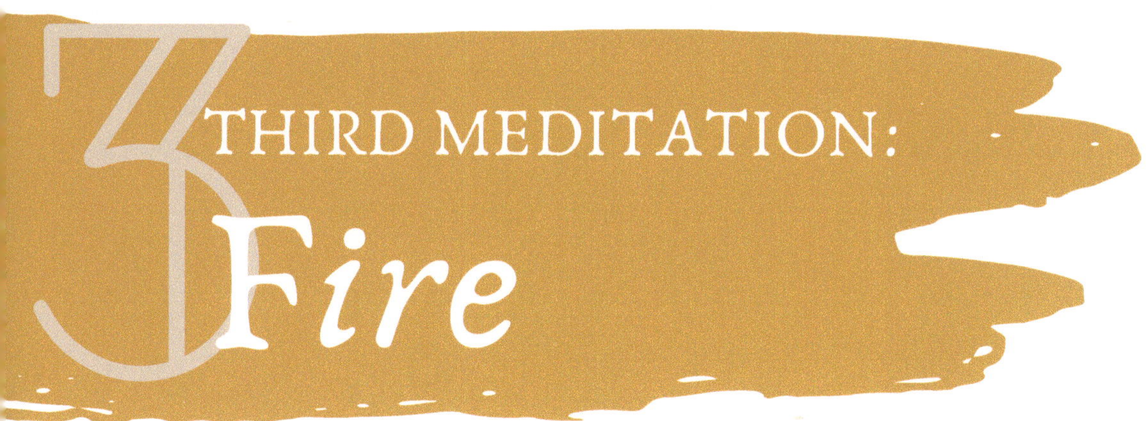

The Solar Plexus Chakra represents Fire, passion, and the power of purpose.

It is important to consider how you show up in the world. Are your actions unconsciously driven by your Shadow, or do your actions reflect personal honor and integrity? Notice your habits and patterns. Where do you focus your time and attention? Transcendence requires an awareness of the behaviors that are no longer serving your growth and evolution. Observe the shadow, but do not allow it to lead. Liberate yourself from the old paradigm.

Sitting in the fire is a spiritual practice.
Burn away anything that keeps you from the expression of your greatest potential.
Allow your Higher Self to rise from the ashes.

What are the biggest disappointments in your life? What are you ashamed of?

"If you think you've blown God's plan for your life,
Rest in this: You, my beautiful friend, are not that powerful." —Lisa Bever

Intention: Find Passion and Purpose
Human experience: Self-definition (insecurity and shame)
Spiritual practice: Self-discovery (self-worth and personal power)

SOLAR PLEXUS CHAKRA:

Power, vision, purpose, direction

ELEMENT: *Fire*

IDENTITY: *Ego*

LOCATION: *Above navel*

INTENTION: *Find passion and purpose*

The Solar Plexus Chakra processes the awareness of self-worth and personal power and is blocked by feelings of insecurity and shame.

"You often feel tired. Not because you've done too much, but because you've done too little of what sparks a light in you."
—Alexander den Heijer

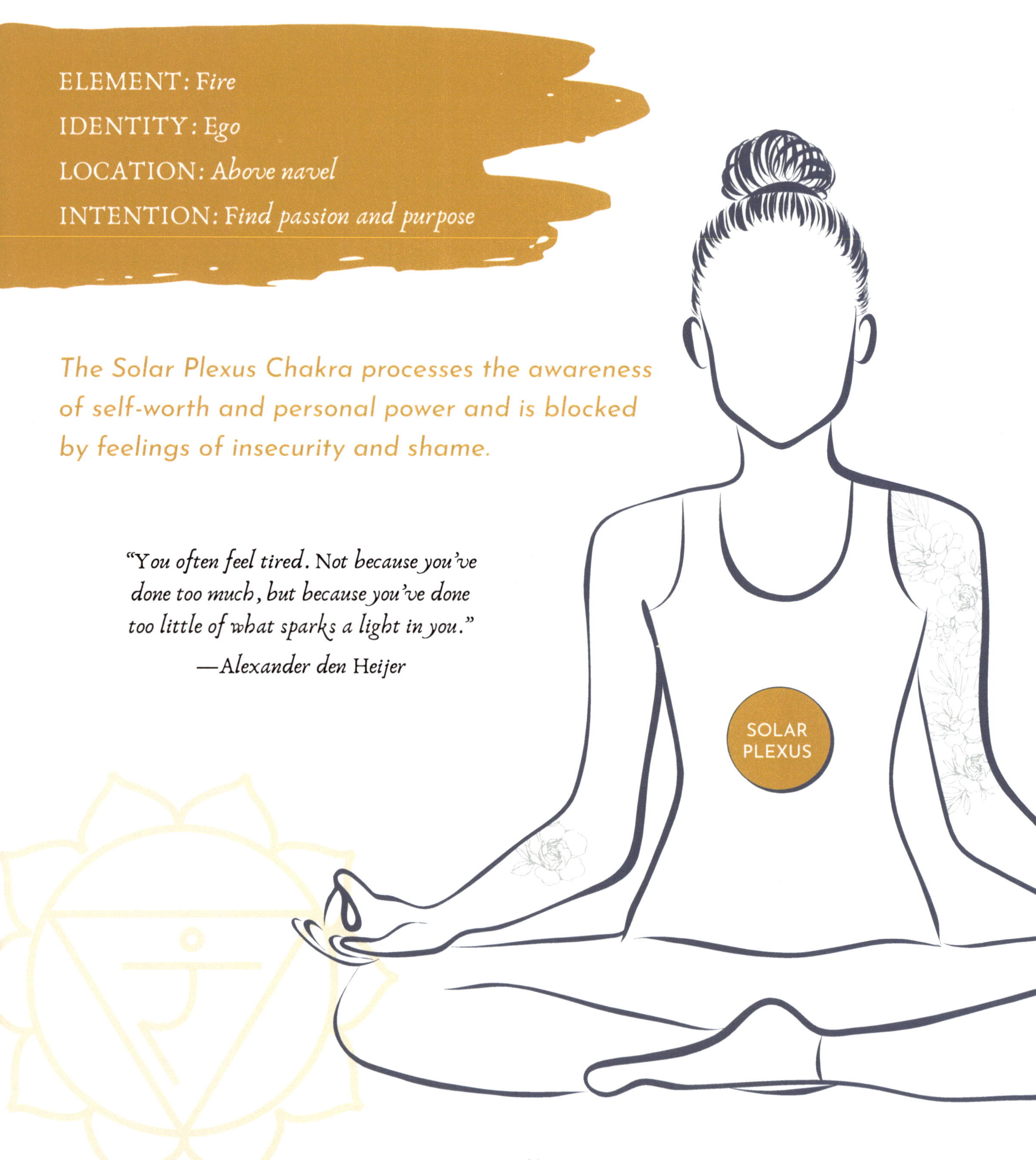

SOLAR PLEXUS CHAKRA:
Liberate yourself

The following deficient and excessive energies carry low-vibrational frequencies. They are collected and stored in the solar plexus chakra, blocking the flow of spiritual energy. If your thoughts, feelings, or behaviors fall into one of these two categories, the healing in this energy center has not yet begun.

Balanced energy in the Solar Plexus Chakra is directly influenced by how closely we are aligned with purpose. We must be willing to shed our skin over and over again as we continue to refine ourselves and reinvent what is possible in our lives. Pay attention to who is asking you to stay small. Those people are not your tribe.

Raise Your Vibration

DEFICIENT ENERGY

- SHAME
- EMBARRASSMENT
- VICTIM MENTALITY
- WEAK WILLED
- CAN'T FINISH TASKS
- HELPLESS
- INFERIORITY COMPLEX
- FEELING POWERLESS
- LOW SELF-ESTEEM
- LOW SELF-WORTH
- LOW ENERGY
- BLAMING
- DISAPPOINTED
- IRRITATION
- NEGLECT
- PASSIVE
- AIMLESS
- INTIMIDATED

BALANCED ENERGY

- COURAGEOUS
- CONFIDENT
- EFFECTIVENESS
- UNDERSTAND WORTH
- SELF-DISCIPLINED
- ACCOUNTABLE
- ENERGETIC
- POWERFUL
- ASSERTIVE
- ORGANIZED
- SPONTANEITY
- DELIBERATE
- PERSONAL HONOR
- PERSONAL POWER
- SELF-CONFIDENCE
- IN CONTROL
- NON-DOMINATING POWER
- CREATE YOUR OWN IDENTITY
- RESPONSIBLE FOR CHOICES

EXCESSIVE ENERGY

- ANGRY
- CRITICAL
- PERFECTIONIST
- DOMINATING
- CONTROLLING
- CONSTANTLY ACTIVE
- STUBBORN
- ARROGANT
- POWER HUNGRY
- DOMINEERING

Intention: Find Passion and Purpose
Human experience: Self-definition (insecurity and shame)
Spiritual practice: Self-discovery (self-worth and personal power)

What makes you feel strong and confident?
What is the vision and mission for your life?

Think through your timeline.
When did you feel small or insignificant?

What did your childhood environment teach you about your worth and purpose in this life? Do you have a fixed-mindset or a growth-mindset when it comes to your ability to live the life of your dreams?

How do you respond when you make a mistake or fail at something?
Do you criticize yourself when you meet challenges?

My Experience with Insecurity and Shame

"Until you make the unconscious conscious, it will direct your life and you will call it fate."
—Carl Jung

Soon after my marriage ended, I dove headfirst into a new relationship. I don't know if I was running away from my reality or running away from myself, but either way, I found refuge with him. Our vibe was cool and authentic, vulnerable and free. It was such an easy connection, so I decided to settle in and get comfortable. But Karma doesn't forget and she was on her way to find me.

"Chemistry isn't enough to build a long-lasting relationship. It makes for a wonderful, fun affair, but for the long term? There's so much more to it than that. I finally realized that a solid relationship isn't between two people who share interests, it's between two people who share priorities. Get that figured out before you give your heart away."
—Unknown

We dated long distance for a year. Because we shared a love for travel and adventure, we would meet up once a month to explore some new destination. We packed as much fun as possible into our weekend excursions before returning to our separate lives in separate states. It wasn't until he moved closer that we realized we had very different ideas of what a full-time relationship was going to look like. I was a single parent with limited time. He was a bachelor with all the time in the world. I worked all day and went home to a child, dinner, chores, to-do lists, and bedtime stories. He worked all day and went home to relax, drink a beer, put his feet up, watch TV, and order takeout. Our lives were as different as night and day, and neither of us were willing to bend. I needed him to be gentle, patient, and supportive; he was aggressive, overbearing, and arrogant. He needed me to be submissive, attentive, and accommodating—I was assertive, distracted, and annoyed. My number one priority was my daughter. Everything else was secondary.

"I hope you find a love that inspires dancing instead of walking on eggshells. I hope you are able to breathe deeply in their presence instead of holding your breath."
—Dr. Thema

I was thirty years old, emotionally drained, and unprepared for what I had gotten myself into. I was pouring all of my energy into creating a consistent routine for my daughter and the only way I knew how to protect her was to keep my life as her mom separate from my life as his girlfriend. As my days continued to be filled with the responsibilities of parenting, he was starting to feel like an outsider looking in. He could not understand why two people who were divorced would continue to talk regularly, but I was committed to collaborating with my ex-husband peacefully for the benefit of my child. He went ballistic if he thought I was being "too nice" to my ex on the phone. He hated when it was my turn to pick up or drop off. What seemed like little things to me, made him explode. There were so many red flags leading up to the nightmare, but I continued to pacify him and make excuses. I kept telling myself that things would calm down eventually—we just needed more time to figure it all out. To be honest, I felt like my back was against the wall. I fully participated in creating this relationship and much had been sacrificed on both ends to make it work. I rationalized to myself that we were in too deep to jump ship. I justified staying as a sign of growth, because my usual response to emotional overload was to disappear. I did love him, and I stayed in it because I believed it would get better. But jealousy and resentment soon turned into rage and revenge.

Truth is, it wasn't our first rodeo. He and I gave dating a shot ten years prior, during our college years. What started out as a pretty cool friendship naturally evolved into a relationship. He was charming and funny, laid back, and unbothered most of the time—an easygoing kind of guy. He grew up in the North, an extreme extrovert and die-hard sports fan. He could carry on a conversation with anyone and loved nothing more than saving freshly printed hundred-dollar bills to add to his collection. His face lit up every time he told a funny story, laughing so hard that tears would fill his eyes and run down his cheeks. That, in turn, made me laugh so hard that tears would fill my eyes and run down my cheeks. He was silly and happy, and I loved that about him. Our college years were packed full of wild adventures. Together, we were fire and ice; passion and rage; a *beautiful fucking disaster*. During the week, I lived on research, painting, and coffee. During the weekends, I lived on cocaine, ecstasy, and adrenaline. We were partygoers and thrill seekers. West Virginia University is in the heart of the peaceful Appalachian Mountains, but the small city of Morgantown does not sleep; Parties, alcohol, and drugs, 24/7/365. Some call it the black hole because once you get pulled into it, it is almost impossible to make it out. Just the other day a friend said to me, "If you can graduate from WVU, you can do anything because the odds are literally stacked against you."

After three years of living and dating in the same city, we decided to move in together. My daughter was a bit older, so I felt comfortable taking a step forward. We found a home in a quiet neighborhood and signed a lease. It was October. I was walking ahead of myself, but I just knew a proposal would be coming soon. On the weekends, he took me to try on rings, and often spoke of wedding plans, and having more children. When I think back on it now, I still can't place the exact time when it all went left. It was a slow and gradual unraveling, even though it all happened in the blink of an eye. He blamed his late nights out on "poker with the guys." His absence all day Sunday was just "football with the boys." Anytime I confronted him about anything that didn't add up, he would turn into a ball of rage—aggressive and mean—just like my father. I would cower and sink into myself, overwhelmed by his energy and his presence. He called me insecure and told me that I was crazy. It didn't take long before I started to question my own sanity. Was I imagining things? Was I making all of this up in my head? The irony was, as long as I pretended like nothing was happening, he pretended as well. We ate dinner together and played board games as a family almost every night after work. He still pulled me close and held my hand and kissed my forehead. He continued to cuddle up next to me at night and tell me how much he loved me.

January.

It was Sunday and I was home cleaning house, doing laundry, and prepping for the week ahead. It was time to switch loads and when I pulled his jeans out of the basket, a yellow sticky note fell out of the pocket. Written on the note, in his handwriting, was a woman's name and a telephone number. It took me the rest of the day to gather up enough courage to call it because I already knew what she was going to say. She confirmed that not only were they dating, but that their relationship began back in September; an entire month before we even moved in together. And just like that, my entire world came crashing down. I knew I had to leave, but it felt wrong. Back in our party days, he watched over me and protected me. He had saved me from myself, many times; cleaned up my vomit, bathed my lifeless body, dressed me, and carried me to bed. During our adulting days, he supported me and cheered me on. He showed up early at events to set up and break down, hauling tents and tables, large paintings, and supplies. He pulled all-nighters with me regularly, pushing me to stay focused and meet deadlines. We cried in each other's arms during some major lows in both of our lives. Since the first time I met him, I have always felt this intense magnetic pull to be close to him. Not necessarily in a romantic way, rather guided by an inner knowing that my spirit had traveled through many lifetimes and many incarnations with his. There was a contentment in our shared vibration that felt like home. I couldn't shake it, no matter how bad I wanted to, or how many times I had tried. I thought he was my best friend. Turns out, as fate would have it, the one person I trusted the most, was the very person holding a knife in my back.

"Everything changes when you begin to love yourself. You no longer send out energy of desperation or need to be filled from the outside. You become a powerful source within yourself that attracts better. The more you love who you are, the less you seek validation and approval."
—Idil Ahmed

Self-definition is our natural desire to be distinguishable in the eyes of others, confirming to the ego, that the story we made up in our head about ourselves, is indeed true. When we don't have a deep sense of purpose in our lives, our worth is defined through the approval and validation of others. When my little world fell apart, I fell apart with it. I could not bathe enough to wash off the shame. My body felt dirty. My soul felt violated. I was so embarrassed that I isolated myself from friends and family so no one would know my secret. I was on my knees a lot those days. It was in the sea of my own despair that I heard God's voice. "Do not attach your worth to anything outside of yourself. See yourself the way that I see you."

"The real challenge for the individual is to practice evolution and to learn the lessons of the old stories so you no longer need to repeat them."
—Dr. Bruce Lipton, PhD

Personal power is key to healing and restoring this energy center. Every experience that has broken you, made you question your worth or ability, made you feel small or insignificant, can be used as fuel to ignite a fire of power, passion, and purpose in your life. Suffering is grace. It is the catalyst to transformation. Go back to those moments with a spiritual perspective. Learn the lessons so you can grow, heal, and evolve. Focus your attention on your dreams and goals, align your actions, think, and feel as if it already is, and watch as miracles begin to show up in your life. Personal power is a choice. You can give it away and play the victim of your life story, or you can harness it and be the creator of a life that is profoundly beautiful.

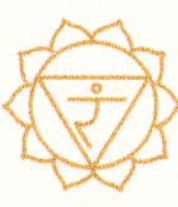

My Experience with Self-Worth and Personal Power

"No, we don't need more sleep. It's our souls that are tired, not our bodies. We need nature. We need magic. We need adventure. We need freedom. We need truth. We need stillness. We don't need more sleep… we need to wake up and live."

—Brooke Hampton

2016. Early midlife crisis. "How the fuck did I get here?!"

For my entire career, I worked my ass off. Full time through the day as a classroom art teacher and part time through the night in my studio. I taught after-school classes three days a week, every fall and spring semester; winter and summer art camps every year; and private and small-group lessons on the weekends. I worked hard; I worked a lot. I was living in the matrix, conditioned by American culture to consume myself to happiness. My focus was on achieving the next best thing, climbing to the next best level, acquiring the next best item. I had been running on the hamster wheel of life for ten years strong, but I had never really stopped to consider whether or not I actually wanted to be there. As I began to look around at my life, I found that I was bored with fake people, fake institutions, fake conversations. I was embarrassed by popular culture. I carried a tremendous grief in my heart for all the hate and violence in the world. I hit this mental wall and I was losing it. "Fuck bullies, fuck the way humans treat nature and animals, fuck the negative cages we build around ourselves, fuck feeling stressed and depressed, fuck the system and fuck this incompetent administration." I was uninspired by life and craving "the sacred" in a way that is hard to describe in words. I needed substance, meaning, depth, purpose. There was so much darkness in the world and my spirit was thirsty for light.

"You cannot breathe the air of anxiety and expect to live in an atmosphere of peace."

—Steven Furtick

Years of working with young people was weighing so heavy on my heart. There was such an overwhelming number of children who were stressed out, lonely, anxious, or depressed. Bullying was out of control. I saw it in classrooms, in the hallways, and on the playground. Self-harm and suicide rates among adolescents and teens were rising rapidly. Having a teenage daughter myself, who had also dealt with some pretty vicious bullying, I read as much research on the topic as I could get my hands on. I found a study from 2010 conducted by the University of Michigan reporting that children were 40% less empathetic today than we were thirty years ago. That's almost half! "So basically, these children are miniature sociopaths?" I found another report from 2014 by the American Trends Panel stating that over the previous three decades, parents saw responsibility and hard work as more important lessons to teach their children than empathy, tolerance, and moral compass. It all made sense. It seemed so obvious, but nobody was addressing it. We needed a deeper approach to education—one that would help students develop the tools that they needed to navigate and manage their own heads and hearts.

> *"When you give birth to that which is within yourself … what you bring forth will save you. If you possess nothing within… That absence will destroy you."*
> —Gospel of Thomas, Saying 70

I was inspired to create a curriculum that taught to the Spirit, full of exploration, discovery, creative expression, and peaceful practice. My goal was to help children become more sophisticated in their thinking and more distinguished in their character, leading to the expression of their greatest potential. It would offer a practical framework for navigating the physical, emotional, intellectual, and electrical identities. In addition to social-emotional learning and mindfulness techniques, it would teach honor and reverence for all expressions of life and a deep appreciation for being alive. Lessons would focus on self-awareness, self-regulation, emotional intelligence, self-healing techniques, social intelligence, moral and ethical decision-making, and global goals. It would inspire collaborative roundtables and innovative design for fighting injustice. It included math, science, and writing integration with differentiated instruction, and met the state and national standards and objectives for visual art.

> *"The answers you seek never come when the mind is busy, they come when the mind is still."*
> —Unknown

In the evenings, over the course of a year, I worked at home developing the curriculum. I prayed every night, asking God to guide me through the process. Then I would sit in meditation and wait to hear from Him. Every night, He answered. Divine downloads were being given to me so quickly, I had a really hard time keeping up. Information was moving through me, but it was not from me. It was the most amazing experience. It was beautiful and powerful and magical. The following school year, I brought pieces of each unit into my classroom for the purposes of research and refinement. My students not only embraced these lessons, they begged me every week for more.

Mid-spring, I presented my work and findings to my boss. My request was to be moved to the middle school the following year so that the impact of this work could be made on the most vulnerable population. Not only was my request denied, she told me it wasn't a good idea to publish because, "You're an art teacher, no one will take you seriously." She then proceeded to tell me a story about a time when she had a business plan that she thought was genius but ended up flopping in the end. "Just because you think it's good, doesn't mean that it actually is." I often wonder why leadership positions are given to managers. Though her intention was to take me down, I left her office with my head held high. I knew that what I had was golden, I just needed to trust God.

I left the building that day with two items on my to-do-before-bed list:

- Submit my work to other educational institutions around the globe
- Create a vision board

I began incorporating my vision board into my meditation practice, every day. I visualized the images in my head, I felt the emotion in my heart, and I practiced feeling the vibration in my body as if all of my dreams were already a reality. Every day, March through June, I turned on Hillsong United, sat on my yoga mat, and dedicated time to stillness and manifestation. Four months later, I received a call about my curriculum and was offered a position in the Bahamas. I put in my notice at work, sold just about everything I owned, packed my daughter, two dogs, and ten suitcases, and jumped on a plane. I had absolutely no intention of looking back.

Self-discovery is the burning away of old beliefs, expectations, people, and ideologies that are no longer aligned with your Highest truth. It is the journey of following your spirit and speaking with your soul, the pilgrimage towards your greatest expression of passion and purpose. I read somewhere that the reason people wake up, is because they finally stop agreeing to things that insult their soul. Look at your thoughts, actions, and behaviors. Look at the people around you. Who is the creator of your daily reality? If you fail to discover and exercise your spiritual gifts, you will soon find yourself apathetic and uninspired by life. Your entire reality will begin to change the moment you choose to empower greatness within yourself and focus your energy in a positive direction.

"The meaning of life is to find your gift. The purpose of life is to give it away."
—Pablo Picasso

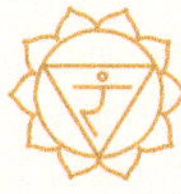

PEACEFUL ✦ PRACTICE
Solar Plexus Chakra

Your true nature is deeper than anything you think you are or what anyone says you are. You are infinite potential; as expansive as the Universe; as sacred as the Divine. You were never meant to be small. When you shrink yourself to fit where you don't belong, you diminish the value of your existence. Create a vision, set your intention, and move forward with purpose.

Imagine the best possible version of yourself. What are your gifts? What would you do with your life if there were nothing holding you back? How would your life unfold if you were writing your own story? Imagine how you would feel living this life. This is who you really are. Unattach from any part of yourself that says otherwise.

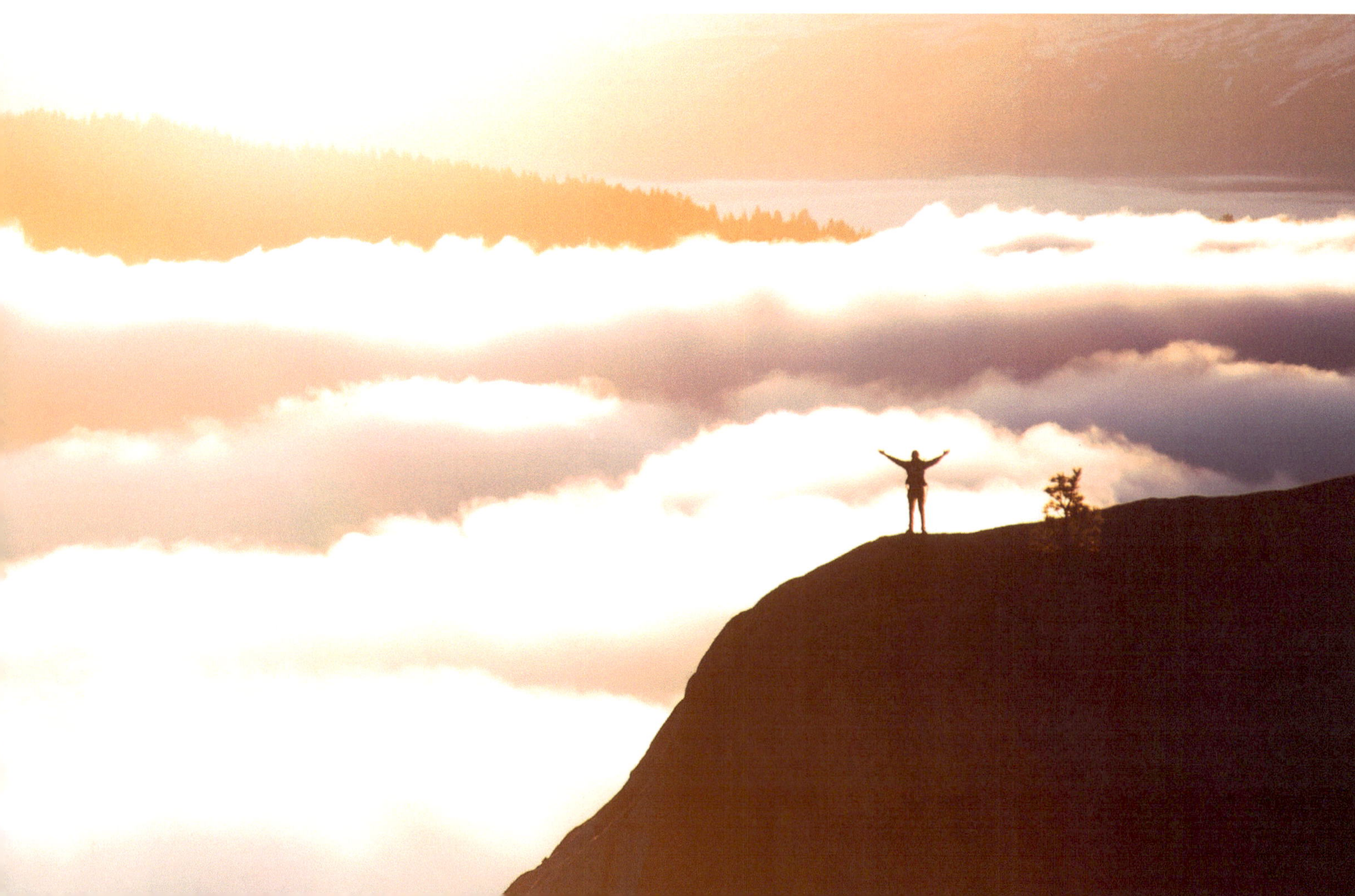

HOLISTIC WELLNESS

Practice Finding Passion and Purpose: Rise from the Ashes

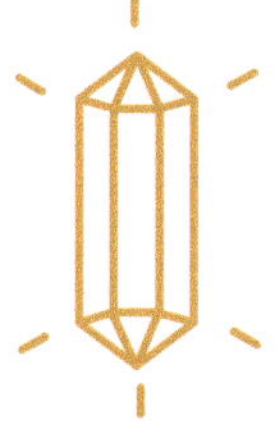

CRYSTALS

Tigers Eye, Citrine, Rutilated Quartz, Honey Calcite

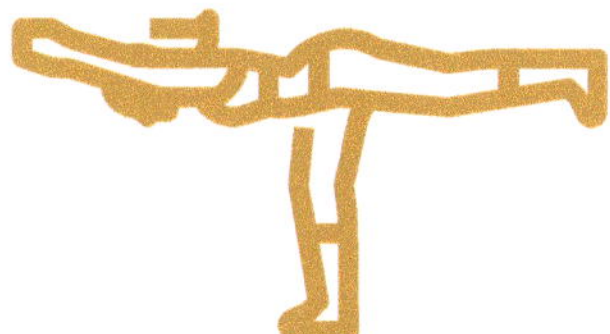

YOGA

Warrior III

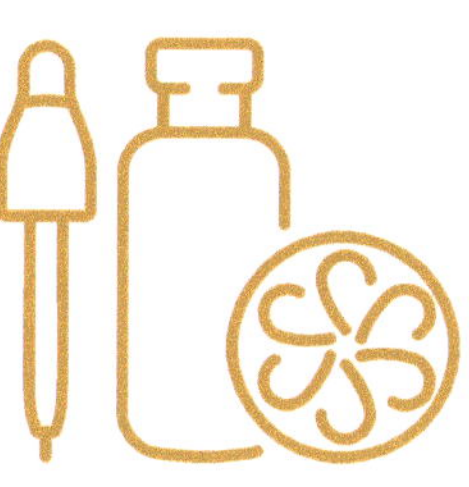

ESSENTIAL OILS

Rosemary, Grapefruit, Lemon, Cardamom, Marjoram, Vetiver

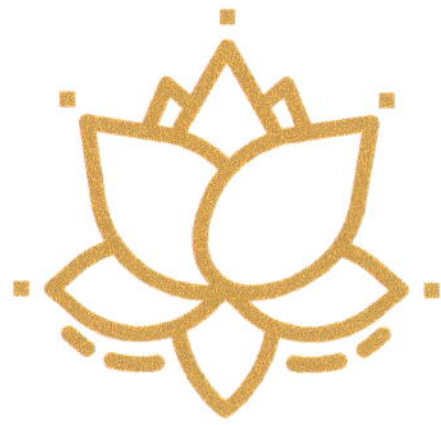

OCCUPATIONAL WELLNESS

Balance work and leisure time, build relationships with coworkers, and manage workplace stress.

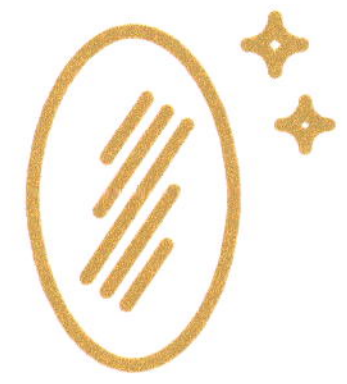

AFFIRMATION

I am confident, whole, and capable of my wildest dreams. I am aligning myself with the Life Force Energy that runs through me. I shine brightly in the world.

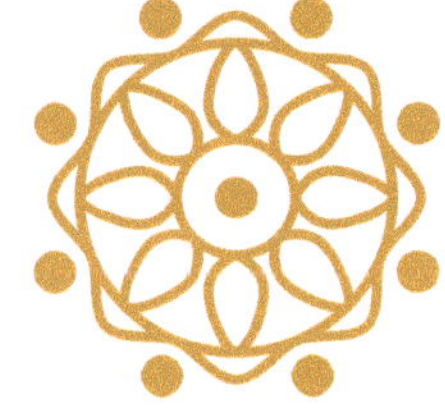

MEDITATION

Close your eyes and imagine the best possible version of yourself and of your life. Experience your visions vividly using all five senses. Feel it as if it is already a reality.

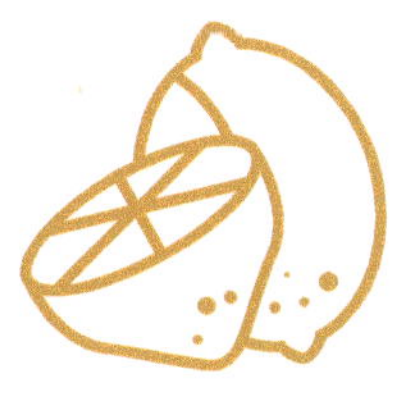

FOOD

Yellow Peppers, Yellow Lentils, Yellow Squash, Oats, Spelt, Bananas, Pineapple, Lemons, Sprouted Grains

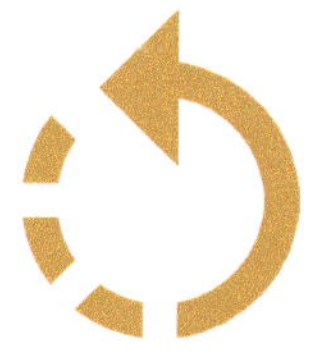

PURPOSE

An intuitive guide pushing your energy in the direction of passion, meaning, and substance.

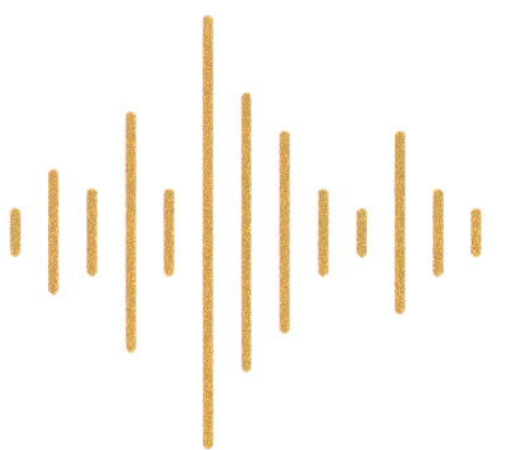

SOUND

Bring transformation and miracles into your life.

528 Hz

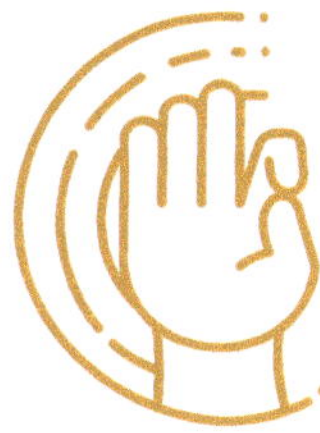

MUDRA

"Will Power"

Place hands between your heart and your stomach. Fingertips touch, thumbs overlap.

Long R-A-A-A-A-M

COLOR

Yellow Increases: Fun, Humor, Lightness, Personal Power, Intellect, Logic, Creativity

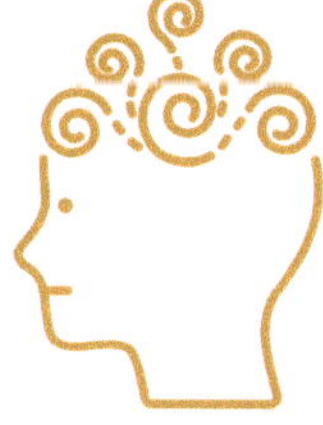

MANIFESTATION

"Hold a thought for 17 seconds and the law of attractions kicks in. Hold a thought for 68 seconds and things begin to move: Manifestation has begun."
—Abraham Hicks

CREATIVE FLOW
Artistic Expression

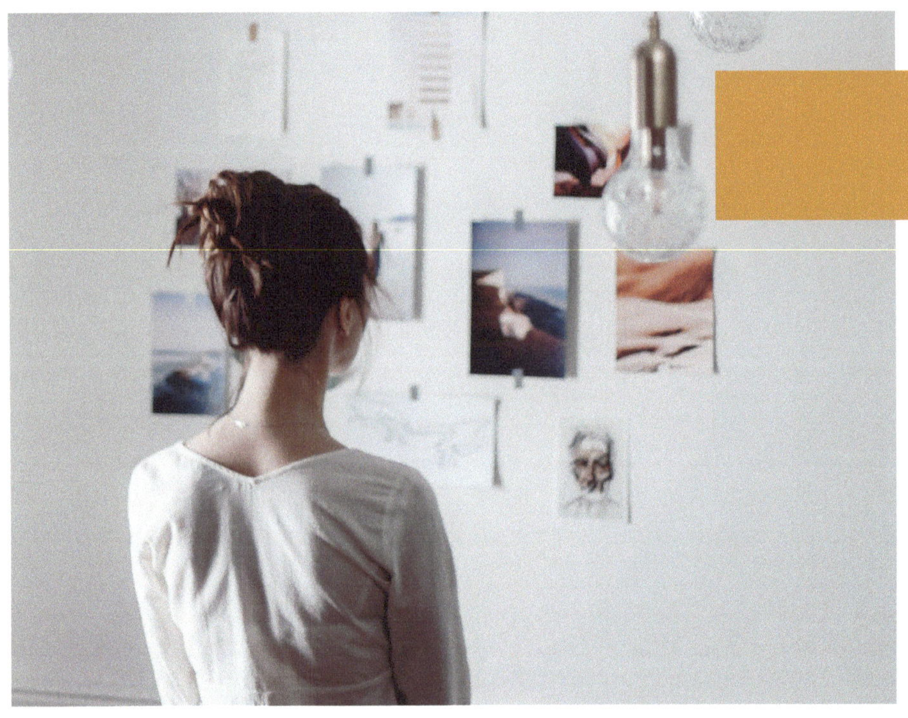

You have the power to change your life—the challenge is to change your mind. Program your mind to believe that you have what it takes to achieve greatness, and watch greatness begin to manifest. Overcome your limiting beliefs, upgrade your vision, and align yourself with purpose.

Materials Needed

Large Board or Canvas

Glue

Scissors

Magazines

"I Am" words/text/phrases

Embellishments (optional)

Sealant

Brush

*"This is the season she will make beautiful things.
Not perfect things but honest things. That speak to
who she is and who she is called to be."*

—*Morgan Harper Nichols*

Intention: Find Passion and Purpose
Human experience: Self-definition (insecurity and shame)
Spiritual practice: Self-discovery (self-worth and personal power)

VISION BOARD

Instructions

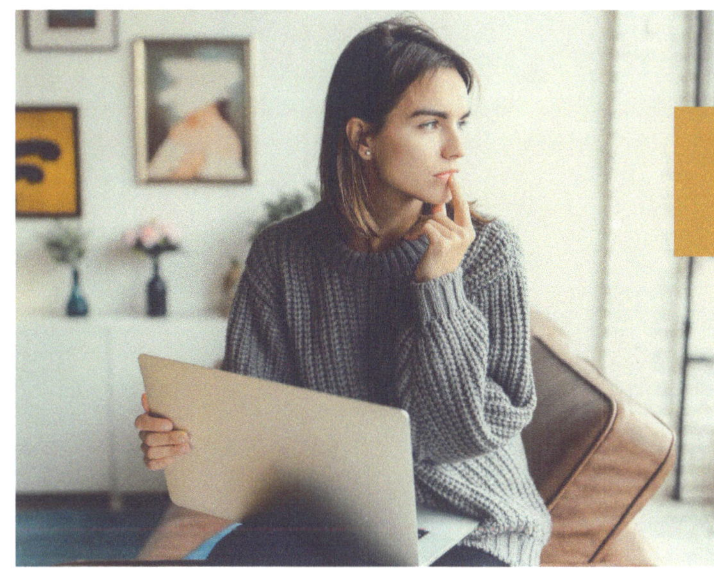

Step 1

Decide what you want to bring into your life over the next three years. Use the categories in Step 2 to help organize and focus your answers; three questions per category. Give yourself permission to dream big!

Ask yourself these questions for each category:
What goals are you moving towards?
Why do you want to achieve these goals?
Why do you deserve them?

Step 2

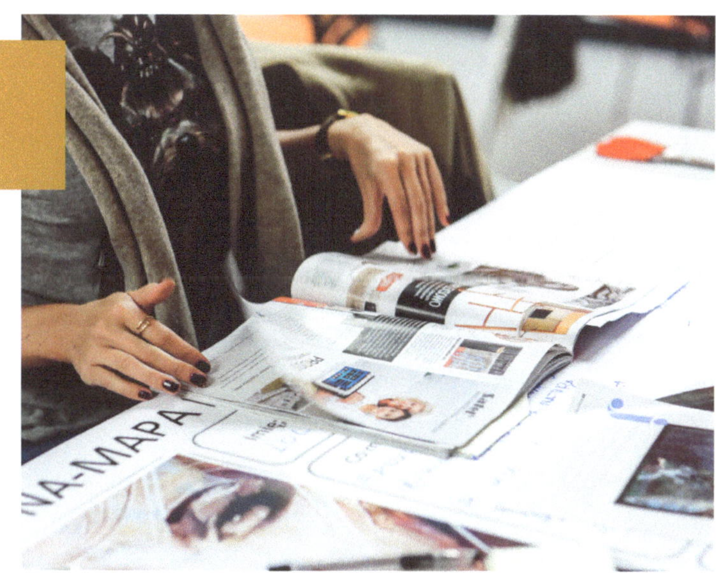

Cut out magazine clippings that represent the following categories for you:

Spiritual	Health
Family	Financial
Career	Travel
Personal Growth	Other
Social	

VISION BOARD
Instructions

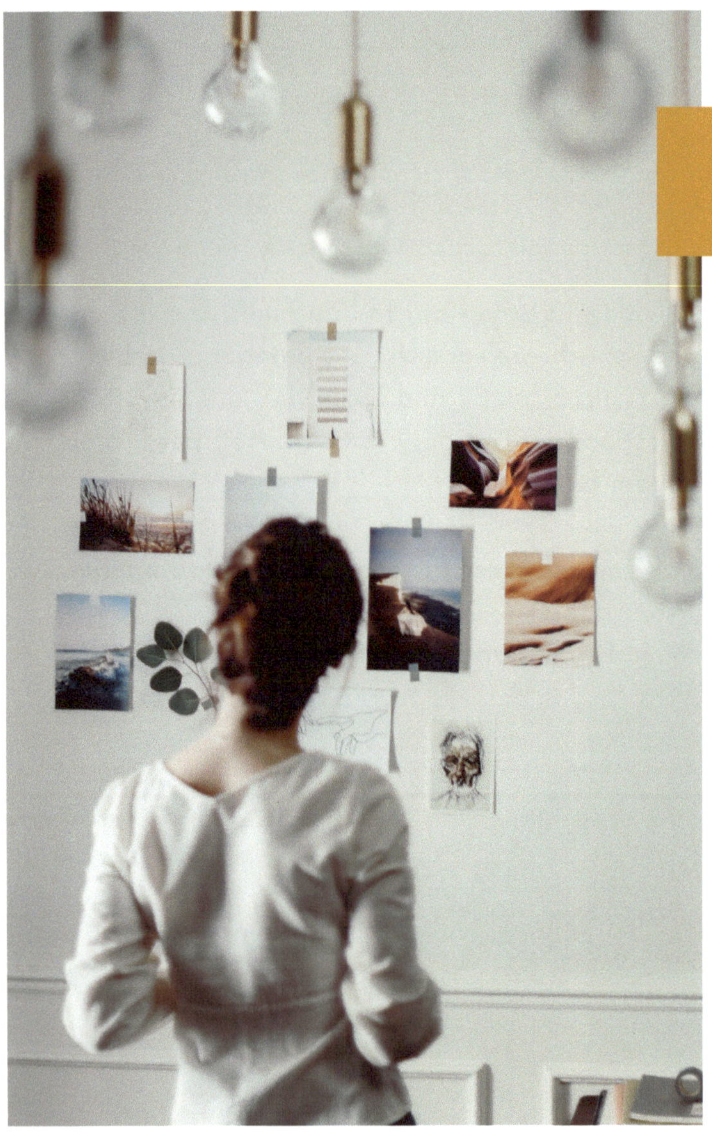

Step 3

Create a beautiful collection of images that represent your answers. Choose "I AM" words that reaffirm your vision. You can print or cut text from magazines. Purchase a canvas or recycle a large board to use as your foundation. Be sure to arrange and rearrange your images and text until you create a balanced composition. Large images first, then smaller images, add words and phrases on top. Finish with embellishments if you want to dress it up a bit! When you are happy with your design, take a picture just in case things shift while you are working. Glue everything on, starting with the background, working towards the foreground. Add a layer of sealant on top to secure your design. Make sure to display your board where you can see it everyday. This practice helps you to be more mindful in your day, focusing your attention and energy towards dreams and goals. Make your vision board part of your daily routine to raise your vibrational frequency and to become a conscious creator of your reality.

"Whatever we plant in our subconscious mind and nourish with repetition and emotion will one day become a reality."
—Earl Nightingale

TIME TO REFLECT

"Finding yourself" is not really how it works. You aren't a ten dollar bill in last year's winter's coat pocket. You are also not lost. Your true self is right there, buried under cultural conditioning, other people's opinions, and inaccurate conclusions you drew as a kid that became your beliefs about who you are. "Finding yourself" is actually returning to yourself. An unlearning, an excavation, a remembering who you were before the world got its hands on you."

—Emily McDowell

TIME TO REFLECT

CONSCIOUS CONNECTIONS

Do good for goodness sake

Create goals to pursue

Level up

Work/Life balance

Align your words with your actions

Try something new

Discover your purpose:
List your top 10 values
List 5 things you love to do
List 5 things you're good at
List 5 things the world needs
List 5 things you can get paid to do
Connect the dots

Listen to podcasts

Read books

DID YOU KNOW?

PSYCHIC ORIGAMI

"Think of someone or something you hate. Now write down everything you despise about them/it in a long list, all the things that enrage you, that make you cry out at the injustice, venality, idiocy, and cruelty of that person/thing. Now take that list and write your own name at the top of it.

Say hello to your Shadow."

"We are not human beings having a spiritual experience, we are spiritual beings having a human experience and Infinite love is the only truth; everything else is an illusion."
—Pema Chodron

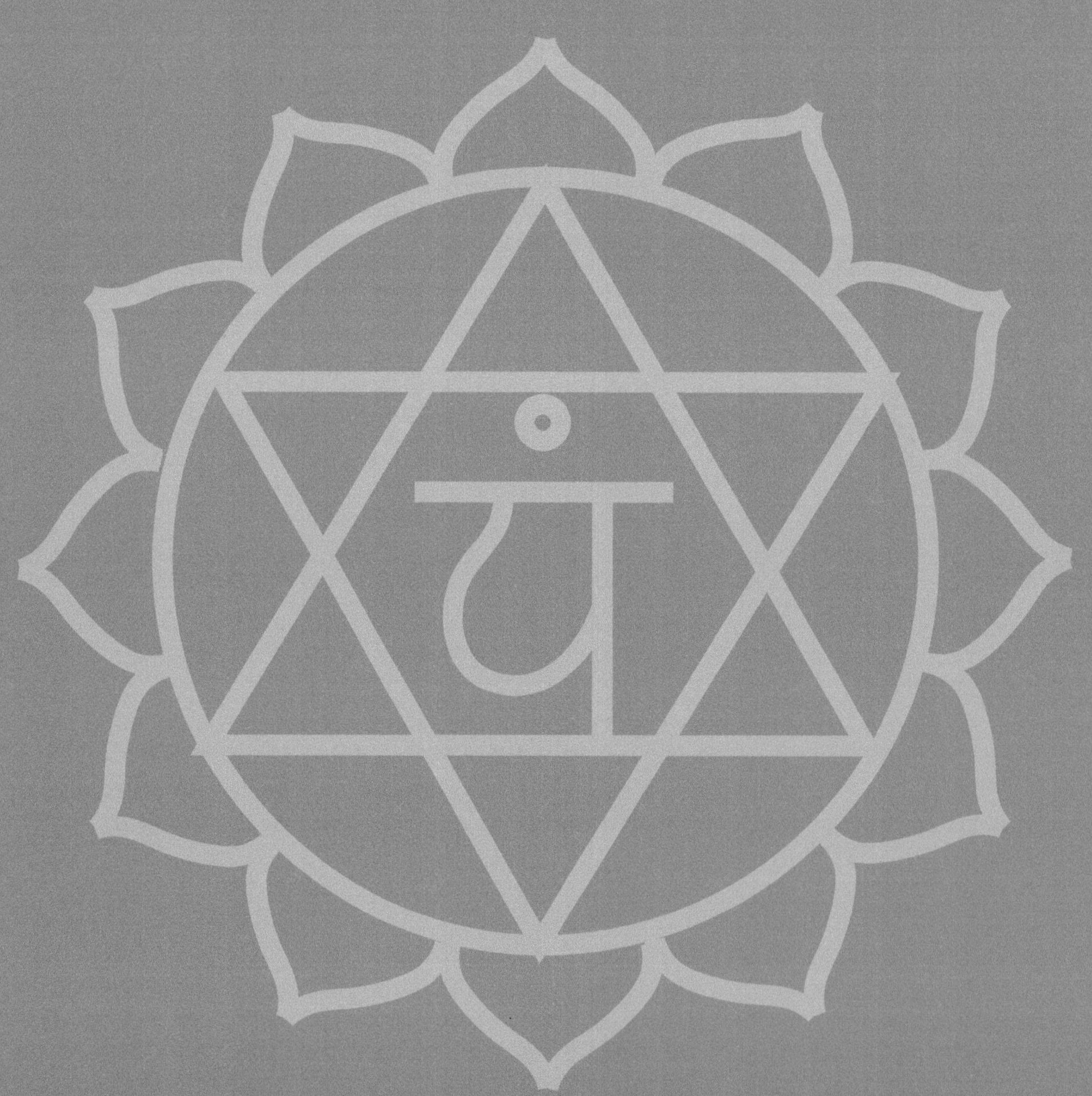

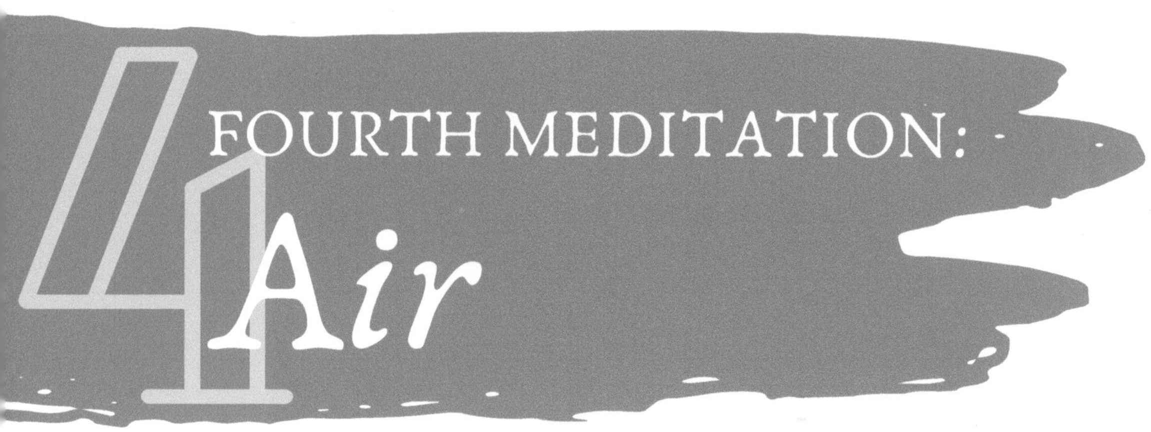

The Heart Chakra represents Air, the breath in your lungs, and is the bridge between your physical and spiritual reality.

Allow your Higher Self to comfort the parts of you that are still hurting. Go inside and mend all of your broken pieces. You are not a victim, you are an alchemist. Pour love into yourself as if it were a sacred offering to the Divine. Breathe in forgiveness and grace. Breathe out love and compassion. Gentle is the only way to the other side.

When you return to Love, the Universe sends Love.

What is your self-love language? Make a list. What are the best ways to pour love into yourself?

"You owe yourself the Love that you so freely give to other people." —Alexandra Elle

Intention: Nourish the Soul
Human experience: Self-acceptance (grief and sadness)
Spiritual practice: Self-understanding (grace and compassion)

HEART CHAKRA:

Love, compassion, balance, inner peace, expansion

ELEMENT: *Air*

IDENTITY: *Social*

LOCATION: *Heart, Lungs*

INTENTION: *Nourish the Soul*

The Heart Chakra processes the awareness of love and compassion and is blocked by feelings of grief and sadness.

"As you awaken, you will come to understand that the journey to love isn't about finding the one. The journey is about becoming the one."

—Unknown

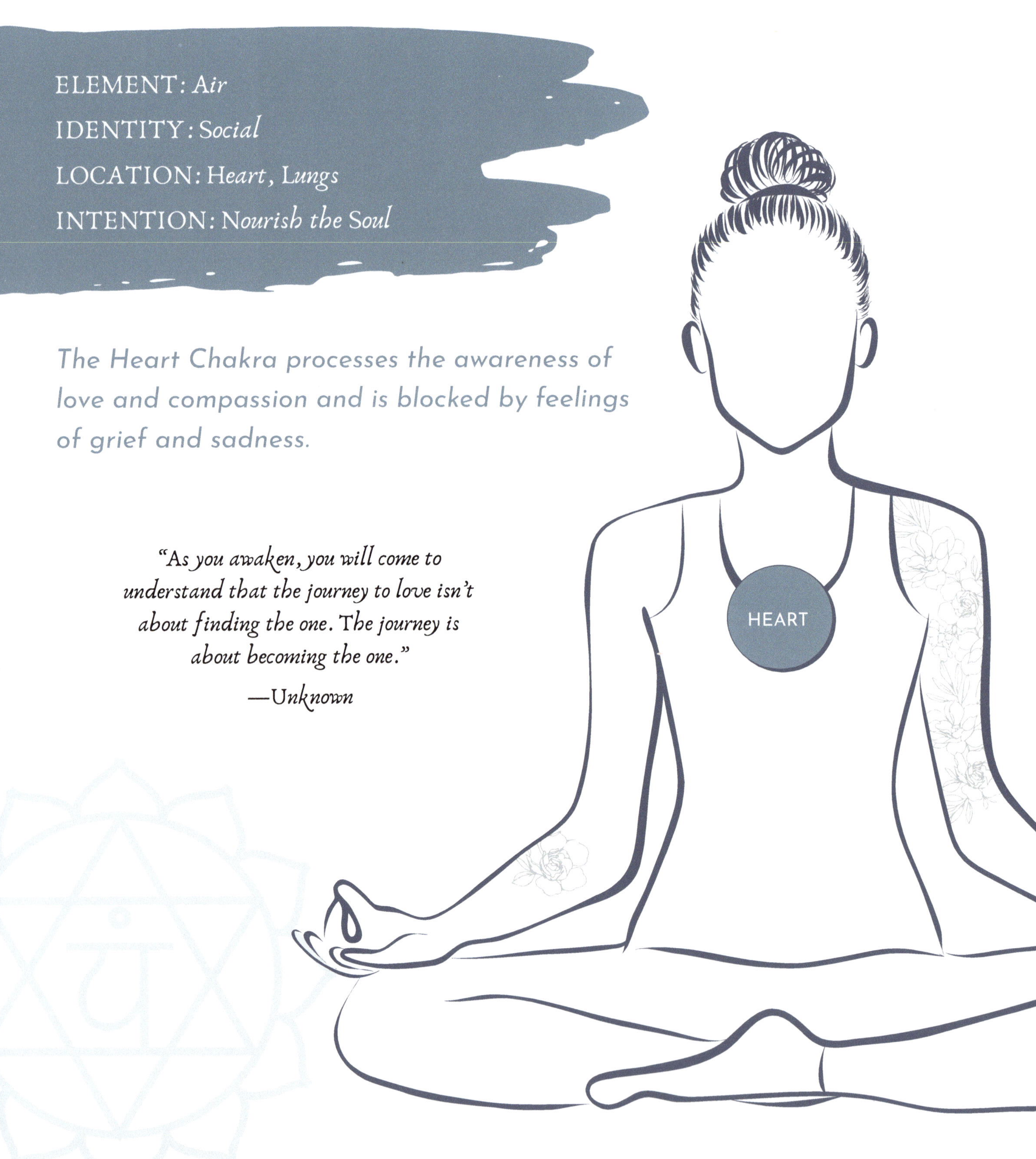

HEART CHAKRA:
Inhale Grace, Exhale Love

The following deficient and excessive energies carry low-vibrational frequencies. They are collected and stored in the heart chakra, blocking the flow of spiritual energy. If your thoughts, feelings, or behaviors fall into one of these two categories, the healing in this energy center has not yet begun.

Balanced energy in the Heart Chakra is learned in many ways through relationship with others. The secret is to fall in love with love. Be in love with yourself, in love with life, in love with people, in love with the Earth, in love with the animals, in love with every experience. It is all an expression of the only thing that is. You have an infinite amount of Love available and accessible to you at all times, as Love is the very essence of who you are. Love is who you are called to be.

Raise Your Vibration

DEFICIENT ENERGY	BALANCED ENERGY	EXCESSIVE ENERGY
• CRITICAL	• OPEN	• NEED FOR ATTENTION & APPROVAL
• INTOLERANT	• WARM	• CLINGY
• ISOLATED	• TOLERANT	• JEALOUS
• WITHDRAWN	• LOVING	• SELF-SACRIFICING
• UNCARING	• UNDERSTANDING	• POOR BOUNDARIES
• LONELY	• JOY	• CODEPENDENT
• EXCESSIVE BOUNDARIES	• COMPASSION	• GIVE TOO MUCH
• INABILITY TO FORGIVE	• FORGIVING	• PEOPLE PLEASING
• ANGER	• LOVE DEEPLY	• DEPLETE SELF
• RESENTMENT	• GENEROUS	
• HATE	• EMPATHETIC	
• DESPAIR	• PEACEFUL	
• LACK OF EMPATHY	• ACCEPTING	
• BITTER	• PATIENT	
• GRIEF STRICKEN		
• UNLOVED		
• BROKEN		

Intention: Nourish the Soul
Human experience: Self-acceptance (grief and sadness)
Spiritual practice: Self-understanding (grace and compassion)

What makes you feel loved? How do you pour love into others?

Think through your timeline. When in your life were you most sad?
What grief do you carry inside of your heart?

How do you respond when someone rejects you or your loving kindness?

What grudges are you still holding in your heart? Who do you need to forgive?

Intention: Nourish the Soul
Human experience: Self-acceptance (grief and sadness)
Spiritual practice: Self-understanding (grace and compassion)

What behaviors did you learn in your childhood in response to a lack of love, that were carried into your adult life?

What lesson is the Universe trying to teach you through those experiences in order to expand your consciousness?

My Experience with Grief and Sadness

"When you cannot be brave or strong, be love. It will lead you back home to yourself."
—K. Azizian

When my daughter was thirteen, she became very sick with pneumonia. She slept around the clock, only waking up for brief moments to take her medicine or go to the bathroom. When she was awake, she was delirious, talking about other worlds and asking questions that scared the hell out of me. It was like someone waking up after surgery, foggy, and confused from the anesthesia, except her disorientation was from fever and dehydration.

"1. You must let the pain visit 2. You must allow it to teach you 3. You must NOT allow it to overstay."
—Ijeoma Umebinyuo

The night before, all was normal. She crawled into bed with me because she wasn't feeling well, but I didn't think that it was anything out of the ordinary. When I woke up a few hours later to check on her, she was drenched in sweat and her temperature was 104. I tried to wake her, but she was lethargic, her words were slurred, and she could barely hold her eyes open. I knew that I had to get her to the hospital immediately—but I was alone and scared. I had never seen her like this, gasping for air, barely conscious. My gut reaction was to call her father. He lived in the same town but on the opposite end, about twenty-five minutes away. Surely, an emergency call at four o'clock in the morning about his sick daughter would sound the alarm and elicit some action! But after a brief conversation, I was forced to accept the fact that he wasn't coming. Tears welled up in my eyes, and an overwhelming sadness welled up in my heart. And there I was, a child again, unsure of my steps.

Funny how trauma will recreate itself over and over again after the initial beating. I was used to being alone. I was used to hard work and dirty hands. I was used to holding myself up with no safety net to fall into. But this was a different kind of alone. This "alone" hollowed out my stomach, took my breath away, made me panic. How was I going to get her lifeless body up a mountain of steps and into the car? How would I get the car turned on and heated without leaving her to lay there alone? How would I deliver her to the front door of the emergency room, park the car, and stay by her side all at the same time? I needed to get her dressed and pack a bag, but all I wanted to do was lay next to her, hold her, and tell her that everything was going to be OK. I wanted to nurture her and comfort her and cover her with the kind of healing energy only a mama can provide.

The next three mornings were exactly the same (i.e., wake up at four o'clock in the morning to a barely breathing child, panic, call child's father, die a little bit on the inside, call my best friend who came to our rescue within minutes every time, hospital check-in, hours of meds, released to go home, repeat).

On the fifth day, after she threw up everywhere, I carried her to the bathtub to bathe her. She sat hunched over and lifeless in the tub, as I gently lifted one limb at a time, cleaning the mess. In that moment, I realized how long it had been since she needed me to care for her in this way. The little girl who used to cuddle up next to me for bedtime stories had quickly turned into a teenager with A LOT of mouth (Lord, give me patience, AMEN!). It damn near breaks my heart watching her grow up and pull away as she becomes more independent and self-sufficient. Life is so fragile, and it passes by too fast, but I am comforted in the knowing that it is a blessing to be a mama, and it is a miracle to experience the immensity of love's vibration.

As I was re-soaping the loofah, she popped her head up, looked me straight in the eyes and said, "Mom, do you think God is a girl or a boy?" Surprised that she was awake, I smiled and said, "I don't know honey, what do you think?" "I think God is definitely a girl." With an amused smirk on my face, I considered her point, then shrugged and nodded in agreement. "Hmm. Really?" I responded, "Why do you think that?" "Well," she said, "Because girls are gentle and kind, and they take good care of you." And just as fast as she opened her eyes and looked at me, she closed them again, leaned against the side of the tub and dozed back off. So, there I was, awestruck by the incredible insight of a barely conscious teenager. I was pretty sure that my child just told me, in so many words, that I was God, and nobody was even there to witness the miracle!

—Heather B. Armstrong, It Sucked and Then I Cried

If I know what love is, it is because of her. She has softened my heart, given me a new set of lenses to view the world through. She teaches me patience, the importance of parenting peacefully, to play and laugh every day. I teach her to be kind and to walk with light, love, dignity, and grace. Her smile fills my heart with the brightest sunshine. Hearing her laugh is the sweetest sound that I have ever heard. She has taught me how to love selflessly and unconditionally. She is my reason to be better, to do better, to change, grow, and evolve. My approach is, "God, she is yours… guide me, so that I can guide her." Then I close my eyes, cross my fingers, sing, dance, hop on one toe, and meditate with the Universe—in the hope that the vulgar and shallow parts of the world will not erode her sense of self, worth, purpose, or direction. As a mother, I am committed to raising a young woman of integrity and substance. I can only hope that I make a fraction of an impact on her life, as she has made on mine.

—Unknown

Self-understanding is the ability to perceive ourselves, in relationship to others. I didn't understand the full capacity of my strength or the depth of my love until I had my daughter. Love is so profound, isn't it? Tears and joy. Sorrow and laughter. Peace and pain. My understanding of love has so much more depth now than it ever did in my younger years. Of course, life is one hell of a teacher. Grief will hollow out the toughest man, it rips the heart wide open. But it also expands our capacity to love. I am so very grateful to God for allowing me to raise and love and care for my daughter. She makes me a better human.

Grace is key to healing and restoring this energy center. To heal your heart, you must release the pain and anger you're holding for the people who have wronged you. From a conscious perspective, consider the offender's story. Hurt people hurt people. You must release the grip you have on some perfect story you made up about how things are supposed to be, and accept the story exactly as it is. Heal the saddest parts of your being with an outpouring of Love.

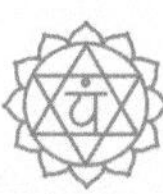

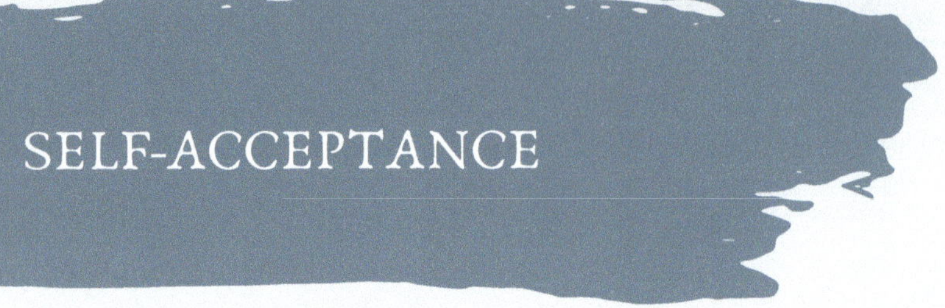

My Experience with Grace and Compassion

"The beginning of love is the will to let those we love be perfectly themselves, the resolution not to twist them to fit our own image. If in loving them we do not love what they are, but only their potential likeness to ourselves, then we do not love them: we only love the reflection of ourselves we find in them."

—Thomas Merton

"Late" is my middle name. The critics shake their heads and click their tongues. They offer love to others only when they see a reflection of themselves. The empaths smile and welcome me, regardless. They offer healing energy because they are beacons of light, givers of love and high vibration.

"She believed she could, so she did… but first she had to put the kids to bed and finish the laundry and make lunches… and figure out what that smell was. So she was late… but still, she did."

—Unknown

I am late for many reasons.

Reason 1: I am an artist. A creative. A wanderer. A dreamer. A constant receptacle of energy and inspiration and thoughts and ideas. I literally stop dead in my tracks to think through new ideas that randomly pop into my head. I get lost in deep reflection, contemplation, and introspection. I move with the wind, often floating away, mesmerized by the kaleidoscope of my own imagination. Then it hits me, "Shit, I'm late…"

Reason 2: I am an empath. I notice and feel all the things. I try to slow down, pay attention, experience each day with presence and mindfulness. I am pulled by a strong inner desire to comfort the hurting and feed the hungry, to give love where there is fear, and offer light where there is darkness. I save the bugs and talk to the animals. I save the animals and talk to the bugs. I am quick to offer a smile and I am generous with praise. One day driving to work, I saw a squirrel that had been hit on the road. It was shivering and scared, broken but still alive. I pulled over to be with it and acknowledge it's suffering because deep in my heart I knew that nothing alive should have to suffer alone. I give honor and respect to every expression of Life, all reflections of Source. Empaths are the healers of everything broken in this world, but we are simultaneously depleted by our calling. Once I am drained of energy, I withdraw from the chaos of the world in order to restore and replenish my vibration.

"DAMN IT, I'M LATE…."

Reason 3: I am curious. I love to explore and discover the world around me. I feel an urgency to take it all apart (how I see it and understand it), then put it all back together with my hands. I am in awe of the bark on a tree (what material would I use to create that texture?), the color green on a leaf (I wonder what blues and yellows I would mix together to get that exact hue?), the shapes of birds (how can I simplify those shapes on paper without losing the subject?).

"WTF KARA?!?! YOU'RE LATE..."

Reason 4: But mostly because I am a single parent with a shit ton of things to do by myself. There's no one to hand the baton to, no one to "tag, you're it," no one to pick up where I've left off, no one to offer a moment of rest when it all becomes too much. I do not rest, I do not put my feet up, I do not take a break, I do not stop moving, sunup to sundown. AND THAT SHIT IS EXHAUSTING. I am the parent, the housekeeper, the dog walker, the grocery collector, the food maker, the errand runner, the homeschool teacher, the business owner, the money earner, the bill payer, the badass superhero—and it's a lot of work for two hands.

> *"When we love and accept ourselves for the way that we are, flawed, broken, beautifully human, we empower others to celebrate their imperfections too. There will always be room for growth, and to love ourselves through the process is where our courage lives. For the right ones, you are enough. You are always enough."*
>
> *—Unknown*

Every day, I have to make a choice. I can live in my head, stressed out in the matrix, chained to someone else's clock. Or I can inhale grace and love, surrender and flow, align myself with Source, and allow my spirit to guide my steps. My Conscious Living mantra is, "grace over perfection." But my shadow is a gangsta, so she usually follows that up with, "Don't stress me tf out, *Karen*!"

> *"Health does not always come from medicine. Most of the time it comes from peace of mind, peace in the heart, peace in the soul. It comes from laughter and love."*
>
> *—Unknown*

Self-acceptance is giving honor and reverence to our Higher self, despite our human deficiencies, flaws, and imperfections. As a young lady, I spent many years holding myself to unrealistic expectations and tearing myself apart when I didn't live up to them. As an adult woman, I have learned to loosen my grip on life and not take myself too seriously. My biggest strength (free spirit, wild at heart, dancing to the beat of my own drum) is also my biggest weakness (I don't make it anywhere on time). Isn't it the most hilarious thing? We are expansive spiritual beings learning lessons through a lifetime of human experiences. We must learn to observe this irony with humor and love.

> *"Love is what we are; we don't get it from somebody, we can't give it to anybody, we can't fall in it or fall out of it. Love is our true being."*
>
> *—Krishna Das*

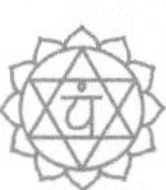

PEACEFUL ✦ PRACTICE
Heart Chakra

Embrace love.

Nourish your soul to restore your Spirit. Align yourself with the frequency of God/the Universe/Your Higher Self by emitting the frequency of Love and Abundance. Stop looking on the outside to be whole. You are every answer you have been searching for.

Close your eyes and bring to your awareness the people that you love. Imagine how you feel when you see them, the moments with them that make your heart full. Experience the feeling of that love bubbling over and filling you with warm Light. Breathe it in. Expand your lungs. Make room for growth and expansion.

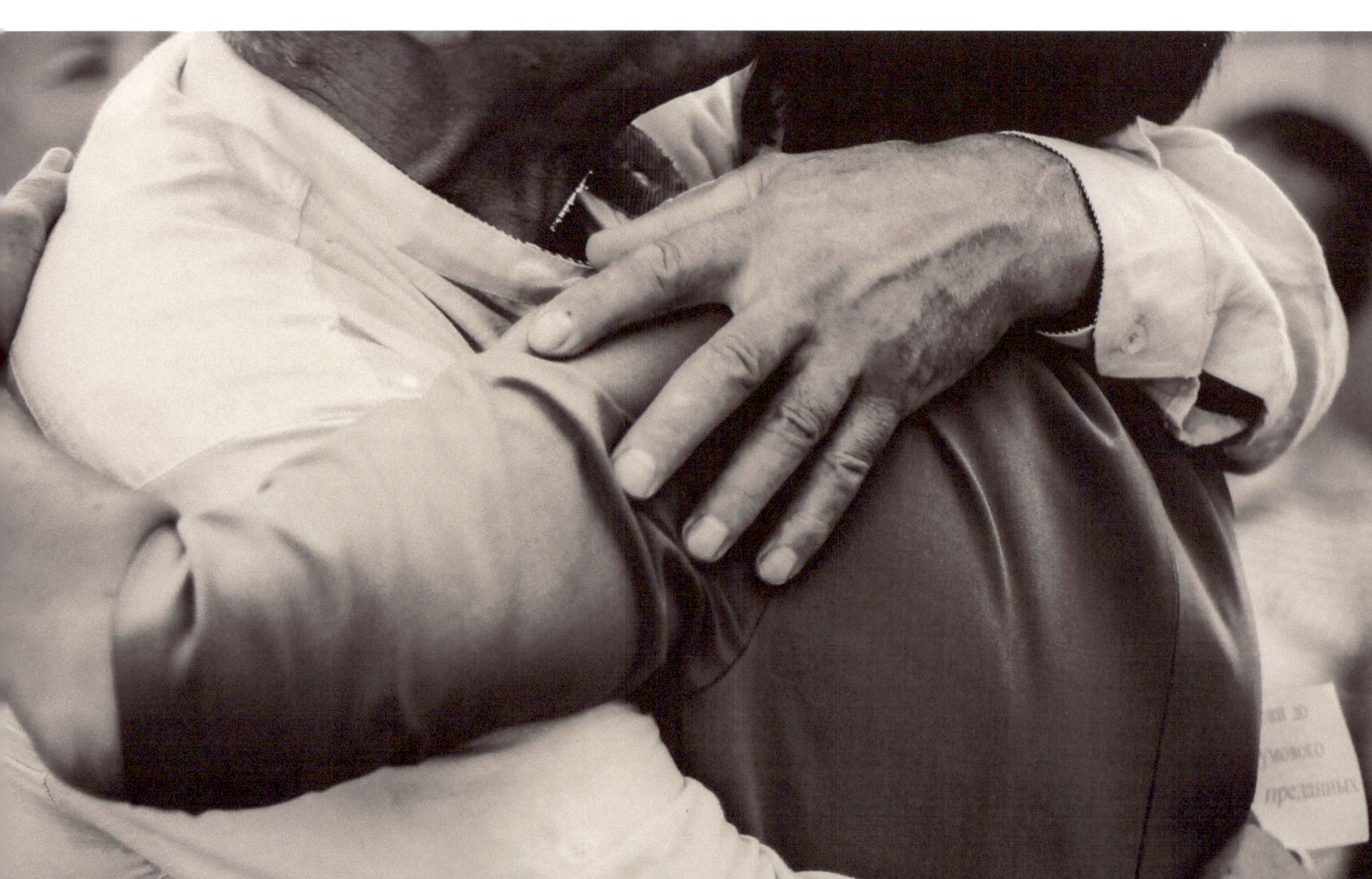

HOLISTIC WELLNESS

Practice Nourishing the Soul: Inhale Grace, Exhale Love

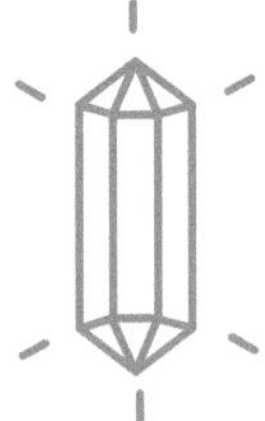

CRYSTALS

Emerald, Green Aventurine, Prehnite, Jade

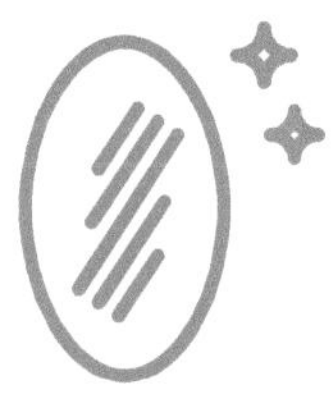

AFFIRMATION

I am kind to myself and others. I allow Grace and Love to guide my steps. I let go of the past and surrender to what is, trusting that the Universe will send exactly what my soul needs to complete itself.

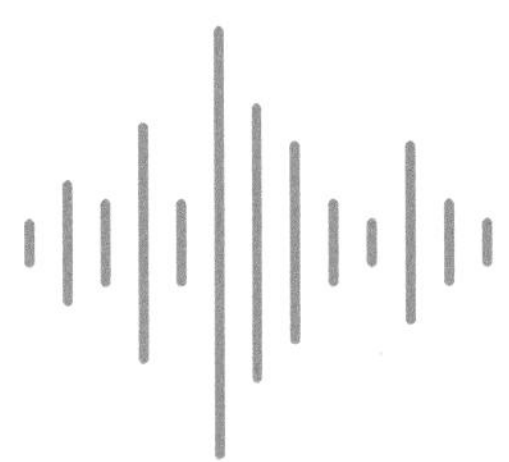

SOUND

Fill up with love and compassion.

693 Hz

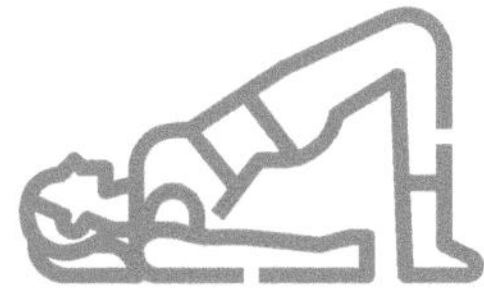

YOGA

Bridge Pose

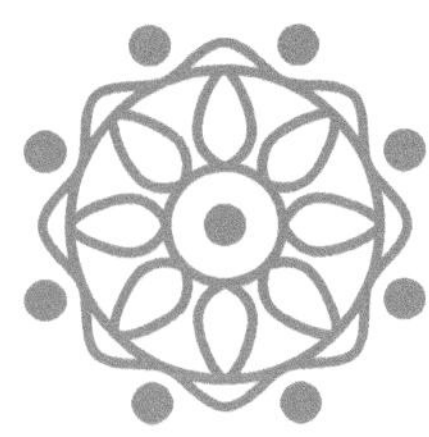

MEDITATION

Envision a person that you truly love. Feel this love expand from your heart and body, filling the room. Rest here. Love is awareness. Offer this expression of love to everyone you meet. Fall in love with being alive.

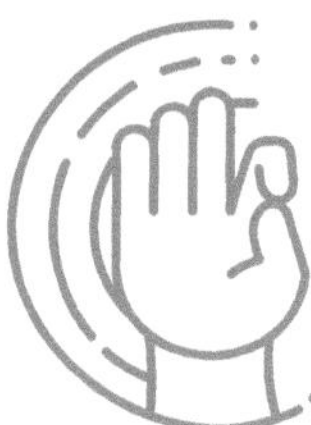

MUDRA

"Love"

Right Hand: Index finger and thumb touching at heart center. Left Hand in same mudra resting on the knee.

Long Y-A-A-A-A-M

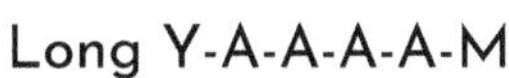

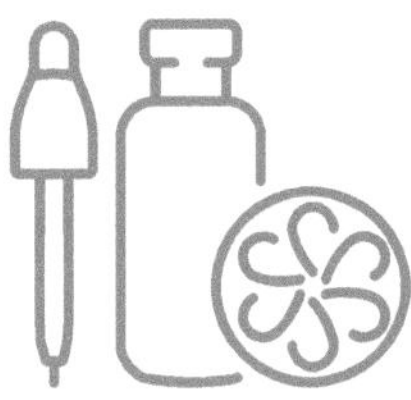

ESSENTIAL OILS

Pine, Eucalyptus, Rose Maroc, Amyris, Geranium

FOOD

Kale, Broccoli, Spinach, Chard, Dandelion Greens, Parsley, Celery, Cucumber, Zucchini, Avocado, Lime, Kiwi, Spirulina, Cabbage, Pears, Green Apples

COLOR

Green Supports: Balance, Harmony, Love, Social, Nature, Acceptance

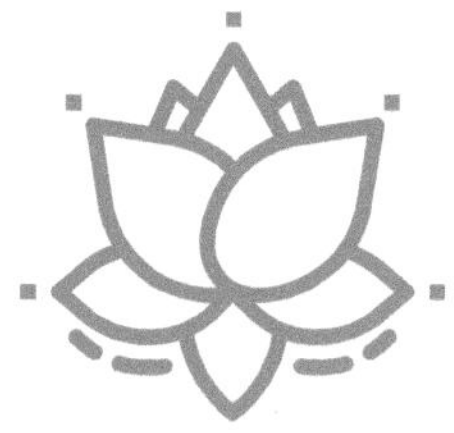

SOCIAL WELLNESS

A sense of connectedness and belonging. Creating positive relationships with self and others.

SOCIAL INTELLIGENCE

Being aware of how your energy affects other people, and how the energy of others affects you.

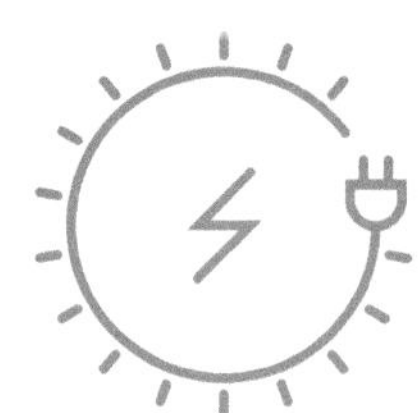

ELECTRIC BODY

50 trillion cells in the human body times 1.4 volts equals 700 trillion volts of electricity. With training and meditation, you can focus this energy and use it for healing.

CREATIVE FLOW
Artistic Expression

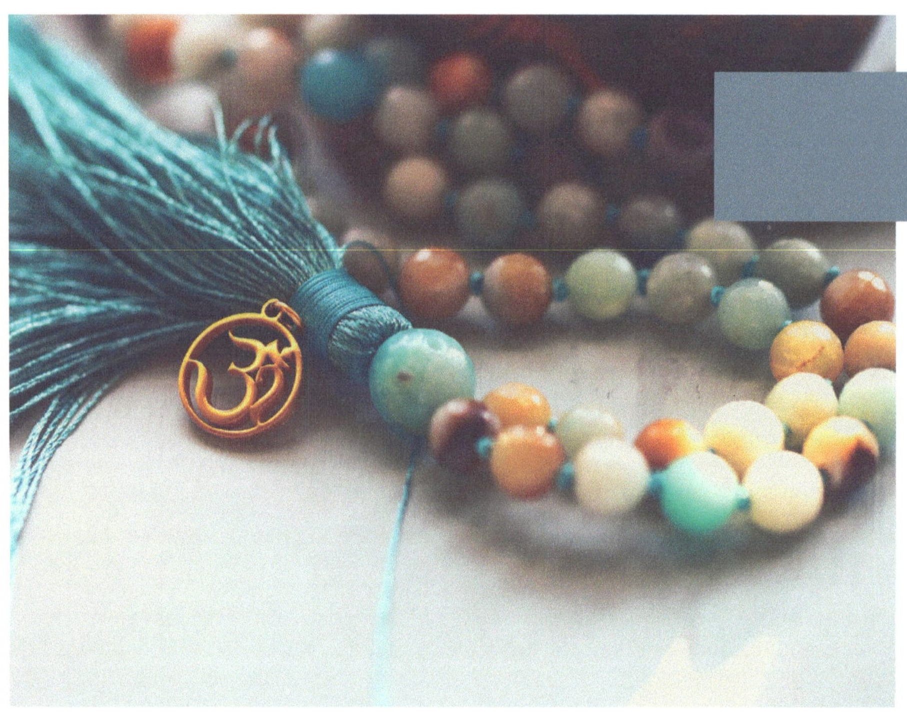

Mala Necklace

Malas are made of 108 beads and count your affirmations (or mantras), helping you to remain focused and present. There are many theories about the sacred number of 108. I am inspired by this one:

(1) = God / The Universe / Your Highest Truth

(0) = Emptying of "Self"

(8) = Infinity and Timelessness

Materials Needed

108 Beads + 1 Guru Bead

66 of color A

26 of color B

12 of color C

4 of color D (marker)

1 of color E (guru)

1 Tassel

3 ft of Beading Wire

Scissors

Bowls to organize and separate your materials

"Healing is an art… It takes time, it takes practice, it takes love."
—*Maza-Dohta*

MALA NECKLACE
Instructions

A Mala is a wearable reminder of your personal
journey and intention.

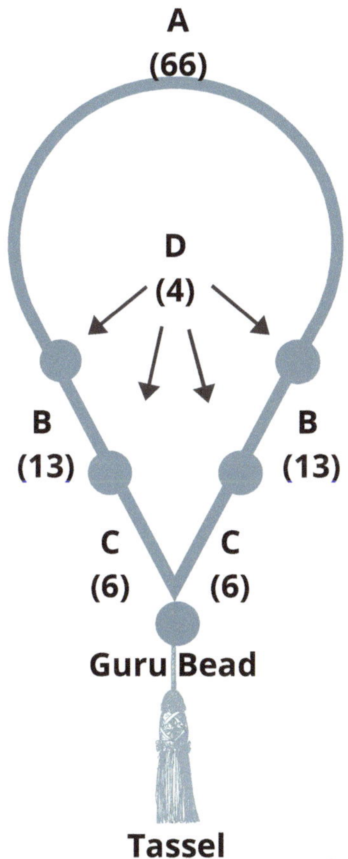

Step 1

Lay your beading wire down as shown. Your Mala
should be symmetrical with 54 beads on one side
and 54 on the other side. String all 66 "A" beads
first. Continue with "B" and "C" beads on the left
side, and then "B" and "C" beads on the right side.
Don't forget to add the "D" marker beads! Tie the
ends of the string together and finish with a knot.
Now add the guru bead and secure the tassel.

Step 2

Sit in practice with your Mala, chanting
your mantra out loud or in your head. Hold
your Mala in your right hand, starting with
the guru bead. Use your thumb to pull one
bead at a time towards you as you recite
your mantra. Do this 108 times, traveling
around the Mala, until you are back to the
guru bead. To continue your practice, reverse
direction and begin again.

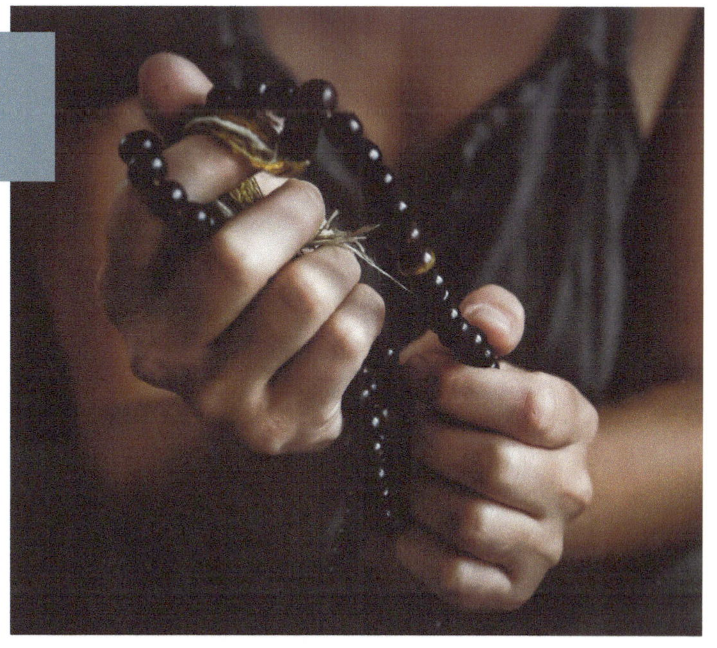

"What do you do when your world falls apart and you must confront the most wounded part of yourself? You hurt. You ache. You throb. You cleanse. You purify. You heal."

—Nikita Gill

CONSCIOUS CONNECTIONS

Set healthy boundaries

Be genuine with others

Pour love into yourself

Make self-care a priority

Build a healthy community around yourself

Offer grace to yourself and to others

Detox from technology and connect in-person

Practice self-acceptance and forgiveness

Love yourself unconditionally

Embrace laughter

Schedule time with family and friends

DID YOU KNOW?

Your heart emits an electromagnetic field that changes according to your thoughts and emotions, and can be measured several feet away from your body. Whether you are conscious of it or not, people, plants, and animals can feel your energy.

The heart is 100,000 times stronger electrically, and up to 5,000 times stronger magnetically than the brain. Master your thoughts and emotions to become a conscious creator of your reality.

"The quieter you become,
the more you are able to hear."
—Rumi

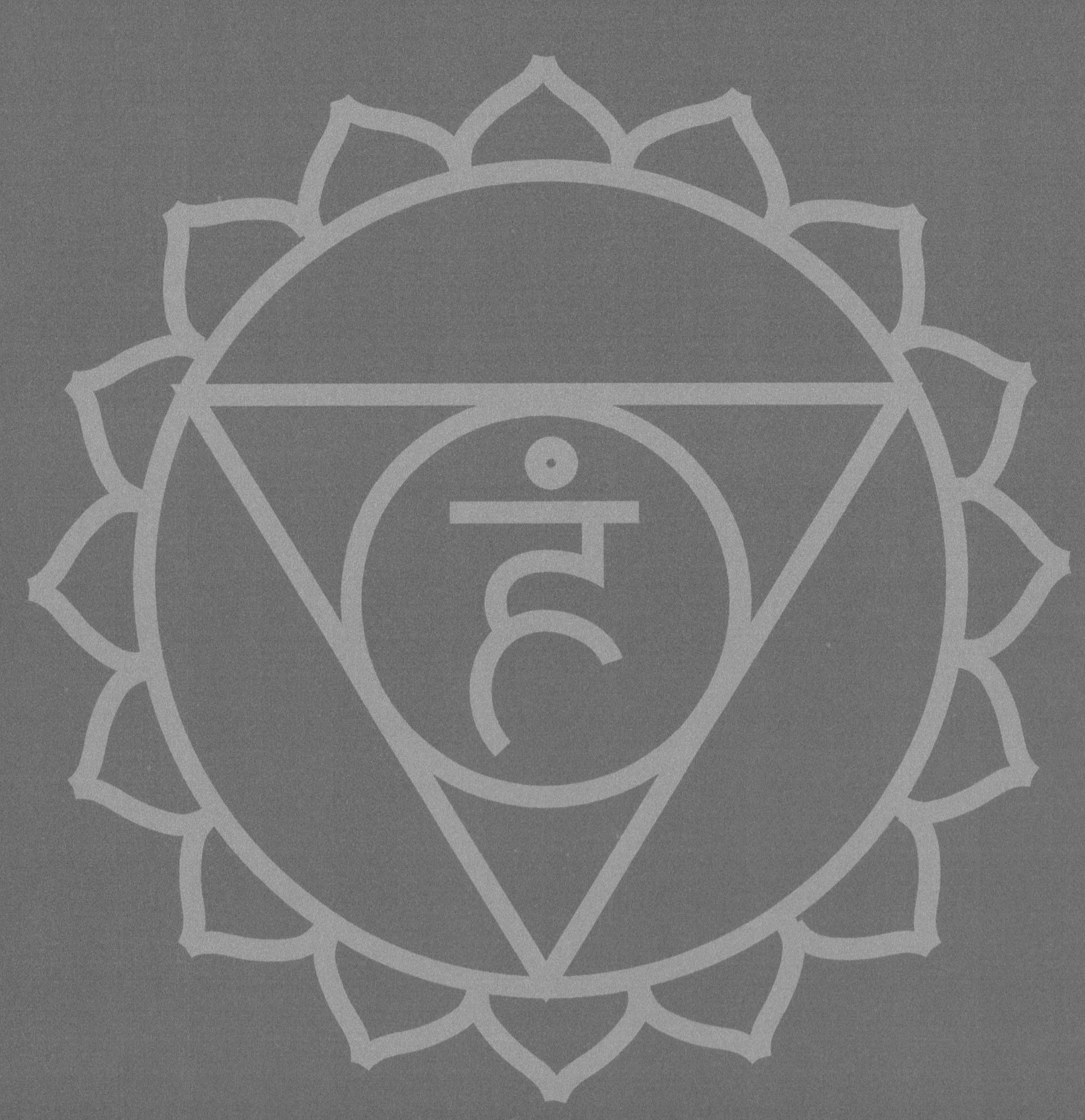

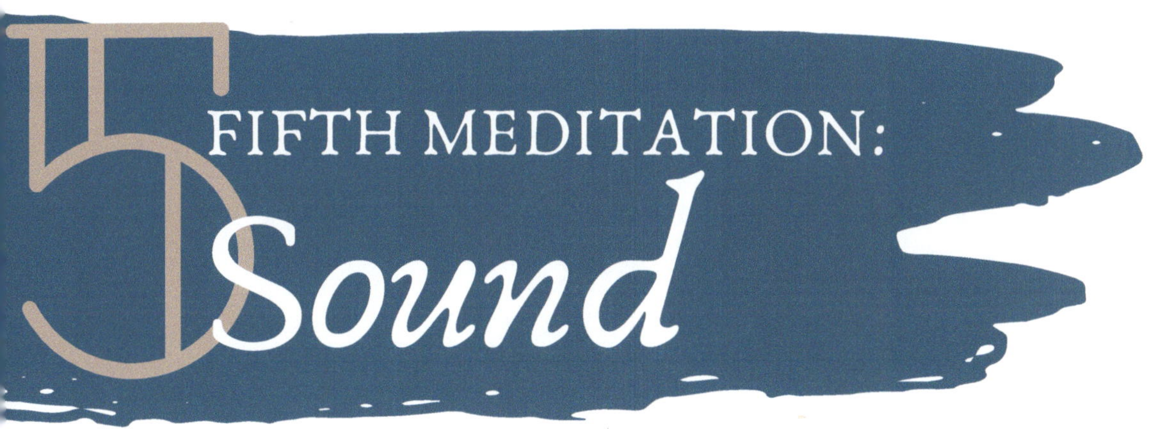

The Throat Chakra represents sound and vibration, the melody of your internal resonance, and the symphony of the Universal Matrix.

Noise and mind chatter will keep you disconnected from the voice of your Higher Self. Quiet the mind. Quiet the environment. Create sacred time to be with your Spirit. Be conscious of what you say and what you listen to. Sound vibrations in and around the body create and attract similar vibrations. Tune yourself to a frequency that is in alignment with peace and you will attract peace into your life.

Be gentle with your words.
Harmonize your energy field by speaking life and truth into yourself and into the world.

What does your self-talk sound like? What names do you call yourself?

"Do not speak badly of yourself, for the warrior that is inside you hears your words and is lessened by them. You are strong and you are brave. There is a nobility of spirit within you. Let it grow." —David Gemmell

Intention: Speak Life
Human experience: Self-Expression (lies and judgment)
Spiritual practice: Self-Love (honor and truth)

THROAT CHAKRA:

Communication, authenticity, truth, resonance, harmony

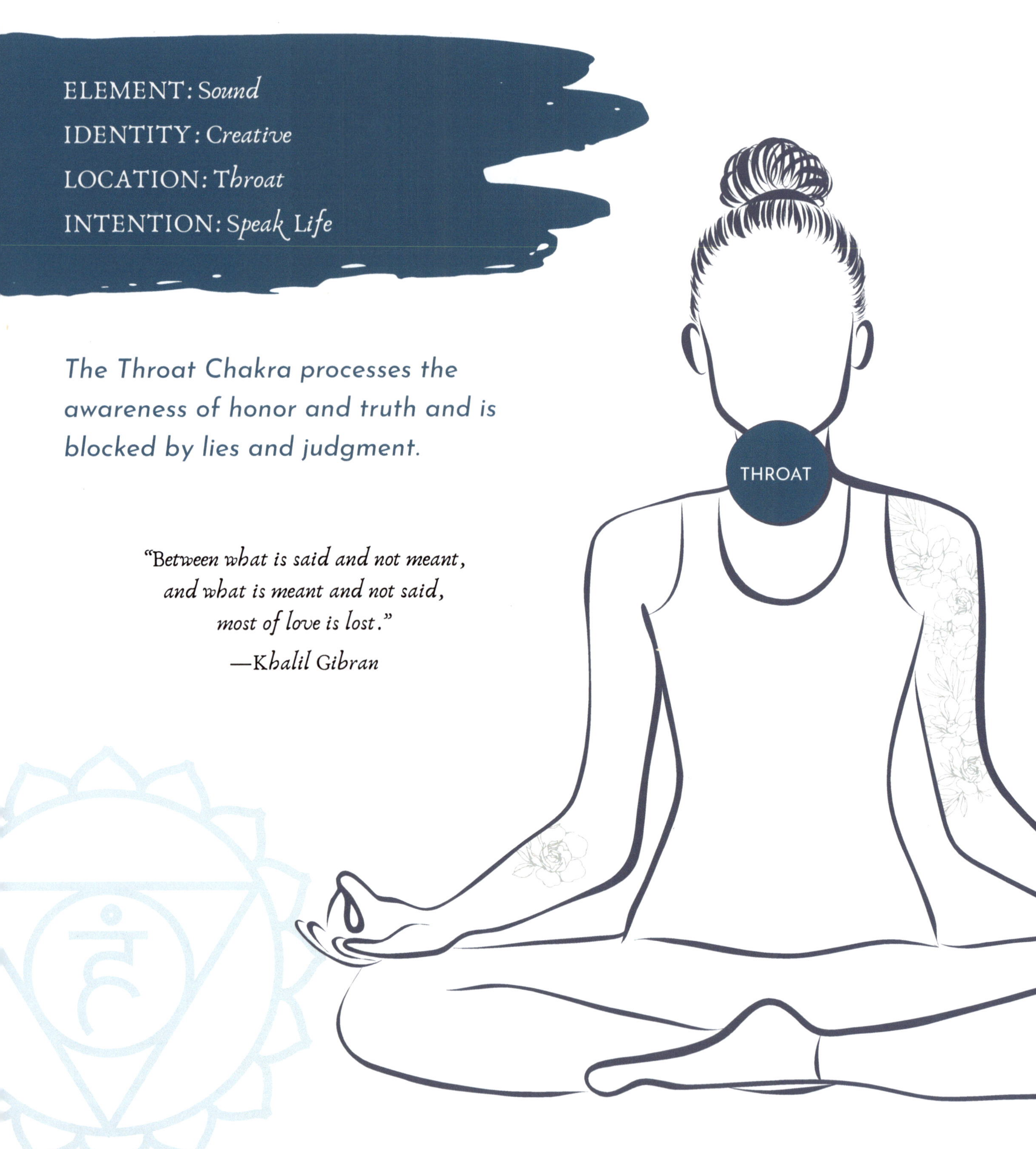

ELEMENT: *Sound*
IDENTITY: *Creative*
LOCATION: *Throat*
INTENTION: *Speak Life*

The Throat Chakra processes the awareness of honor and truth and is blocked by lies and judgment.

*"Between what is said and not meant,
and what is meant and not said,
most of love is lost."*
—Khalil Gibran

THROAT CHAKRA:
Internal resonance

The following deficient and excessive energies carry low-vibrational frequencies. They are collected and stored in the throat chakra, blocking the flow of spiritual energy. If your thoughts, feelings, or behaviors fall into one of these two categories, the healing in this energy center has not yet begun.

Balanced energy in the Throat Chakra is influenced by our commitment to peace and harmony. The most important thing you can do to honor your sacred self, keep your mind stable and your spirit healthy, is to protect your peace at all costs. Speak your truth. Set up boundaries. Find solace in solitude. Get to know your spiritual nature.

Raise Your Vibration

DEFICIENT ENERGY	BALANCED ENERGY	EXCESSIVE ENERGY
• INDECISION	• HONESTY	• GOSSIPY
• NEGATIVE SPEECH	• TRUTH	• LOUD
• SECRETIVE	• AUTHENTIC VOICE	• CRITICAL
• AFRAID TO SPEAK UP	• IN HARMONY WITH SELF AND OTHERS	• OPINIONATED
• MISUNDERSTOOD	• CLEAR AND CONCISE COMMUNICATION	• HARSH WORDS
• CAN'T EXPRESS SELF	• KNOW YOUR OWN TRUTH	• TALK OVER OTHERS
• SELF-CONTAINED	• CONFIDENT IN SELF-EXPRESSION	
• SMALL WEAK VOICE	• CREATIVE	
	• DIPLOMATIC	
	• GOOD LISTENER	
	• FULL VOICE	

Intention: Speak Life
Human experience: Self-Expression (lies and judgment)
Spiritual practice: Self-Love (honor and truth)

What is your truth? What is your purpose?
Are you living an authentic life?

Think through your timeline. When were you silenced or taught that your opinion was invalid?

Do you engage in conversations that are critical or judgmental of others?

How do you respond when someone judges you, makes fun of you, or calls you an offensive name?

Intention: Speak Life
Human experience: Self-Expression (lies and judgment)
Spiritual practice: Self-Love (honor and truth)

When did their perception of you become your perception of yourself ?

What negative words have been said to you or about you, that you continue to hear in your head?

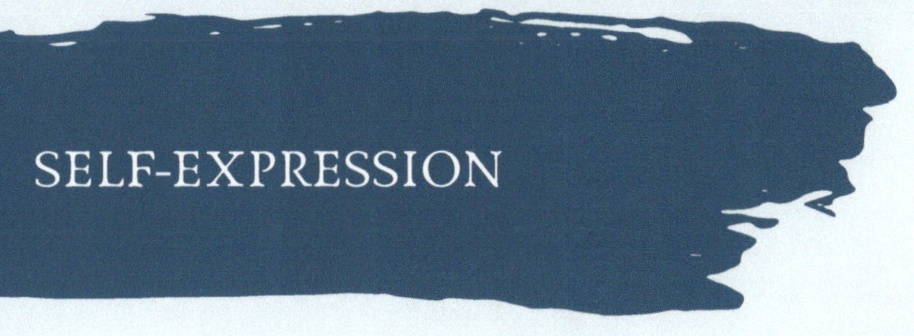

My Experience with Lies and Judgment

"Before children speak, they sing. Before they write, they paint. As soon as they stand, they dance. Art is the basis of human expression."
—Phylicia Rashad

As a kid, I loved to draw. By the time I was in the seventh grade, I carried my sketchbook with me everywhere. All of my thoughts and ideas, inspiration, and curiosities were kept safe in those pages. It was a visual representation of my life and experiences during that time. For me, drawing was my peace in the midst of insanity, freedom in the midst of chaos, therapy in the midst of an ever-persistent sadness.

I was not a fan of art class that year. The projects were fun, but the teacher was mean as a snake. She sat at her desk from the beginning of class right through to the end. We knew if Ms. Medea stood up, something was about to go down. One day in particular, something caught her eye. She was up and was staring in my general direction. I was on task, so I didn't think anything about it. I was really into the assignment and my project was coming along well. We were asked to make a 3D animal out of clay, and I chose to create an elephant—an elephant bowl, to be exact; carefully, thoughtfully. With superb craftsmanship, might I add. I hollowed out the trunk with precision to allow for perfect air flow and measured and cut out a small hole on its back for the screen. As a certified stoner (and non-certified artist), I was pretty proud of my work.

"You never know how long your words will stay in someone's mind even long after you've forgotten you spoke them."
—Unknown

But there she was, for no good reason that I could think of, walking towards me. I forgot all about my sketchbook that was sitting on my desk, secured under my arm. Ms. Medea came right up to me, grabbed it, and began carelessly flipping through the pages. Through clenched teeth, I pleaded with her to give it back. She glared at me, shrinking me down to nothing. "Where did you get this?" she asked. Her voice was harsh. I lowered my head, embarrassed that our conversation was now a show in the middle of the classroom. "It's mine," I said, "That is all of my artwork." She looked back through the pages, then back at me. "This is not artwork, and you are not an artist. Artists do not draw these types of things." She pulled the pages out, crumpled them in her hand, and dropped them into the trash can. I was mortified. Tears welled up and burned my eyes before falling down my cheeks. I digested all of her mean hateful words that day. And I believed them.

I stopped carrying my sketchbook. I didn't take another art class for seven years—the rest of middle school, all of high school, and the first two years of college. During my third year of college, studying forensic psychology, I enrolled in an art class to meet the elective requirement. What I initially wrote off as a "bird class," ended up calling me back home to myself. The following semester, I switched my major to fine art, and started over.

Self-expression is an outpour of subjective thoughts, feelings, and ideas by way of creation; An offering of who we are. My natural inclination as a young person was to draw and create. I didn't consider myself an "artist," or try to measure up to anything. I simply expressed myself in a way that felt like truth.

Walking in your truth is key to healing and restoring this energy center. When we allow the perception of others to become our perception of ourselves, we adopt their vibrational reality. Over the years, I have learned that hurt people, hurt people. Hate and viciousness are just symptoms of pain and suffering. Their actions define their state of consciousness and expose their struggle with shadow. Observe, but don't attach. Your power and your strength are in your growth, in your truth, in your light.

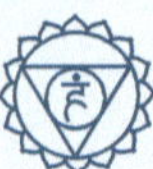

My Experience with Truth and Peace

"May every word that is ever spoken by our mouths or typed by our fingers be words that lift up, and never words that tear down."

—Unknown

Middle school is hard for most girls. For one reason or another, the middle school experience is one that we all remember: juggling the load of new responsibilities, trying to navigate the friend groups, the mean girls, the gossip, the bullies, changing bodies, unexpected feelings and emotions, different challenges, new experiences. As an adult, I can still remember moments from middle school that make me cringe.

"Be they type of woman who fixes another woman's crown, without telling the world that it was crooked."

—Unknown

My daughter started being bullied her first year in. One girl made school life hell for her and for many other girls in her class. At the time, I was unaware of the bullying that was taking place within a community that I had grown to love and care for. What I did know was that out of nowhere, my daughter started setting her alarm to wake up two hours early every morning to straighten out her naturally curly hair and pile on foundation. "But you are beautiful," I would say to her. "There is no reason to change your hair or hide under makeup. People love you for who you are honey and if they don't, they're not your people." She despised that answer. I could see the pain in her eyes, the frustration in her body language. "Talk to me, love." She would just stare at me and say, "Nothing Mom…I'm fine." I had no idea what she was dealing with every day. One morning in particular, she came out of the bathroom with her hair brushed down over her face, a baseball cap on, big baggy clothes—I couldn't even see her eyes. She rushed past me, straight to the car, loaded her things, and hopped into the front seat.

"Darling, you feel heavy because you are too full of truth.
Open your mouth more. Let the truth exist somewhere other than inside your body."

—Della Hicks-Wilson

On our way to school, I pulled over into an empty lot. I took her hand and moved her hair from her eyes. "I know something is wrong, honey, please talk to me. I love you. I can't help you of I don't know what is going on." And there it was—tears began falling from her eyes like they had been stored there for a lifetime. I held her close while she sobbed in my arms. We sat there for a long time while she told me everything—the pain, the anger, the embarrassment, the loneliness—that she had been holding all of this on her shoulders for months without any support from anyone. How? My heart ached for my baby. Over the last ten years of her life, she had been playing dress-up and catching frogs. She was full of life and all the sweet things. And now, here she was, carrying a weight on her back so heavy, it was crushing her into something I didn't recognize. I could not comprehend how I was one building away loving and teaching hundreds of other children while mine was repeatedly unprotected by the people "in charge." The irony was that my daughter still wanted to be her friend. She justified that because this girl was going through a hard time at home, she needed to be there for her. She had already decided that she would endure the depletion of herself, in order to continue to pour into someone else.

> *"Mama Bear is such a sweet way to describe the fact that I'd tear you open and eat your insides if you hurt my child."*
> *—Unknown*

It is heartbreaking to watch your children suffer. A fierce rage began to stir in my gut, a wild visceral instinct to protect her. But I am an alchemist, and I was determined to transform that pain into love. I wanted to offer healing to my daughter in a way that would honor her essence and give reverence to her existence. I created a series of watercolor portraits, a collection of beautiful, brown women. I wanted my daughter to see herself, her family members, and her ancestors when she looked at them. I wanted her to see the essence of beauty in all its glory; full of color, full of magic, full of inspiration.

> *"Ego says, 'Once everything falls into place, I'll feel peace.'*
> *Spirit says, 'Find your peace, and then everything will fall into place.'"*
> *—Marianne Williamson*

Self-love is the act of loving oneself by prioritizing your own well-being and happiness. It took many years of adulting before I gave myself permission to truly love myself. I was taught to pour into everyone else's cup, to give of myself to the point of exhaustion. I watched all the women in my life work their fingers to the bone taking care of bills, and homes, and husbands, and children. I watched them carry the weight of the world on their backs while lugging around an immense amount of exhaustion in their hearts. The more women I've talked to and shared stories with, the more I have found it to be true. We continue to pour, even after our own cup has been depleted. What a beautiful discovery it was to find that self-love nourishes the soul and is the essential ingredient to loving others. In that case, we should all make it our first priority.

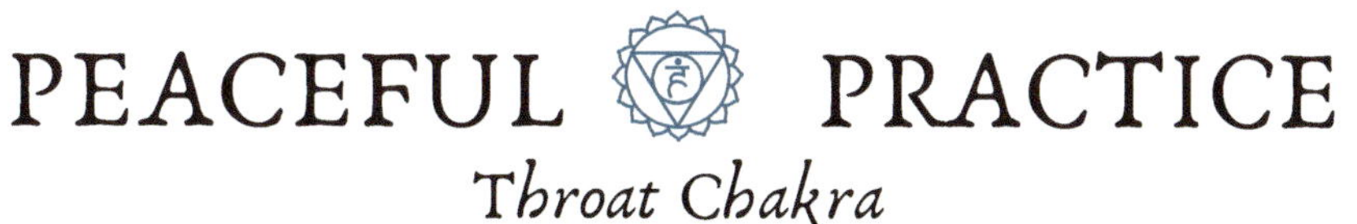

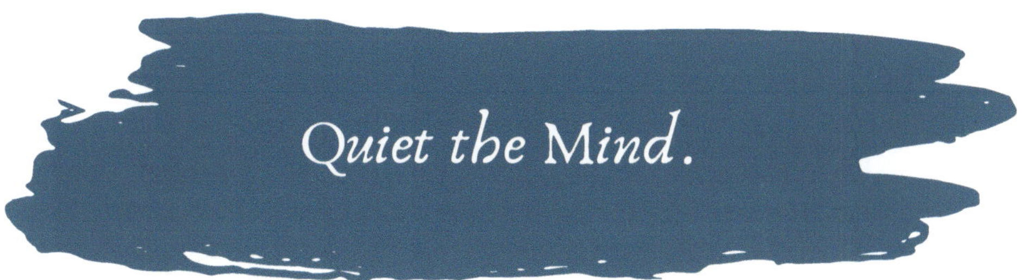

Sound vibrations that are in harmony with sacred geometry, have profound effects on the expression of molecular biology. Sound is a powerful tool for healing the mind, tuning the body, harmonizing the energy field, and connecting Spirit to the frequency of Source.

Quiet the mind chatter and sit in silence. When you notice that your mind begins to wander, gently bring it back. The outer world is an illusion. Listen for the peaceful sound of your internal resonance. This is who you really are, who you have always been. The peace of your Spirit is always present, available to you at every moment of every experience. When you begin to honor your true nature of calm and absolute peace, reality shifts and miracles begin to show up at your doorstep.

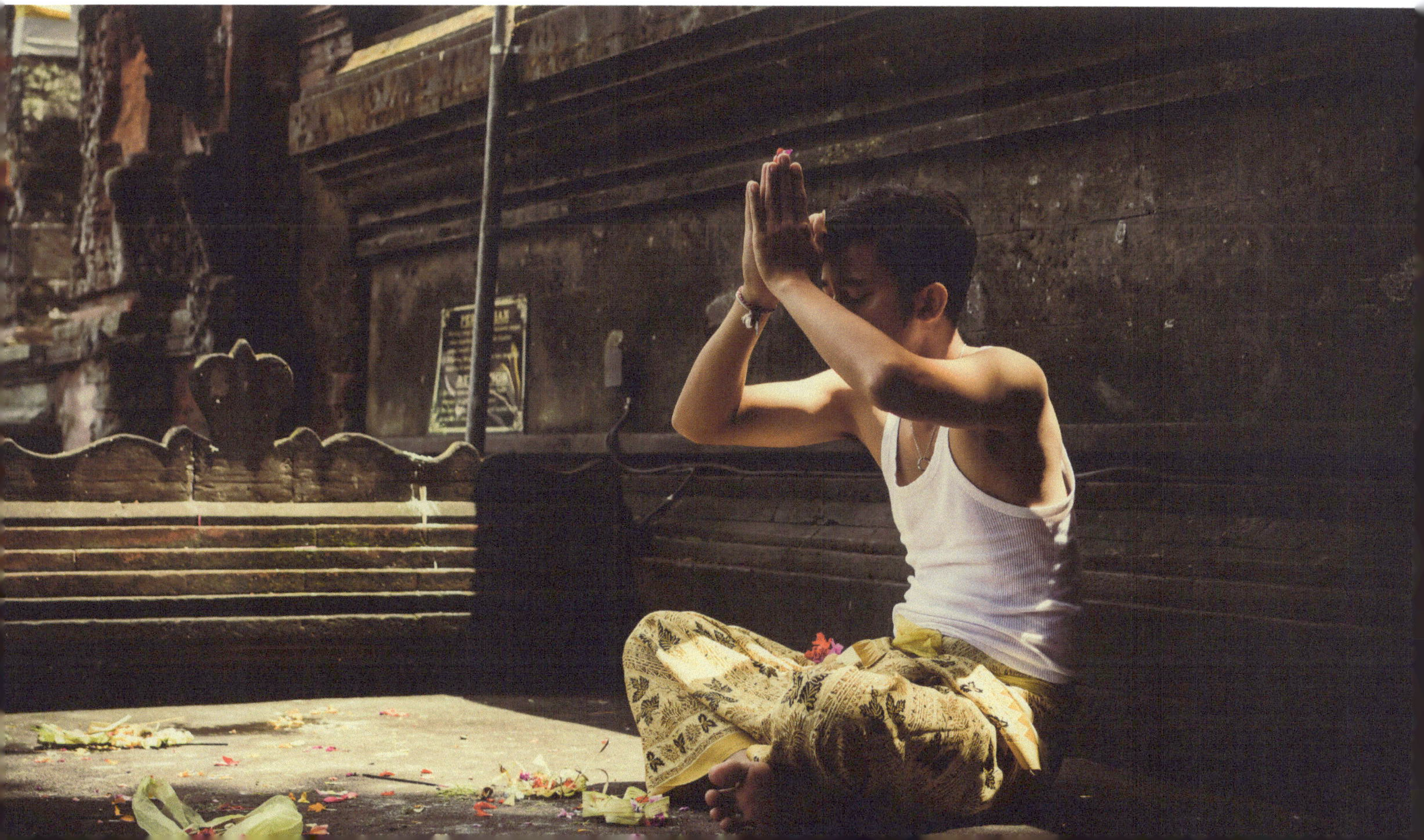

HOLISTIC WELLNESS
Practice Speaking Life: Internal Resonance

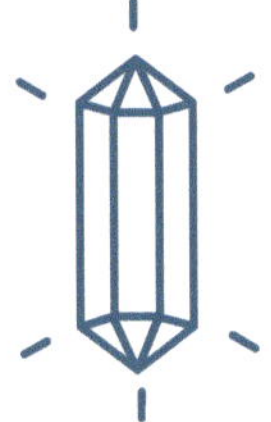

CRYSTALS

Blue Kyanite, Blue Apatite, Blue Lace, Chrysocolla, Turquoise, Aquamarine

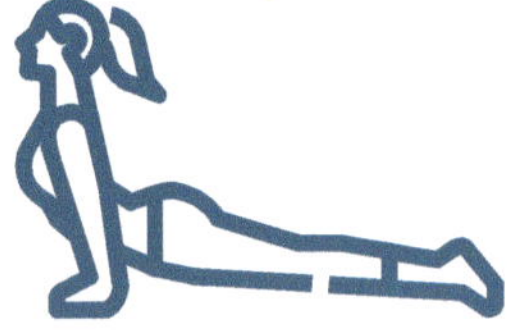

YOGA

Upward Dog

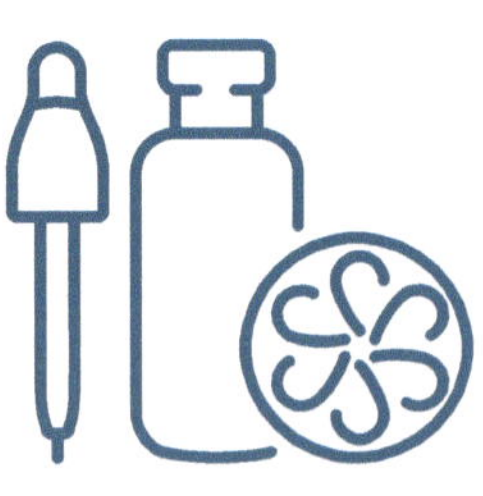

ESSENTIAL OILS

Peppermint, Sage, Clove, Cypress, Spearmint, Fennel

ENVIRONMENTAL WELLNESS

Recognize how your overall well-being is directly connected to your inner and outer environment.

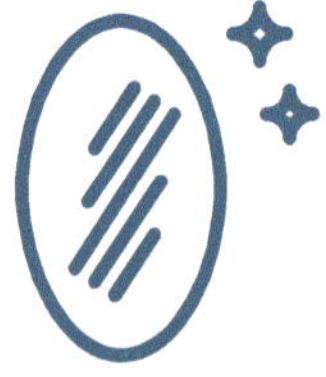

AFFIRMATION

I am aligned with my highest truth. I communicate with honor and speak life into the world.

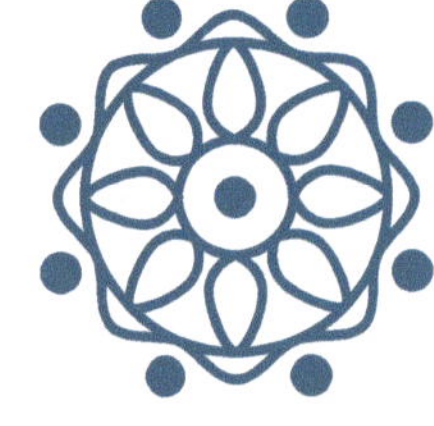

MEDITATION

Practice the art of sitting quietly with yourself. Notice the voices that you hear. Is your shadow louder than your Light? This exercise reveals which of the two you pour into.

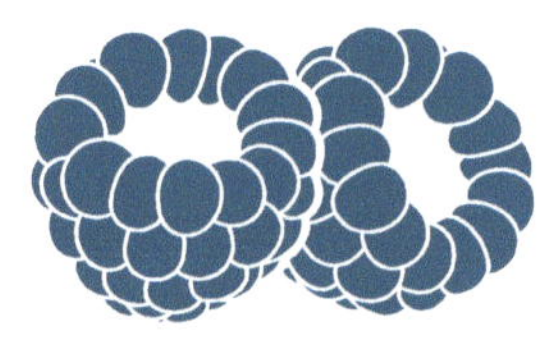

FOOD

Blueberries, Blackberries, Blue Raspberries, figs, Kelp, Coconut Water, Herbal Teas, Raw Honey, Lemon, Apples, Plums

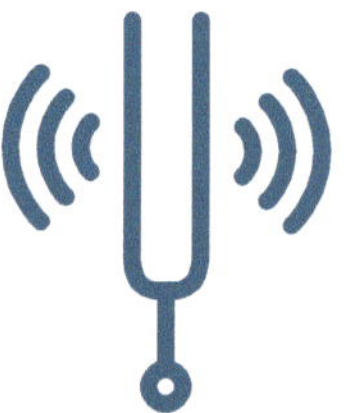

INTERNAL RESONANCE

"Our entire biological system, the brain and the Earth itself, work on the same frequencies."
—Nikola Tesla

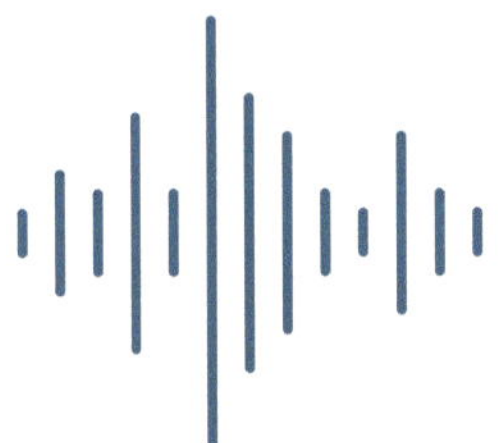

SOUND

Cleansing and purification.

741 Hz

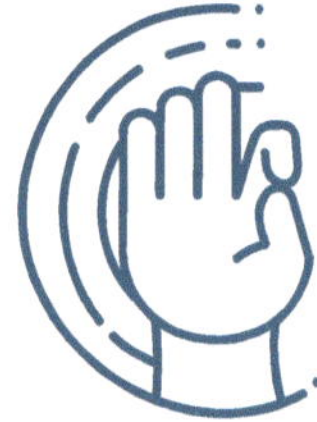

MUDRA

"Expression"

Hands by stomach, fingers interlaced, and thumb tips touching. Focus on throat.

Long H-A-A-A-A-M

COLOR

Blue Increases: Calmness, Communication, Honesty, Self Expression, Appreciation for Beauty

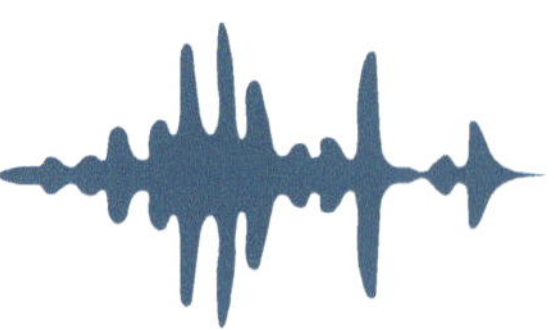

VIBRATION

"The vibration of good words has a positive effect on the brain and body. The vibration of negative words has the power to destroy."
—Masaru Emoto

CREATIVE FLOW
Artistic Expression

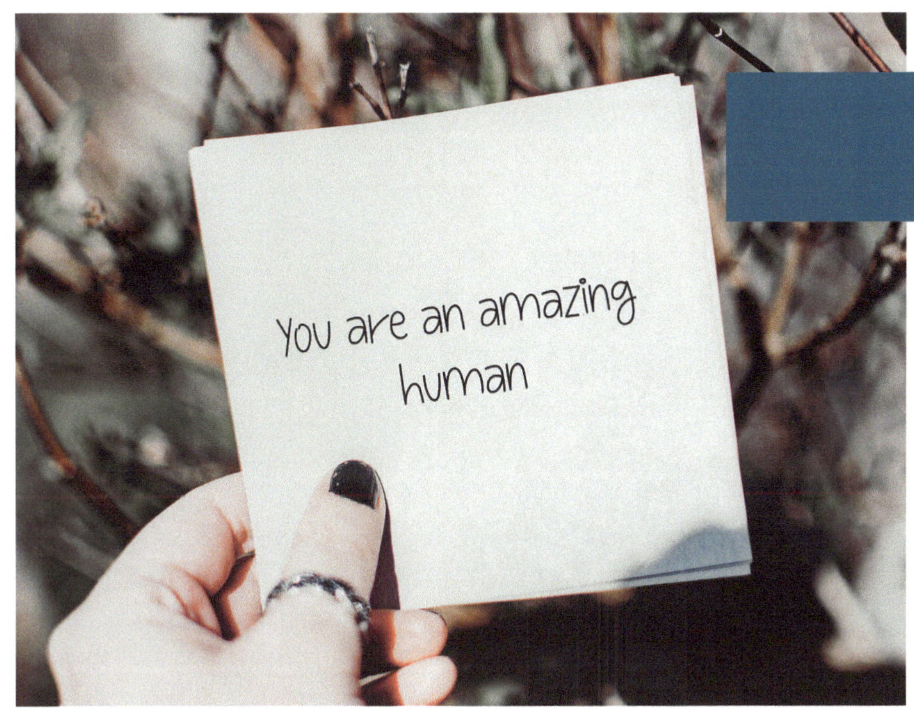

Art Abandon

Words are vibrations that create in real time. Every time a word is read, thought, typed, or said, it is either building up or tearing down.

Materials Needed

Mat Board

Scrapbook or Decorative Paper

White Cardstock

Beautiful Quotes/Words/ Phrases

Scissors

Glue Stick

Optional:

Small Transparent Gift Baggies

Ribbon or String

Fancy Tags

Hole Punch

Miniature Easels

""Be kinder to yourself, and then let your kindness flood the world."

—Pema Chodron

Intention: Speak Life
Human experience: Self-Expression (lies and judgment)
Spiritual practice: Self-Love (honor and truth)

ART ABANDON
Instructions

Step 1

Stack and glue the foundation in 3 layers.

For example:

Mat Board: Large (5″ x 7″)
Scrapbook Paper: Medium (4″ x 6″)
White Cardstock: Small (3″ x 5″)

Step 2

Cut out a beautiful quote or phrase and lay it down as the fourth layer, one word at a time. Arrange and rearrange the placement of each word until you are happy with your design, then glue it down. Sticker quotes work great as well (no need to cut or glue)!

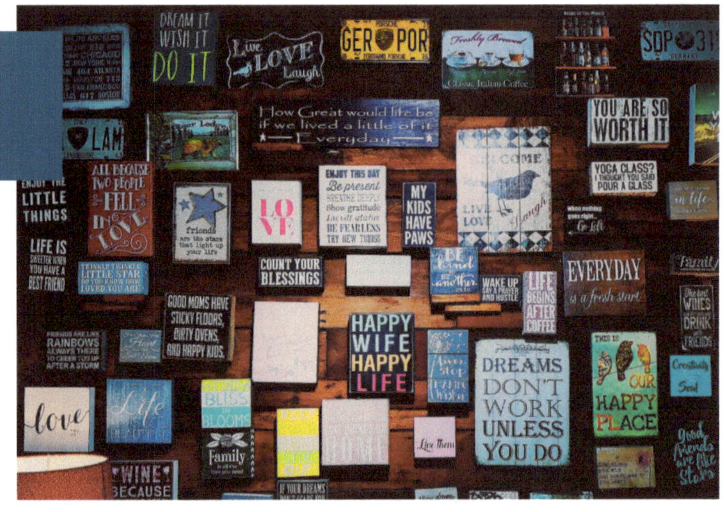

Step 3

Keep these around your house or office where you can see them. Every time you look at them, read them (out loud or in your head). What lovely little offerings of healing to your Spirit.

Or, package them up in little gift baggies, add a fun tag with a little note, and leave them around town for strangers to find! What a beautiful way to offer healing to the world.

TIME TO REFLECT

"Silence is essential. We need silence just as much as we need air, just as much as plants need light. If our minds are crowded with words and thoughts, there is no space for us."

—Thich Nhat Hanh

TIME TO REFLECT

CONSCIOUS CONNECTIONS

Unclutter your space

Be honest

Spend time alone

Share your voice

Sit in meditation

Stand up for what you believe in

Stay away from people who drain your energy

Avoid gossip and drama

Speak kindly to yourself

Do not compare yourself to others

Practice listening

DID YOU KNOW?

The Solfeggio frequencies are an ancient 6 tone scale used to create sacred music (including the Gregorian Chants!). Each Solfeggio frequency can be used to balance energy in your mind, body, and spirit. When played in harmony, they are believed to open a portal to the Divine Matrix, unlocking miracles and spiritual blessings.

396 Hz: Liberating Guilt and Fear	417 Hz: Undoing Situations and Facilitating Change	528 Hz: Transformation and Miracles (DNA Repair)
639 Hz: Connecting/Relationships	741 Hz: Expression/Solutions	852 Hz: Returning to Spiritual Order

Intention: Speak Life
Human experience: Self-Expression (lies and judgment)
Spiritual practice: Self-Love (honor and truth)

"Only when we are brave enough to explore our darkness
will we discover the infinite power of light."
—Brené Brown

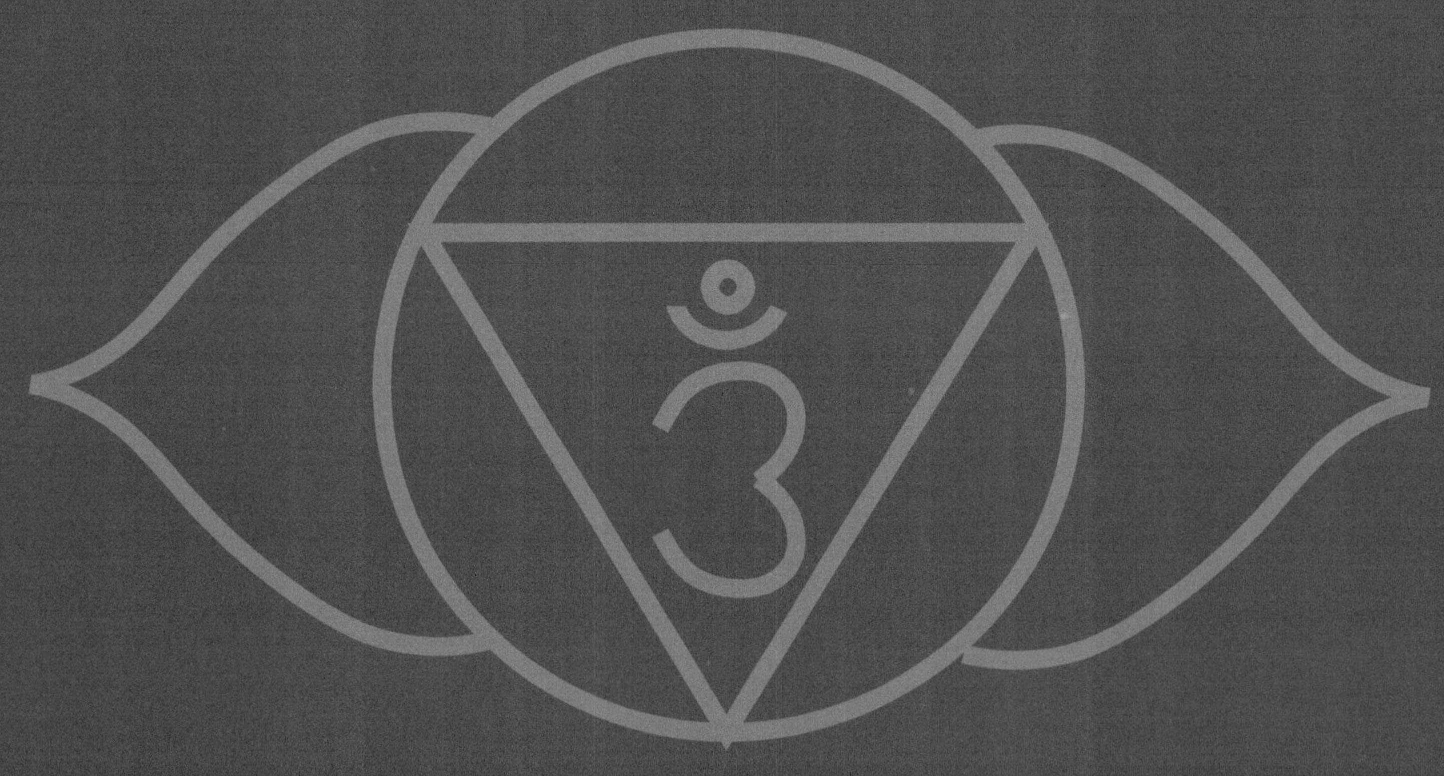

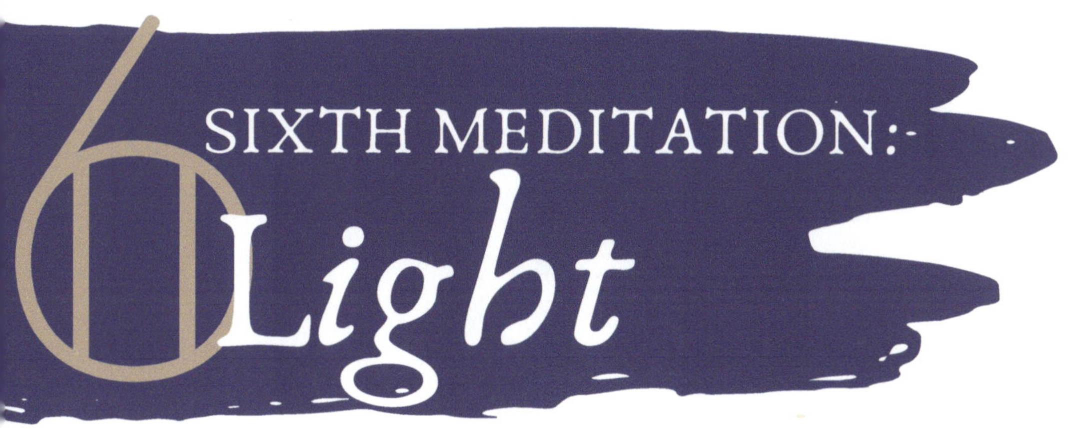

The Third Eye chakra represents Light, the ability to illuminate our reality, widen our perspective and see more clearly.

When the third eye is open, there is a primal knowing that all is connected, all is an extension of the only thing that is. You will see your own reflection in the faces of others. No longer will you turn away from the injustices of the world. No longer will you sit in comfort while others suffer. When you identify with Spirit and connect yourself to Source, you will be drawn to all paths that lead to the Light. You will help the hurting and feed the hungry. You will mend the damaged and restore the broken.

You will become a beacon of Light, illuminating all that is shrouded darkness.

Do you treat all forms of life with the same degree of honor, respect, reverence?

"All beings tremble before violence. All fear death. All love life. See yourself in others. Then who can you hurt? What harm can you do?" —Buddha

Intention: Illumination
Human experience: Self-reflection (privilege and separation)
Spiritual practice: Self-transformation (perspective and insight)

THIRD EYE CHAKRA:

Intuition, wisdom, perspective, illumination

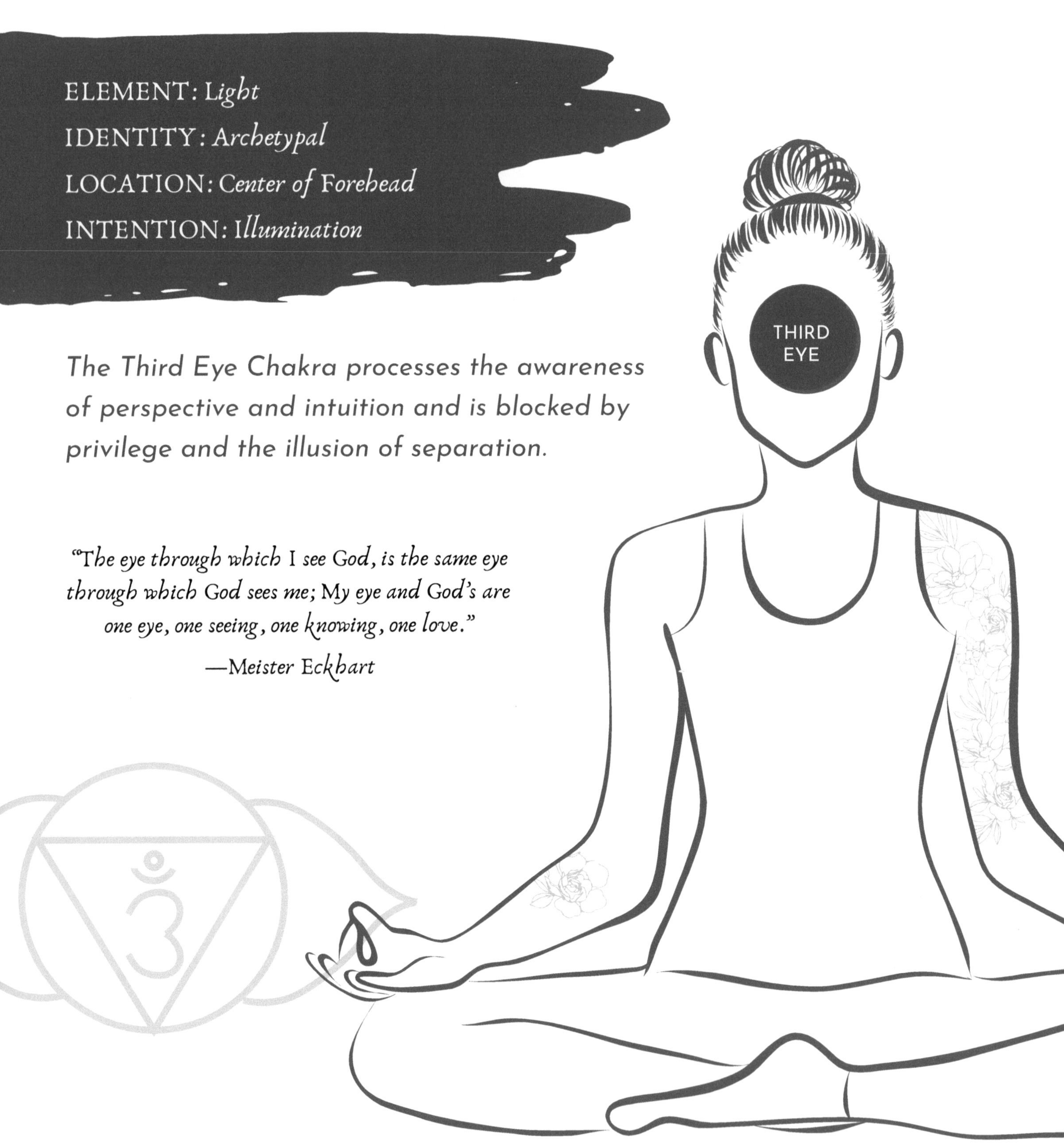

ELEMENT: *Light*

IDENTITY: *Archetypal*

LOCATION: *Center of Forehead*

INTENTION: *Illumination*

The Third Eye Chakra processes the awareness of perspective and intuition and is blocked by privilege and the illusion of separation.

"The eye through which I see God, is the same eye through which God sees me; My eye and God's are one eye, one seeing, one knowing, one love."

—Meister Eckhart

THIRD EYE CHAKRA:

Open your eye

The following deficient and excessive energies carry low-vibrational frequencies. They are collected and stored in the third eye chakra, blocking the flow of spiritual energy. If your thoughts, feelings, or behaviors fall into one of these two categories, the healing in this energy center has not yet begun.

Balanced energy in the Third Eye Chakra is the result of a shift in perspective. Widen your lens from a single point of view to the collective. You are but one string in the tapestry of life. The fullness of life is available to those who choose to live outside of the realm of their own existence. Empty yourself of yourself. Trust your intuition. She will set you free.

Raise Your Vibration

DEFICIENT ENERGY	BALANCED ENERGY	EXCESSIVE ENERGY
• POOR JUDGMENT	• IMAGINATIVE	• DIFFICULTY CONCENTRATING
• LACK OF FOCUS	• INTUITIVE	• NIGHTMARES
• POOR IMAGINATION	• INSIGHTFUL	• DELUSIONAL
• CAN'T SEE BEYOND PHYSICAL	• CLEAR THOUGHTS	• HALLUCINATIONS
• INSENSITIVE	• A VISIONARY	• OBSESSIVE
• NO DREAM RECALL	• SEES BEYOND PHYSICAL	• SELFISH
• DENIAL	• CALM	• SELF-CENTERED
• BLIND TO THE TRUTH	• DETACHMENT	
• POOR MEMORY	• WISDOM	
• LOST	• SEES BIG PICTURE CLEARLY	
• POOR JUDGMENT	• ACCEPTS TRUTH	
• JUSTIFYING	• OBJECTIVE	
• CONFUSION	• A DEEP SENSE OF PEACE AND CENTEREDNESS	
• DEPRESSION		

Intention: Illumination
Human experience: Self-reflection (privilege and separation)
Spiritual practice: Self-transformation (perspective and insight)

How often do you honor your insight and intuition?

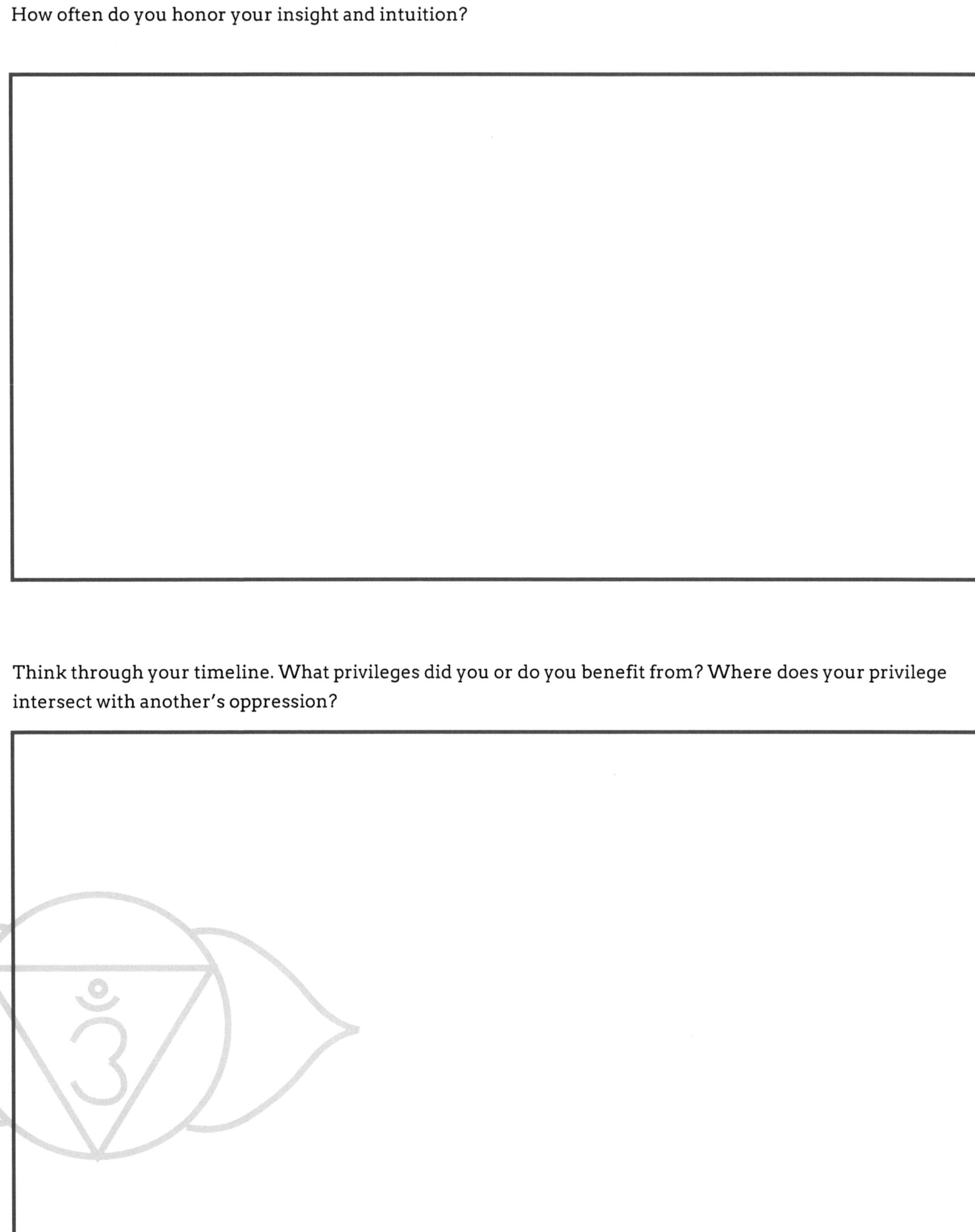

Think through your timeline. What privileges did you or do you benefit from? Where does your privilege intersect with another's oppression?

Which injustices in the world do you feel most compelled to speak out against?

Which injustice in the world do you ignore because it doesn't directly affect your everyday life?

Intention: Illumination
Human experience: Self-reflection (privilege and separation)
Spiritual practice: Self-transformation (perspective and insight)

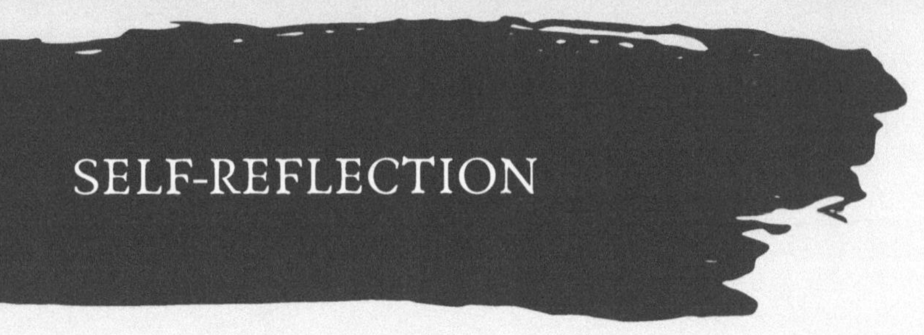

My Experience with Separation and Privilege

"We live in a culture where people are more offended by swear words and middle fingers than they are by famine, warfare, and the destruction of our environment."

—Unknown

I traveled to South Africa during the summer of 2015 and again in 2017, both times with a small American group of teachers and high school students. "Life changing" doesn't begin to describe how profound those experiences were. Although there was a palpable energy and vibration in the air that excited my spirit, I was repeatedly slapped in my face by my own privilege. This is exactly what every American should have to experience within their lifetime. We are a spoiled and entitled group of humans—and perspective is everything.

After a long journey in the air, we arrived at Port Elizabeth, a small city in South Africa's Eastern Cape Province. It was similar to any other small city; congested buildings and store fronts, traffic, hundreds of people moving about the streets. We knew it was their winter season, but I was not prepared to be so cold. Before leaving the airport, we stopped by the currency exchange booth. I handed the clerk $500 US dollars and in return, she handed me $8,000+ South African Rand. PRIVILEGE CHECK.

The hostel was a cute little house in a quaint neighborhood close to town, but the first night there was miserable. Because the winters are short, most homes in South Africa are not built with central heating. I slept in a hoodie, sweatpants, three pairs of socks, my winter coat, gloves, a toboggan, under two blankets and I was still cold. I bitched and moaned the whole night, too uncomfortable to get much sleep. The next morning, I crawled out of bed, body stiff, hoping to warm up in the shower. But there was a water shortage, so we each had two minutes on the timer to jump into freezing water, wash, and jump back out into a cold room to dry off and get dressed. After three days of this routine, I was tired, irritable, and underwhelmed.

"Lower income, less educated voiceless people are so much easier to control. Poverty is not by accident, it's by design."

—Unknown

On the fourth day, we packed the car with suitcases full of donations, and our backpacks with an abundance of supplies, food, and water. We were off to Joe Slovo township, about fifteen minutes outside of the city. It was our first day on the job and we were so excited to meet the children. Leaving the city was like driving through a portal into a completely different world. The change in landscape and infrastructure was mind-boggling. Nothing could have prepared me for what I would see that day.

"Becoming aware of privilege should not be viewed as a burden or source of guilt, but rather, an opportunity to learn and be responsible so that we may work toward a more just and inclusive world."

—Unknown

When we arrived, we were greeted by a sea of children with big beautiful smiles and warm welcoming energy. They were just as excited to meet us as we were to meet them. Distracted by the interactions, it took me a moment to recognize the disparity of it all. The American group was decked out, head to toe, in designer winter gear, while many children standing around us were barely dressed at all—shorts and t-shirts, some without shoes. All I could think about was my own child. I couldn't get the knot out of my throat. PRIVILEGE CHECK.

During art class, I was teaching at the board in the front of the classroom. When I turned around, I saw that a group of children were casually passing my water bottle around, each taking a turn to drink from it. I was horrified and quickly rushed over to retrieve it. They didn't understand why I was taking it away, but I didn't understand why they were drinking out of it. "You all share the same bottle?" I was confused. My intention wasn't to offend, but we did not do that back home in America. As a matter of fact, I was taught not to ever put my mouth on any surface where someone else had theirs. I was such a germaphobe, the idea of passing a bottle around and sharing lip space with anyone, anywhere at any time made my stomach feel queasy. "Yes," a little boy answered, "We share our water." "Damn!" I thought to myself, "We don't share anything." PRIVILEGE CHECK.

At the end of class, a bowl of beads fell to the floor and scattered in every direction. All at once, every child in that room was on the floor retrieving them. They did not stop until every single bead was found. All 500 of them. Back home in America, I spent thirteen years teaching in various public, charter, and private schools. When beads fell to the floor, a few students would join me in picking up a handful of them, but many would have probably been left for the janitor to sweep into the garbage. PRIVILEGE CHECK.

"If you are more fortunate than others, build a longer table, not a taller fence."

—CMCP

During lunch break, the children lined up in a single-file line, waiting their turn to be served. The American group was taken to a different room in the school to eat, away from the children. We pulled out sandwiches, chips, fruit, and chocolate. Cold water bottles were passed to each of us. We sat around laughing and talking and sharing about our day, as we were each teaching in different classrooms and working with different children. When we finished, we trashed our leftovers, as usual, then joined the children again. Every child there had the same lunch, a small bowl of beans and rice. There wasn't any fruit or chocolate, no water bottles, and there certainly wasn't enough for seconds. The Americans were full, standing among children who were hungry. I learned later that day, that most of those children would not eat again until the next day's lunch serving of beans and rice. PRIVILEGE CHECK.

Recess followed. One child used a rock to draw a giant square grid into the dirt to use as a game board. A large group of children stood around the outside of the grid singing a song in their native Xhosa language, using their hands and feet to create the rhythm. Two children stood inside the grid, each foot in a different square, dancing and moving around the grid on beat. If one of them messed up, he would be replaced with a new opponent, and the game would continue. The whole setup was pretty creative and the Americans could not help but dance along, even though we had no clue what they were saying. I asked a boy standing next to me to translate the lyrics, so he sang to me in English. "I'm hungry, I'm hungry, I'm hungry." That was it. That was the entire song. The entire game. Goosebumps ran across my arms and scalp. I looked around at these resilient kids, everyone smiling, full of joy, choosing to be happy despite the discomfort. PRIVILEGE CHECK.

The next day, we participated in a Narrative4 project. The assignment was to share a life-changing story with one partner, and then present the partner's story to the group, in first person. The purpose of the program was to teach radical empathy and give us each a glimpse into the world of someone who lives on the other side of the planet. We each had an hour or so to meet and share with our partners before coming together for presentations. While the American children told stories of bad grades, broken friendships, divorce, and lost soccer championships, the African children told stories of rape, abuse, death, disease, and famine. PRIVILEGE CHECK.

After the school day ended, we were taken on a walking tour through the township. I saw homes nailed together using wood and metal scraps, with no foundation and no floors. I saw piles of newspaper shavings, on the cold dirt, used as beds. I saw children without parents, living in conditions unacceptable for human life. I saw poverty on a scale so unimaginable, I could not believe that it even exists. That night, I sobbed myself to sleep. Convicted. My spoiled ass actually had the nerve to complain about the weather. PRIVILEGE CHECK.

We popped in and out of many restaurants during our stay. Every restaurant owner that we encountered was white, every server black. The servers bowed their heads when they talked to us, they did not make eye contact, and they addressed us individually as sir or ma'am. One day at dinner, an American man seated at our table barked orders at the servers, and if he didn't understand their accent, he made a joke by mocking them, then told them to start again. I was embarrassed to be sitting so close to him. It was disgusting to watch, offensive to hear. When I asked the students to help clean up our tables, he smirked and told them not to. "These people get paid to do that." A self-righteous white male treating black servers like they were beneath him, in the most hideous display of power and entitlement. They couldn't even defend themselves for fear of retribution. PRIVILEGE CHECK.

"I don't know how to save the world. I don't have the answers or The Answer. I hold no secret knowledge as to how to fix the mistakes of generations past and present. I only know that without compassion and respect for all of Earth's inhabitants, none of us will survive – nor will we deserve to."

—Unknown

Self-reflection is the practice of deep introspection about how we deal with the complexities of life, the way we cope with difficult truths. School and church taught me that humans were separate from and superior to all other expressions of life. Culture taught me that humans were separate from each other. This is an illusion. Every living thing on this planet is an expression of Divine Source, and therefore should be treated with honor and reverence.

"Our greatest cruelty is our casual blindness to the despair of others."

—Unknown

Widening your perspective is key to healing and restoring this energy center. It is imperative that you look closely at the injustices of the world, and to examine where your privilege intersects with someone else's oppression. There is a multitude of sadness and suffering that needs your attention. Poverty, hunger, inequality, child-trafficking, factory farming, environmental destruction, animal extinction, water crisis, ocean dead zones, the list goes on. Do not bury your head. Do not look away. Acknowledge the darkness in the world. Allow it to break your heart wide open.

"She asks me to kill the spider. Instead, I get the most peaceful weapons I can find. I take a cup and a napkin. I catch the spider, put it outside and allow it to walk away. If I am ever caught in the wrong place at the wrong time, just being alive and not bothering anyone, I hope I am greeted with the same kind of mercy."

—Rudy Francisco, Helium

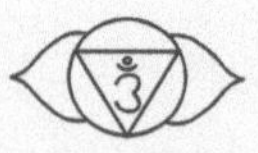

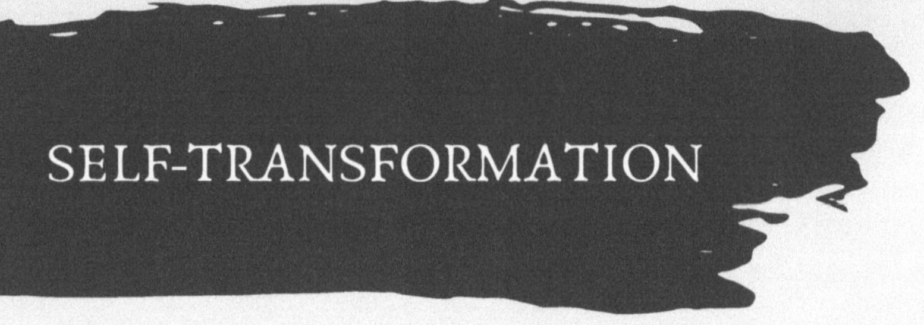

My Experience with Insight and Intuition

"Purify your mind from clutter, your heart from sorrow, your soul from past pain.
Your sacred space from energy and vibration that does not serve you."
—Unknown

Two dogs, six suitcases, and one angry teenager made the ten hours of travel on three planes with two layovers, an experience that I never wanted to have again. I was running on fumes and I could not wait to get there and settle in. The three weeks leading up to our move was packed full of teaching and moving out and packing bags and vet checks and paperwork and an expense list that didn't end. But to me, it was all worth it. I was so over American culture and I wanted nothing more than to be immersed in nature, living a simple life, in communion with the natural world. I wanted my daughter to experience more than iPhones and beauty commercials and pop culture. I was offered a teaching position, so we were off to the island of Eleuthera, in the Bahamas, to live for a year. Secretly, I was hoping that my daughter would fall in love and never want to return.

As soon as we stepped off the last plane, I felt a giant relief wash over me. We made it, and all I could think about was taking a nap. Waiting at the gate was the assistant principle and another new teacher who had just arrived thirty minutes prior. After collecting all our gear, we realized that one of our suitcases was missing. Of course, it was the one that had all my daughter's personal items, including pictures of her family and friends, comfy clothes, and her favorite toiletries. Why, Lord? She was already pissed that I took her away from everything she knew, and now on top of that, all of her keepsakes were gone.

"Your anxiety acts up around certain people because their energy
disturbs your spirit and the ancestors within you."
—Unknown

Our first stop was in front of a sketchy apartment building to drop off the other teacher. He was fairly young, just out of college. I learned later that all the young teachers were assigned to this specific complex. As we pulled away, the assistant principal laughed and said, "He has no idea what he is in for." She went on about how badly infested those apartments were with bugs, and how Americans, new to the island, were never prepared for it. "Bugs? What kind of bugs?" I could feel the anxiety taking over. "No one said anything to me about bugs?" My daughter and I looked at each other, a little concerned, then back at her. She warned of the creepy crawlers that live in all the homes. She told us to keep our eyes open for spiders "the size of your hand" hiding under the pillows and in between the sheets. She told us stories of small dogs being eaten alive by the feral dogs on the island. The entire ride was one terrifying story after another. Was she serious? Was this the way she welcomed new families to the island? You could have heard a pin drop the rest of the ride. When I caught a glimpse of her in the rear-view mirror, she had a creepy little smirk on her face that immediately warned my spirit. I knew in my gut that she was not to be trusted.

"I'm stuck somewhere between humbled and hell nah."
—Unknown

We finally pulled into the driveway, in front of the little concrete block house that we would call home for the next twelve months. It was not what we were used to, but I was convinced that the awesome adventure ahead would far outweigh the accommodations. I could not wait to get out and into our new space. My daughter? Not so much. Our two dogs, a cockapoo and a shih-poo, who were groomed to perfection before leaving, were now covered in little briars just from walking across the yard. Inside, multiple surfaces in the bedrooms and kitchen were covered in ants. Giant cockroaches came out of both drains in the bathroom when we brushed our teeth or took a shower. When I asked about fresh drinking water, we were told to drink from the tap, which by the way, smelled like rotten eggs. Just to be clear, I don't consider myself a snob, but dirty water is where I draw the line.

"I am presently experiencing life at a rate of several wtf's per hour."
—Unknown

The next day (and every day following), we were picked up three different times and taken to campus for community meals. At some point, I happened to see the young teacher from the previous day. He had dark circles under his eyes and an expression on his face of both shock and regret. He sat alone and didn't say a word to anyone. It was as if he had seen a ghost, or perhaps a giant spider "the size of his hand" in his sheets. The third day was worse, if you can even imagine. We were outside, mid-afternoon, out of nowhere, surrounded by a pack of wild dogs. I quickly retrieved my own dogs, one in each arm, and stood in front of my daughter as a shield to protect her. The pack was growling, teeth exposed, close enough that I could feel their breath on my leg. I knew if they decided to attack, I would not be able to protect us. I was terrified. Thank goodness a few of the locals chased them away. They were adamant that we carry rocks and sticks to defend ourselves anytime we walked outside. They told us that dog attacks were common and having two small dogs would make us a target. They could not believe that the school did not warn me of this fact before we arrived.

After such a terrifying experience, I immediately put a request in to be moved to campus. I did not feel safe outside and I certainly did not move to an island to sit in the house. The school campus was gated, the accommodations were beautiful, and all the other expat families lived there. I was a single woman with a teenage daughter and two lap dogs. It made sense that my little tribe live there too. But, for some reason, they put us out in the middle of nowhere, surround by thick bush, unprotected from potential dangers on the island.

My request was approved for June of the following year, as they didn't have any available units on campus until that time. It was September. They tried to reassure me that all would be fine and continued to imply that we were perfectly safe where we were. The assistant principal even suggested that I leave my daughter at the house alone while I attend faculty meetings and teacher trainings, but the locals had already warned me not to leave my daughter alone at the home at any time, for any reason, because it wasn't safe. When I told her that I was warned otherwise, she became angry and accused me of going behind the back of "my leader." (My Shadow Self: "I grew up in the hood. If you think for one second that I would be led by a blonde, blue-eyed 20-something white girl from America in the heart of the Bahamian islands, you have me all the way fucked up.") "Hell nah. Not today, Satan." There were so many things about her that seemed manipulative and unethical, but really, she was the least of my concerns. I had to decide if we were going to wait it out, in the bush, until June. Or if it was time to cut ties. "Tai, pack your things, we're going home."

The next day, I went in to meet with the administration to terminate my contract. The principal was shocked by my decision and called me disrespectful. She said that I should be grateful to have an opportunity to live and work in the Bahamas (*as if I couldn't live and work anywhere in the world?!*). I'm not sure if they were just used to power-tripping young people fresh out of college or what, but I had already been in the game for many years and I was not easily manipulated. God, family, work. In that order. Every. Single. Time. "Integrity over everything" is how I roll.

As soon as I signed the paperwork, poof—we didn't exist. They left my daughter and I at that house, with no communication, no food and no transportation for two days. When the locals caught wind of the news, they immediately came to our rescue. They wrapped their arms around us, took care of us, treated us like family. They were some of the most beautiful people I have ever met. One sweet friend offered her car to me the following day so my daughter and I could explore the island. Another sweet friend offered to be our tour guide for a personalized adventure. Another sweet friend invited us over for family dinner and then took us to the beach for a bonfire under the stars. The next day, we packed our bags, and said our goodbyes. More sweet friends showed up to the airport to help cover travel expenses and see us off. What was supposed to be a one-year contract ended up being a two-week vacation.

"And so she learned that love was something you couldn't force; you had to trust that the universe would bring you exactly what your soul needed to complete itself."
—Mark Anthony

We arrived at Greensboro, homeless. I was without a job, my daughter wasn't enrolled in school, and I had already sold most of our belongings. Almost everything I worked for over the course of my career was gone. I felt like a horrible parent and a total failure. My Mom took us in. My daughter and I, two dogs, and a pile of suitcases, all stuffed into one room. She didn't have much in material offerings, but she held us tight, loved on us, and prayed over us. It was exactly what we needed. As I ran in circles, trying to figure out my next move, I heard God's voice, loud in my ear. "Peace child. Be still. Everything is already taken care of." Then, like magic, angels started to appear everywhere.

"Focus on the powerful, euphoric, magical, synchronistic, beautiful parts of life, and the universe will keep giving them to you."
—Unknown

The very next day, I got a call from my first angel. Without my knowing, she had organized a GoFundMe, exceeded the goal, and was ready to transfer the funds to my account. An entire community of angels contributed to that fund. Three days later, I received an email from another angel. She offered accommodations in the west wing of her home, for "as long as we needed to stay." Four weeks after that, I met the next angel. He offered to lease me his beautiful condo, even though I had no job and no prospects. He said, "You taught my wife and my daughter. They love you so I trust you." I moved in that following weekend. I used the GoFundMe account to cover first and last month's rent, deposit, utilities, food, toiletries, and house supplies. The very next week, another angel called. She owned a business in town and needed a studio manager. She heard I was back and called to offer me the position right on the spot.

*"The moment I realized we don't attract what we want, we attract
what we are, I became the greatest version of myself."*
—Unknown

Blessings continued to pour in, one after another. There was an incredible favor over my life. Doors were opening and angels continued to show up. I continued to pray, and God continued to answer. I spent the next five months taking entrepreneurial classes and launched a business upon completion. Almost two years in, my business is growing and thriving.

*"When your energy vibrates at a frequency that is within direct alignment
to what the Universe has been attempting to deliver your entire life, you
begin to live in the flow and true miracles start to happen."*
—Panache Desai

Self-transformation is the direct result of a shift in perspective. I learned to acknowledge my setbacks, challenges, and obstacles from a place of total acceptance. All those things weren't happening to me, they were happening for me. When I look back through the timeline of events, I can see clearly that all of it was necessary to get me exactly where I am supposed to be. For years, I prayed for freedom to build my own dream, make my own schedule, have more time with my daughter, more time in my studio. It turns out, the very story that I thought would break me, ended up setting me free.

*"It's funny how we outgrow what we once thought we couldn't live without, and then fall in love
with what we didn't even know we wanted. Life keeps leading us on journeys we would never go
on if it were up to us. Don't be afraid. Have faith. Find the lessons. Trust the journey."*
—Akshara Shrivastava

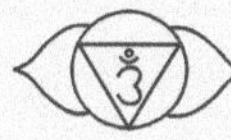

PEACEFUL ✧ PRACTICE
Third Eye Chakra

When you are disconnected from your true spiritual nature, you will feel a sense of loneliness or emptiness deep within your core. You will identify as separate from the Natural World and become distracted by your own privilege.

Illuminate your Spirit by extending prayers and blessings to all things; The Universe, The Earth, People, Animals, Bugs, Friends and Family, Strangers, and to all who have caused you pain. Offer prayers for a collected healing, a revolution of consciousness, that all life may live in peace and be free from suffering.

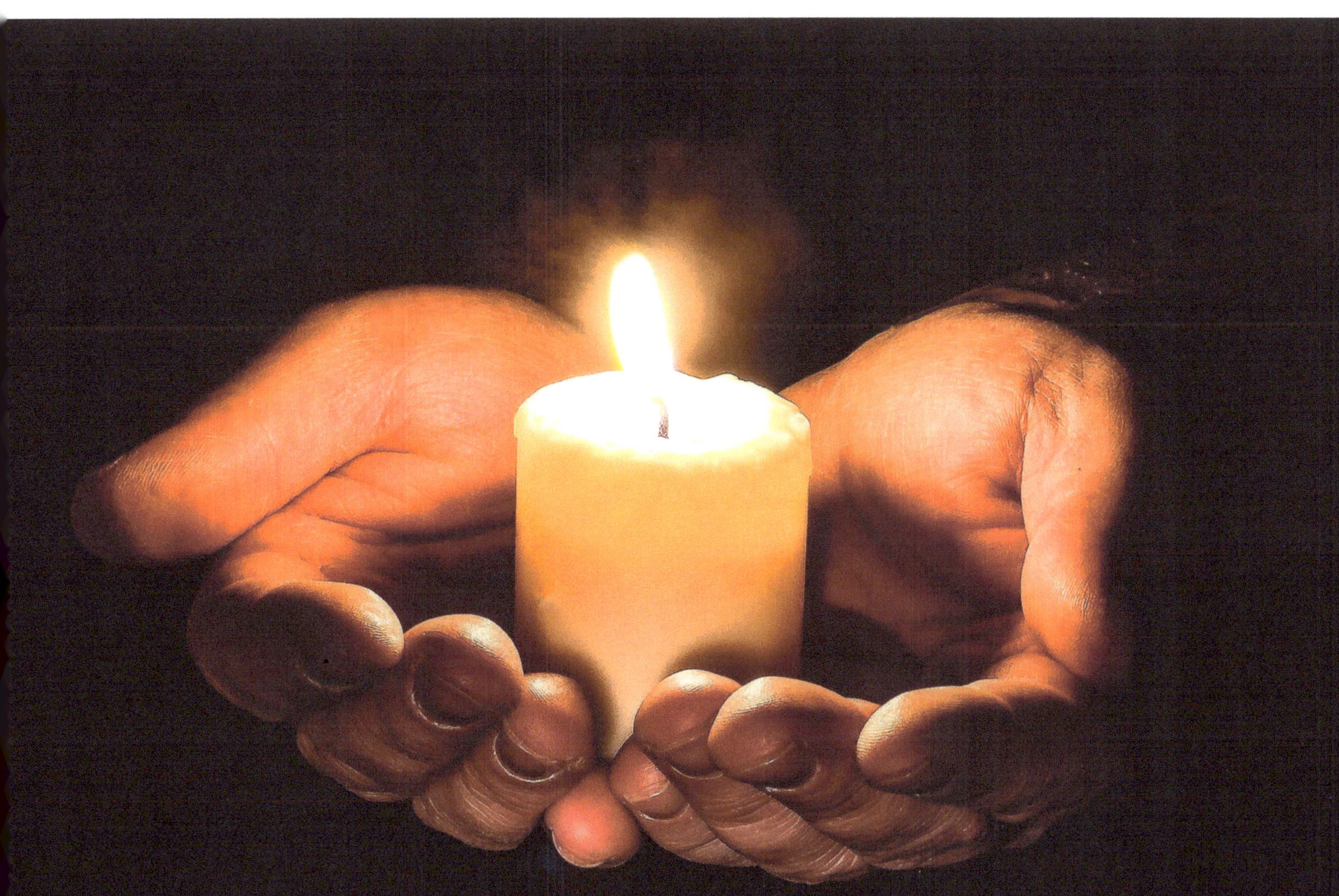

HOLISTIC WELLNESS
Practice Opening Your Third Eye: Illumination

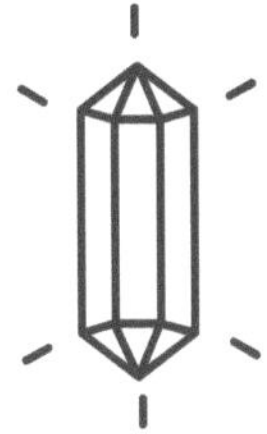

CRYSTALS

Amethyst, Labradorite, Lepidolite, Lapis Lazuli

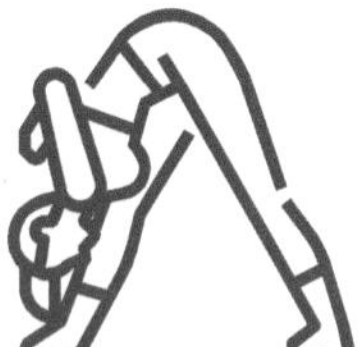

YOGA

Pyramid Pose

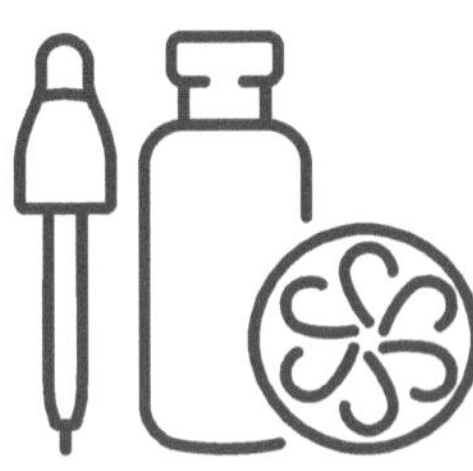

ESSENTIAL OILS

Frankincense, Jasmine, Myrrh, Star Arise, Patchouli

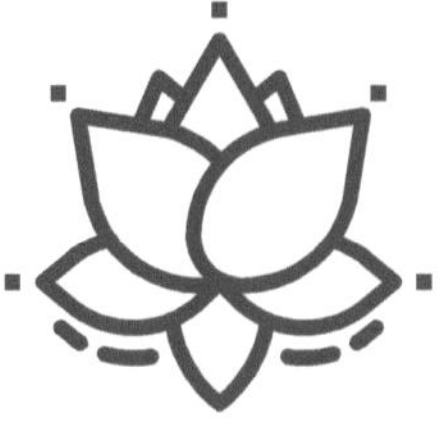

INTELLECTUAL WELLNESS

Intelligence isn't knowing everything. It is the ability to challenge everything you know.

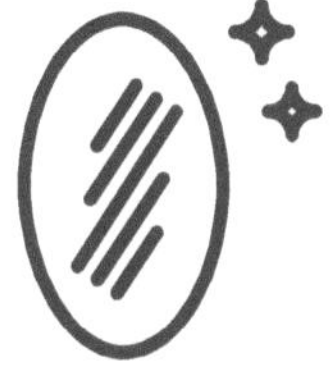

AFFIRMATION

My spiritual vision is clear. I honor my intuition and see divine Light in all beings. I will act with moral courage, justice and self-control.

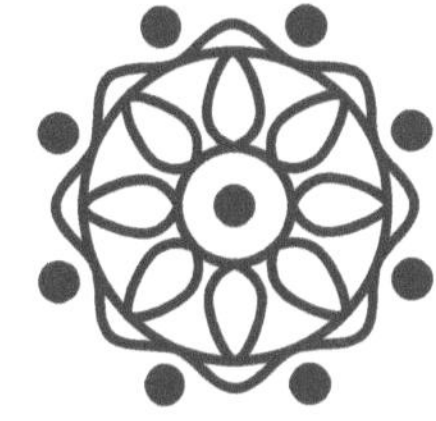

MEDITATION

Offer blessings to all living things on the Earth. Pray that all may live in peace and be free from suffering.

FOOD

Purple Grapes, Purple Kale, Blueberries, Purple Cabbage, Eggplant, Purple Carrots, Purple Potatoes, Blackberries, Plums, Cacao

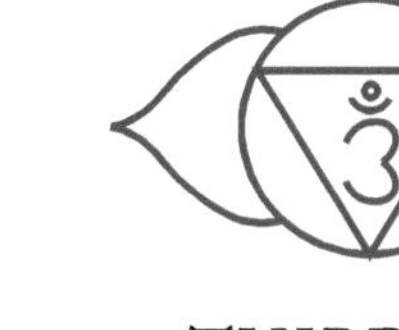

THIRD EYE

Located deep in the center of the brain and is connected to Light. It serves as a metaphysical connection between the physical and spiritual worlds.

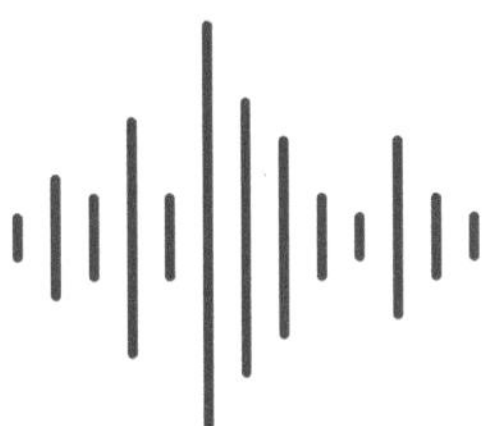

SOUND

Activate crystal clear intuition.

852 Hz

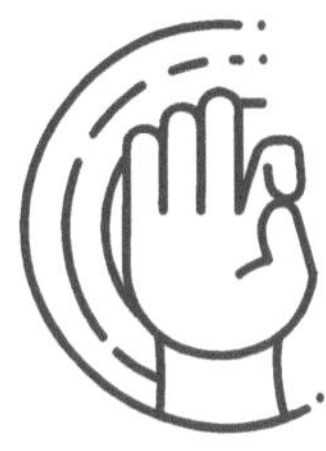

MUDRA

"Intuition / Wisdom"

Hands in front of the lower part of your breast. Middle fingers stand up tips touching, other fingers bend at first joint.

Long A-A-A-U-U-M

COLOR

Indigo Stimulates: Self-Responsibility, Inner Strength, Creative Visualization, Intuition, Calmness, Clairvoyance, Beauty

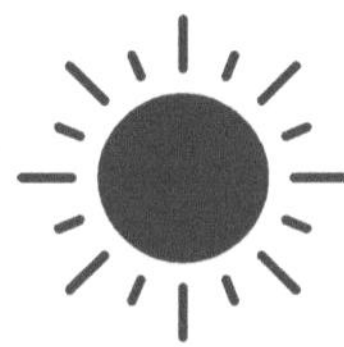

SUN GAZING

Many ancient cultures used this practice to heal illnesses, obtain psychic abilities, and charge the brain. If done correctly, at the right time of day, there are many benefits.

CREATIVE FLOW
Artistic Expression

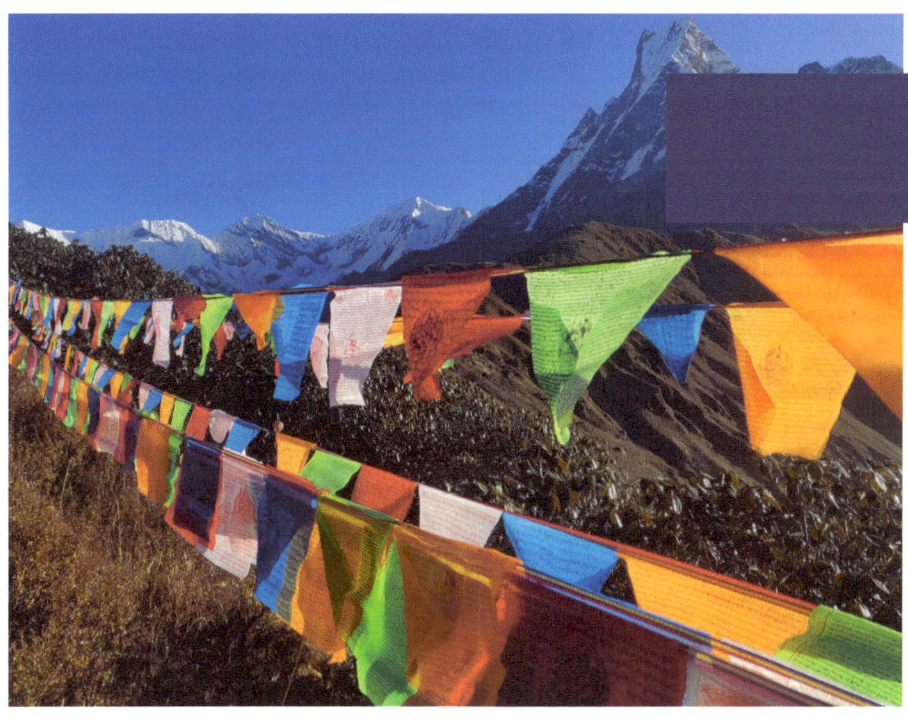

"Peacemaking does not mean passivity. It is the act of interrupting injustice without mirroring injustice, the act of disarming evil without destroying the evildoer, the act of finding a third way that is neither fight nor flight but the careful, arduous pursuit of reconciliation and justice. It is about a revolution of love that is big enough to set both the oppressed and the oppressors free." –Shane Claiborne

Materials Needed

Watercolor Paper

Watercolors

Colored Pencils

Sharpies

Hole Punch

Ribbon/String

Scissors

Masking Tape

"I imagine one of the reasons people cling to their hates so stubbornly is because they sense, once hate is gone, they will be forced to deal with pain."

—James Baldwin

Intention: Illumination
Human experience: Self-reflection (privilege and separation)
Spiritual practice: Self-transformation (perspective and insight)

PRAYER FLAGS
Instructions

Prayer flags are traditionally used to promote peace, strength, well-being, and wisdom. They are intended to spread goodwill and compassion by sending prayers out into the world. The practice of hanging prayer flags quietly harmonizes the environment, increasing happiness and love.

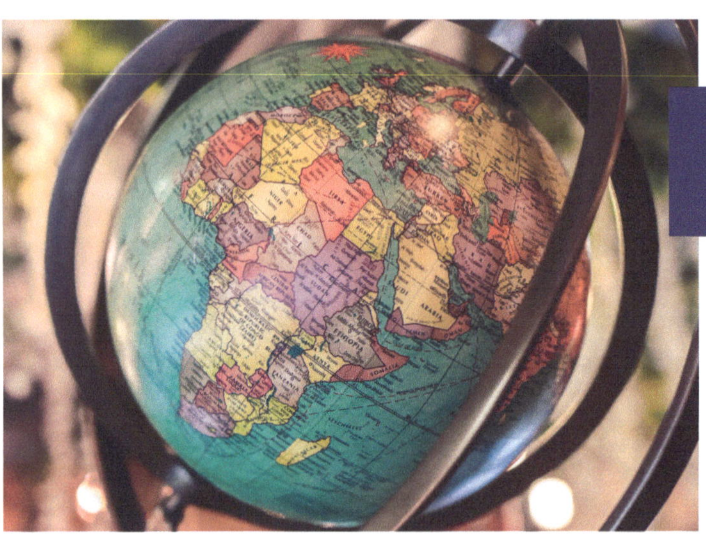

Step 1

Check out globalgoals.org to learn about the 17 Global Goals for sustainable development. Come up with seven beautiful words that you would like to use on your prayer flags as an offering of hope and healing.

Step 2

Lay down a rectangle shape of masking tape in the center of each piece of watercolor paper. Use colored pencils to draw simple organic lines and shapes, filling in the negative space around the tape. Use watercolors to add details around the colored pencils.

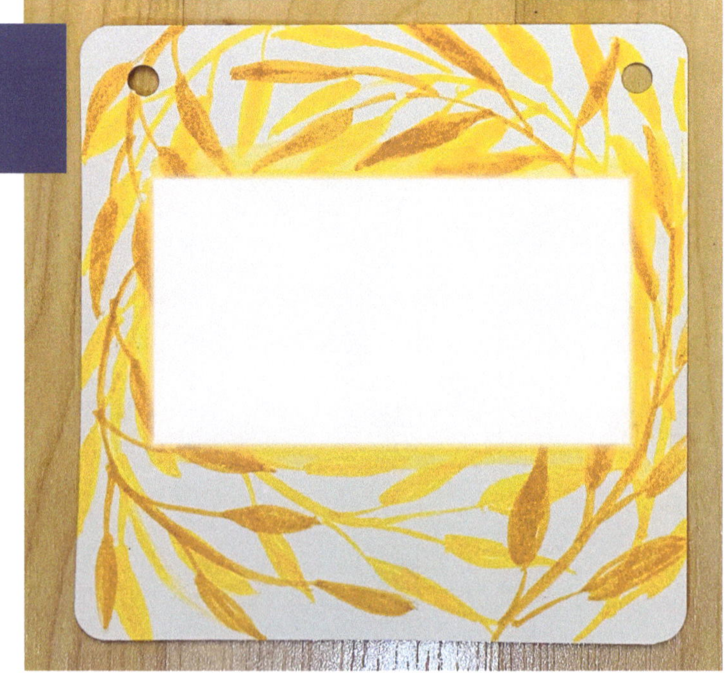

PRAYER FLAGS
Instructions

"When we heal ourselves, we heal our ancestors from wounds that run deep in our family. When we heal our ancestors, we heal the world from wounds that run deep in humanity."

—Miriam Rose

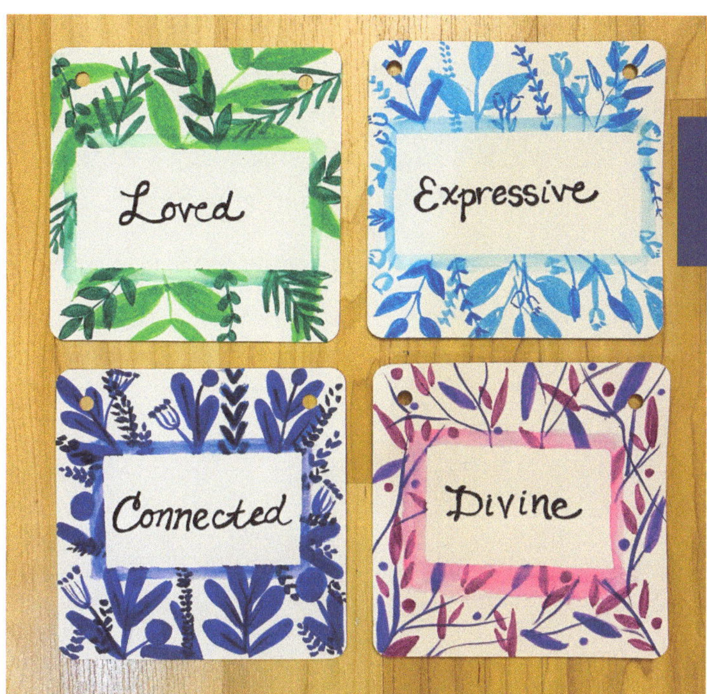

Step 3

Once the paint is dry, remove the tape. Use a pencil to write one word in the center of each flag. Trace with a sharpie.

Step 4

Punch holes in the top-left and right corners. Use a beautiful ribbon to string the cards together.

And voila! They are ready to hang!

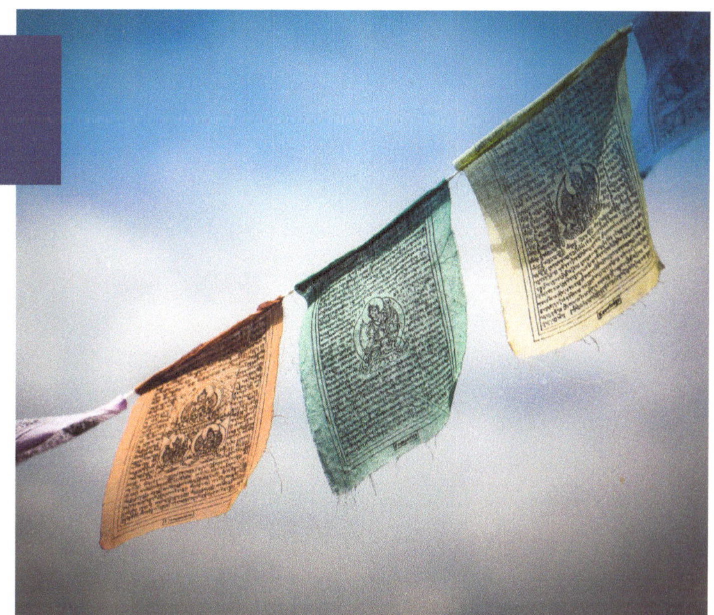

Our world is not divided by race, color, gender, or religion. Our world is divided into wise people and fools. And fools divide themselves by race, color, gender, or religion.

—Nelson Mandela

CONSCIOUS CONNECTIONS

Open your Mind

Explore different points of view

Experience and learn from different cultures

Decalcify your pineal gland

Do not ingest fluoride

Widen your perspective

Cultivate your own thoughts and ideas

Listen to your intuition

Practice the art of Sun Gazing

DID YOU KNOW?

Humans can only see 1% of the visual light spectrum. That means that 99% of reality can not be seen with the human eye. We are only able to perceive a tiny fraction of the world we live in. The majority of existence is invisible!

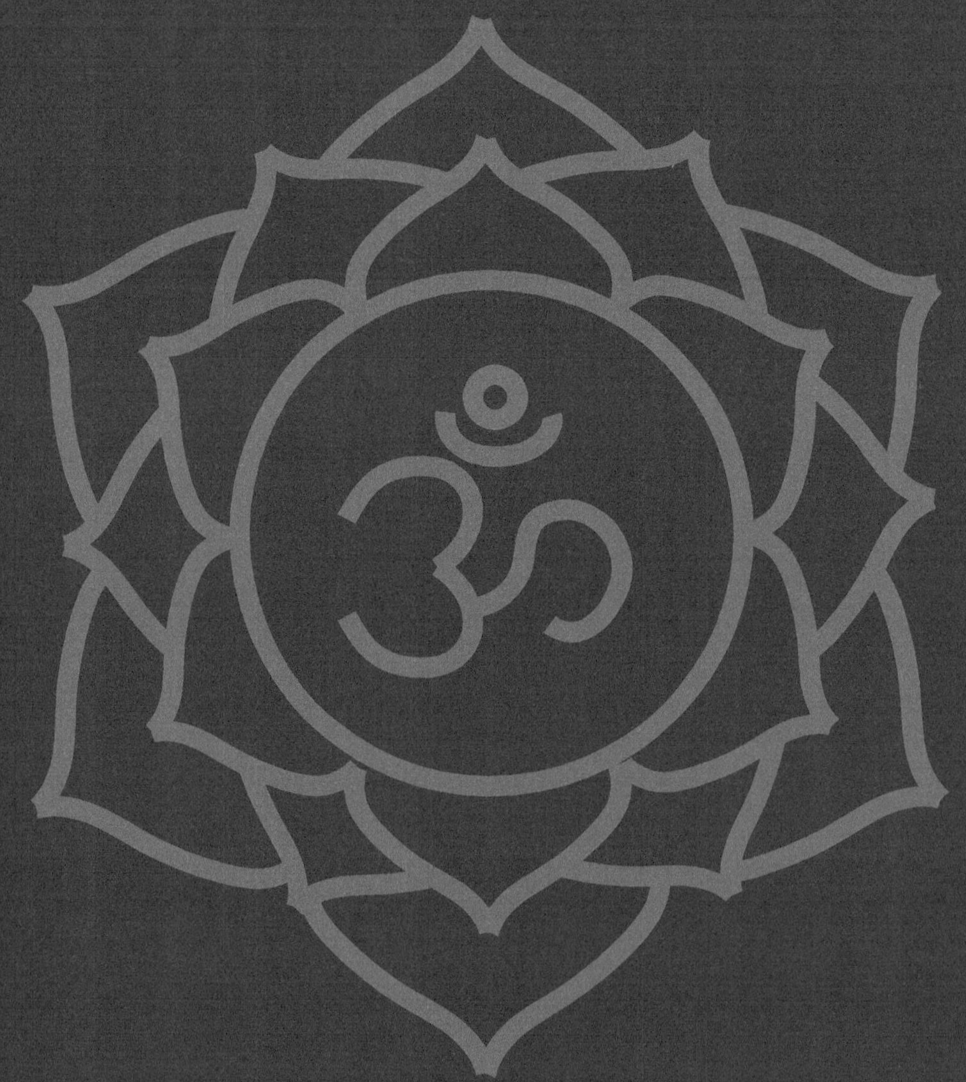

"There is nothing more important to true growth than realizing that you are not the voice of the mind— you are the one who hears it."
—Michael A. Singer

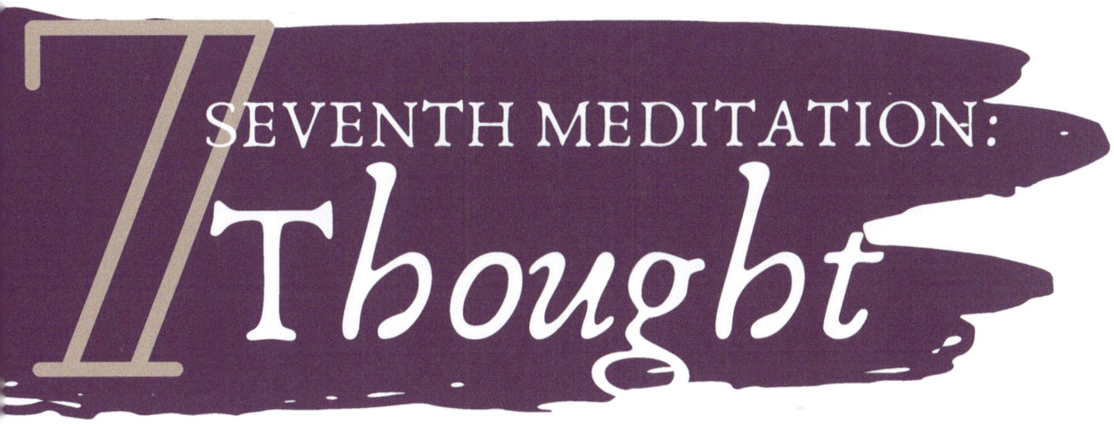

The Crown Chakra represents Mindfulness, Your Higher Self, and the Awakening of Consciousness.

Think of your Higher self as the great big expansive sky and your thoughts as the clouds passing by. Learn to observe your thoughts, without identifying with them. They are not who you are. Become sensitive to the awareness within that can guide you to truth and to Light. Consciousness is wise. It is the voice of patience, love, and grace. It is the awareness connected to the Divine.

Who are you?
(Do not use labels to define your religion, belief, ideology, gender, sexuality, race, age, nationality, etc.)

"And if you become aware that you are not your thoughts, the life of those thoughts will begin to grow weaker, they will begin to become more and more lifeless. The power of your thoughts lies in the fact that you think they are yours."
—Osha

Intention: Connect to Source
Human experience: Self-knowledge (attachment and materialism)
Spiritual practice: Self-mastery (consciousness and spirituality)

CROWN CHAKRA:

Consciousness, connection, spirituality

ELEMENT: *Thought*
IDENTITY: *Universal*
LOCATION: *Top of Head*
INTENTION: *Connect to Source*

The Crown Chakra processes the awareness of consciousness and spirituality and is blocked by attachment and materialism.

"God is a frequency
that exists within you.
Tune In."
—Unknown

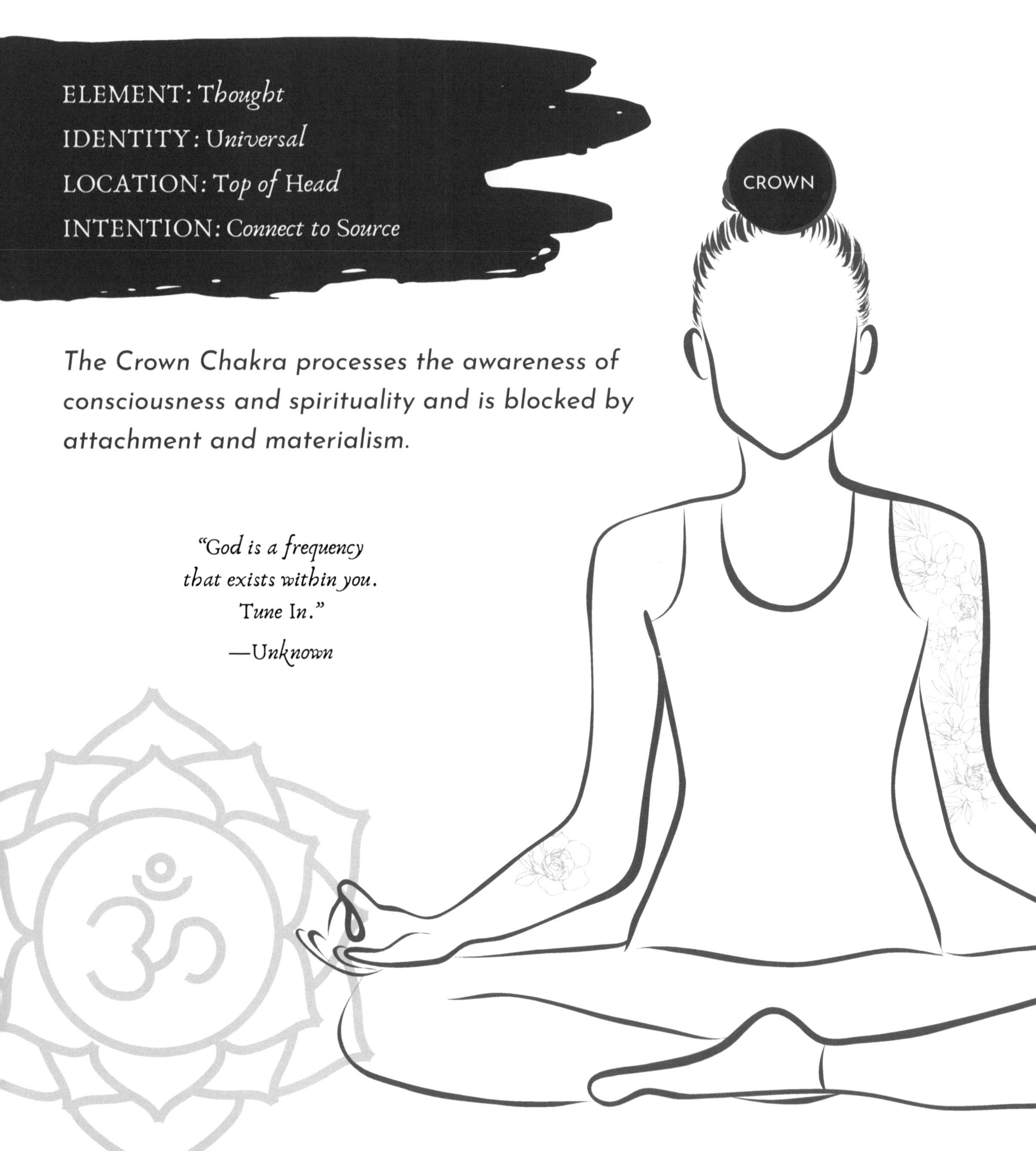

CROWN CHAKRA:

Connect to source

The following deficient and excessive energies carry low-vibrational frequencies. They are collected and stored in the Crown Chakra, blocking the flow of spiritual energy. If your thoughts, feelings, or behaviors fall into one of these two categories, the healing in this energy center has not yet begun.

Balanced energy in the Crown Chakra is influenced by how often we connect with the God frequency. It is vital to your spiritual health to pour into your Spirit on a daily basis. This practice strengthens the voice of your Higher self and weakens the voice of your shadow. High vibrational frequencies connect you to Source and help you to create and attract from higher levels of consciousness.

Raise Your Vibration

DEFICIENT ENERGY

- DEPRESSION
- CYNICISM
- DISREGARD FOR THE SACRED
- CLOSED-MINDED
- DISCONNECTED FROM SOURCE
- ALIENATED
- APATHY
- LIMITED BELIEFS
- MATERIALISM
- ANGER AT DIVINE
- LONELINESS
- ALIENATION
- DEPRESSION
- WEAK FAITH
- HOPELESSNESS
- SELF-INDULGENCE
- RIGID BELIEF SYSTEM
- BRAIN FOG
- APATHY
- CONFUSION

BALANCED ENERGY

- STRONG FAITH
- UNIVERSAL LOVE
- AWARE/AWAKE
- WISDOM
- CONSCIOUSNESS
- SPIRITUAL CONNECTION
- AWARE
- INTELLIGENCE
- KNOWLEDGE
- UNDERSTANDING
- BLISS
- PRESENCE
- OPEN MINDEDNESS
- ENLIGHTENMENT
- INSPIRED
- EQUANIMITY
- AT PEACE

EXCESSIVE ENERGY

- JUDGMENTAL
- DOGMATIC
- GRANDIOSE
- SPIRITUAL ADDICTION
- OVERLY INTELLECTUAL
- RIGHTEOUSNESS
- EXCESSIVE PURITY
- STRONG ATTACHMENT
- DISSOCIATED FROM BODY/WORLD

Intention: Connect to Source
Human experience: Self-knowledge (attachment and materialism)
Spiritual practice: Self-mastery (consciousness and spirituality)

What is your Highest truth?

Think through your timeline.
What were you taught about spirituality or spiritual practices?

What are the first thoughts that you have when you don't get what you want?

Which of your thought patterns could use a good dose of consciousness?

Intention: Connect to Source
Human experience: Self-knowledge (attachment and materialism)
Spiritual practice: Self-mastery (consciousness and spirituality)

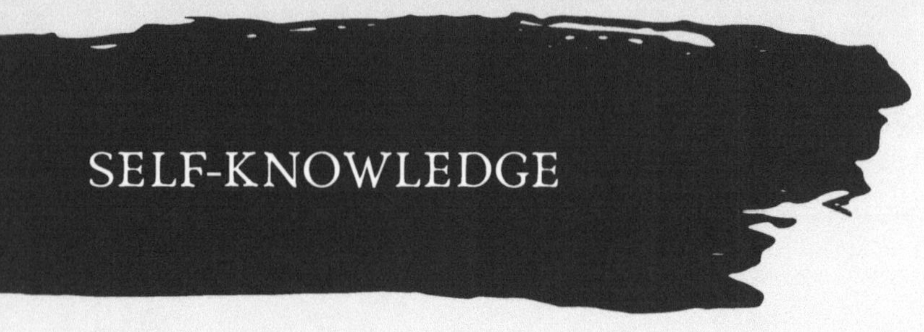

My Experience with Materialism and Attachment

"Children do learn what they live. Then they grow up to live what they've learned."
—Dorothy Nolte

My mother was a single parent of four. She was a no-bullshit kind of lady, tough as an ox. She was the type of Mom who taught us to think critically about our decisions so we wouldn't be surprised by the consequences, good or bad. She wanted us to make logical choices, not because "mommy said so," but because we knew better. Any time I had a meltdown, she would look at me, hand on her hip, no-bullshit face, and say "Kara, calm down. You got this. Let's think logically here." She was always teaching, always encouraging, always coaching us along. She was a nurse by trade, often picking up extra shifts to keep food on the table and the bills paid.

When she was home, she was on the move. Music turned up, cleaning, cooking, making beautiful notes of affirmations, prayers, and quotes to hang on the walls around the house. She used colorful markers and wrote in flowy organic font. She taught me that letters are art and that beautiful words are like music to the ears. The only time she stopped moving was to perch back and smoke a cigarette. To me, she represented power, strength, resilience, and grit. I never saw anything shake her. She was the type that would suck it up and get it done, and she expected that from her children as well. It didn't matter how far out in the deep end she would find us. Her response was, "You took your ass out there, now figure out how to get back." It was always about the work ethic. She would say, "As long as you try your best, that's all that matters. I don't care if you bring home a C as long as you worked your ass off for it. But if you bring home a C when you were capable of an A-, I'm whooping your ass." And she meant every word. You can't do anything but respect that.

She was cool. "Aunt Sandie" to all the neighborhood kids, she took everyone in. She had the mouth of a sailor and a heart of a saint. She used to say, "Always look for the kid who doesn't have any friends—your smile will change their life." She signed us up for camps, programs, and after-school activities, and if there wasn't a coach to do the job, she would take the position. She taught us to keep going no matter what. "You have to be able to pick yourself back up and try again." She taught me that I could do anything if I worked hard for it, and I believed her. I was driven and focused. I pushed myself to the max at everything I did. Her take-no-shit-AND-I-love-you approach to parenting created a warrior spirit. I was determined to succeed.

My father was in and out of prison most of my childhood. We were either visiting him in prison or he was visiting us at home—but either way, I missed him terribly. He was my daddy and I loved him something fierce. He was raised by an alcoholic, and as a child himself, was beaten relentlessly. That violence created a monster, fueled by grief and rage. He spent his teenage years running the streets with criminals, and by the time he was an adult, he was a ticking time bomb. No one knew when he would explode so everyone tiptoed around him, terrified of being targeted. His ability to incite fear made him feel powerful and his cultural conditioning kept him prisoner to the illusion of his own ego.

He was a villain in the streets, but he wasn't all shadow. The depth of his rage was equal and opposite to the height of his joy. On a normal day, if he was home, he was the life of the party. We had one large stereo system that was always up loud enough to fill every room in the house with music. The smell in the air was usually a mixture of food cooking on the stove and a bucket of bleach water in the bathroom. Good music, good food, and a clean house was all it took to make my dad a very happy man. He would dance around the living room all lit up with joy.

I would just sit and stare at him with so much love in my eyes and in my heart. He would bow and take my hand, gently pull me up onto his feet, and then twirl me around the living room in the most formal fashion. He made me feel like a princess, but deep down there was always a tinge of uneasiness in my body. He was naturally loud and aggressive, and I was the definition of a gentle heart and sensitive soul. He could sense that his presence made me shutter and I could sense that that broke his heart. I was a mirror that forced him to look at his own reflection. He didn't know how to be any different, but with me, he tried. He would often kneel down on one knee next to me and soften his voice, reassuring me that everything was OK. He would wipe my tears with his massive hands, while fighting to hold back his own. The only time I saw gentleness in his eyes was when he looked at me. For this reason, I learned to be a peacemaker and a people pleaser. I wanted to avoid conflict at all costs.

My Aunt Marsha lived at the top of a mountain, with acres upon acres of land. To me, she was the definition of work hard, play hard. She was either on the mower, tending to the flowers, picking fruit from the trees, or berries from the bushes. She loved to cook and bake and host family get-togethers. There was always an abundance of everything at her house. I spent much of my childhood there, swimming during the day and off in the woods riding horses in the evening. My Uncle Jack was a hunter, so there was often a freshly killed deer hanging upside down in the garage, above a pool of its own blood. He used to let us choose our guns from the gun cabinet then take us out back for target practice. Every holiday, Aunt Marsha pulled out the photo albums and we would all sit around together looking through family pictures and listening to stories. I loved spending time with her. All the kids did. She acknowledged us and spent real quality time with us. She was fun and spontaneous. She taught me that everything in life is an adventure.

"Children learn more from what you are, than what you teach."
—W. E. B. Du Bois

My Aunt Karla was only 5'2", but her presence was regal. "Grace and poise, Kara. Grace and poise." She reminded me of a queen. With white blonde hair and bright blue eyes, she was confident, sophisticated, educated, and refined. She was the type to eat dessert first because "you only live once." She never raised her voice but was assertive and matter of fact about her rules and expectations, a no-nonsense kind of woman. She loved to build large furniture items with her power tools, and if I was there; she would not allow me to stand around idle. "More hands, less work." She taught me that I was strong enough and smart enough to build anything, and how to have fun while I was doing it. She created a beautiful garden in her yard that could be seen from the kitchen window so while she washed the dishes, she could enjoy the view. She would say, "The to-do list is always going to be there, you might as well whistle while you work."

"There are places in the heart you don't even know exist until you love a child."
—Anne Lamott

As a child, I spent a lot of time with my grandma. We drank tea and played rummy more than we did anything else. She loved to pull out the old-school slides and projector. She would aim it at the wall in the living room and turn off all the lights. She told stories of her life as a military wife, living in Europe, raising children. When I was a young girl, she made it very clear that I wasn't allowed to play outside, in her neighborhood, with the "nigger" kids. I didn't know what that meant at the time, but later found out that when my mother told her that she was pregnant with me, she was ostracized from the family for being a "nigger lover." Isn't it funny how the Universe sends us children that push against the boundaries and parameters that we cage ourselves in? They are our teachers of what it means to love without conditions. Over time, she softened. There was never any doubt in my mind that she loved us with all of her heart. She was fighting her own demons, and we were exactly the experience that she needed to heal some of them.

"Show me your friends and I'll show you your future."
—Unknown

As soon as I became a teenager, my entire life changed when I was thrown headfirst into a harsh and unforgiving reality. My relationship with my Mom was shattered, and I was spiraling out of control. I felt abandoned at home, so I ran to the streets in search of love and connection. We were wild, feral children. We didn't know boundaries, we didn't follow rules, and we damn sure did not respect authority.

I was on the fast track to nowhere. My Mom wanted desperately to preserve our relationship. She wanted to keep me close and know that I was safe, so she gave up her role as my parent and adopted a new role as my friend. At fourteen years old, I started taking her car to run errands, pick up friends, and cruise around town. At fifteen, she signed for body piercings and took me to get my first tattoo. She was by my side the first time I went to a nightclub because she wanted to teach me how to "protect myself around drunk men."

My friends and I often partied at the house, coming and going as we pleased. My mom bought our cigarettes and her friend at the time let us play paper football for bags of weed. He would hold his hands in the air, thumbs together, pointer fingers up, about five feet from the table. You could see the sweat on our foreheads as we steadied the football, lining it up with the target. We only had three shots to score. If we failed, we were out. Those were the rules, and there were no second chances.

I was, like all children, a byproduct of my environment. Although I had many experiences that fed my spirit, I had many more that fed my shadow. The unconscious program that was given to me, I did not choose for myself. So, I observe it, without attachment. Your shadow's voice will always be there, but through daily spiritual practices, the quieter it will become. The mind will grow what you choose to cultivate. Keep the flowers, pull the weeds, and never stop planting new seeds.

> *"The first step toward success is taken when you refuse to be a captive of the environment in which you first find yourself."*
> —Mark Caine

When I was a teenager, the conditions were perfect for my shadow to take over and lead the way. My conscience knew better but the voice of my Higher self was beyond my perception. Self-knowledge is an excavation of the mind. The goal is to uncover the truth about how our experiences and interactions growing up, influenced our motives and character. It is digging through the patterns of thoughts that have been hardwired into our subconscious mind and are now running on autopilot and directing our lives.

Shadow work is key to healing and restoring this energy center. Through intentional daily practice, I continue to refine my moral compass and search for magic in the Light. Ram Das taught that our human experience is the curriculum and spirituality is the high.

> *If you look at the people in your circle and don't get inspired, then you don't have a circle. You have a cage."*
> —Nipsey Hussle

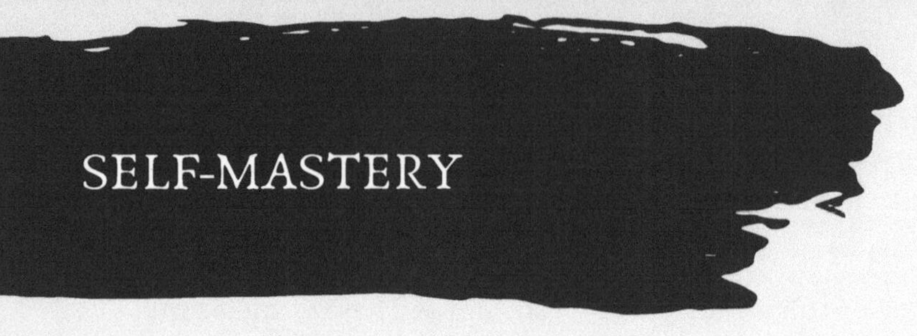

My Experience with Consciousness and Spirituality

"Train up a child in the way he should go and when he is old, he will not depart from it."
—Proverbs 22:6

I grew up "Christian." I didn't really know what that meant early on, but I really didn't have a choice in the matter. I knew to listen to my mother or suffer the consequences. My Mom always kept us connected to a church even though we were never regular customers. We popped in here and there, some years more than others, depending on where we were and what was going on in our lives at the time. Still, we prayed before meals and read bible stories at night. My Mom loved to make beautiful little scripture cards and hang them around the house. She was no saint and she definitely had a slew of demons that haunted her, but her intention to keep God in our lives and in our hearts was genuine.

"Remember that your perception of the world is a reflection of your state of consciousness."
—Eckhart Tolle

There was something about church that felt unnatural to me, and something about the teaching that felt forced. I asked so many questions because there was much that just didn't make sense, didn't resonate within the depths of my Being. I was eleven years old the day the preacher asked me to come up after service to be saved. I remember the alarm sounding off in my gut in response to a prayer that went something like this:

"Lord Jesus, I was born a sinner. I believe you died on the cross so God would forgive my sins. I believe the only way to get to the father is through you, Jesus. I receive YOU as my Lord and Savior. Amen."

What I heard was:

"Jesus is God. I am born of darkness. Jesus is the only way to reach God. Jesus is God. Heaven is only attainable after death if I profess 'Jesus is God' in this life. Amen."

These were my questions:

- If I call anyone God, other than God, isn't that idolatry?

- If God was in Jesus, isn't he in all of us?

- If my spirit is an expression of God, wasn't I born of Light?

- Aren't all paths that lead to God accomplishing the same goal?

- Why do you keep saying Jesus is God?

- Didn't a group of men throw out numerous books from the bible and reconfigure the entire thing based on their own agenda?

"Unthinking respect for authority is the greatest enemy of truth."
—*Albert Einstein*

I remember looking around at all of the "nice" people, wondering how on earth they were buying into this bullshit. I couldn't rationalize a loving God using humans as pawns in a game of "guess the one right religion out of 4,000+ or burn in hell for eternity. Oh, and by the way, you have roughly eighty some years to figure it out, if of course nothing happens in between. Good luck!" What kind of sick shit is that?!

In addition to the questionable teaching, I could not, for the life of me, figure out why we were congregating in a building to get closer to God. The Natural world was pulsating with a Life Force Energy so powerful and miraculous, it damn near takes your breath away. One only needs to stand back and take in the absolute perfection of the design to see that God is ever-present in Nature. Why would we go anywhere else if we wanted to be next to him? All this disparity was constantly spinning around in my head, but anytime I asked a question, I was scolded and told to have faith. I spent my entire childhood in nature, and nothing about this experience came close to that vibration. I did end up getting saved that day, but it was a decision based in fear and obligation.

"The search for truth is a search for identity, that in finding Truth, we find ourselves."
—*Neil Sutton*

I carried the Christian label through my teenage years and young adult life, even though my lifestyle was the farthest thing from holy. The day I decided to drop the label was the day that I decided to go on my own journey, in search for Truth. I collected books on religion and spiritual teachings, asked questions, did a ton of research, obsessed with finding the answers. The more I read, prayed, and studied, the clearer the path became. I decided that my spiritual practice would be inspired by the heart of Jesus and the mind of Buddha. I would follow all paths that lead to the Light and seek the face of God by going deep within myself.

I started meditating regularly. I began each day on a yoga mat in my living room, Hillsong United playing quietly in the background, working towards stillness in my body and in my mind. I would pray and talk to God, then sit in meditation to listen. The more I practiced, the easier it became to quickly fall into a deep state of relaxation and peace.

And then one day, I found Him. I was about ten minutes into my meditation when my consciousness was transported through a tunnel of magnificent colors racing past my head, moving at incredible speed. I came to an abrupt stop when the tunnel opened to the most beautiful landscape I had ever seen. It was a slow-motion view of lush green fields that extended far out into the distance, mountains, water, a giant expansive blue sky. I was almost invisible within this enormous space. I felt small and vulnerable, but there was a noticeable presence that was comforting and reassuring.

Before I could settle in, I was jerked into high acceleration over the landscape, then dropped "at His feet." The presence was so large that I can only think to compare it to what an ant might feel like standing in front of a General Sherman tree. It wasn't like I was looking at toes, but I knew without a doubt that I was standing before the presence of God. It was so magnificent that I felt this weird sensation to bow my head. But my head was pulled back up and an immediate vibration of Love and Grace fell over me. It was an offering so pure and so full; I could barely contain all of it within the confines of my body. It filled my heart and poured out of my eyes. I could feel all of the guilt and shame that I had been carrying around for years, being absolved. I was instructed to tune myself to this vibration, apply it to myself, and to every soul I encounter along my path.

Self-mastery is the journey of mastering the experience of this reality, through the awakening of consciousness. Living consciously means choosing each day to quiet the shadow and lead with the Higher self. It is the consistent practice of being accountable for your energy and vibration. It is the creation of Light where there is darkness, peace where there is chaos, stillness where there is noise—in the mind, body, and spirit. What do you often see throughout your day? Ladybugs? Bluebirds? Butterflies? I see number patterns everywhere so that became my daily reminder to pray. Anytime I see a pattern of numbers, I immediately close my eyes, give thanks, and raise my vibration to match the frequency of the Divine Matrix, giving honor and reverence to my Creator.

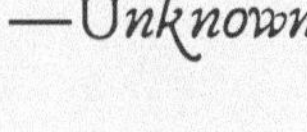

PEACEFUL 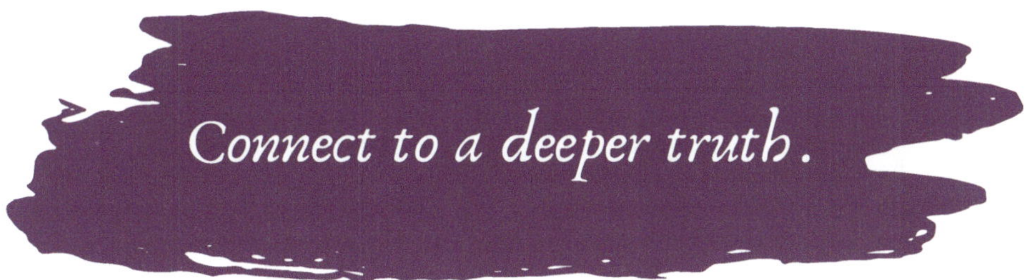 PRACTICE
Crown Chakra

Connect to the deeper truth of who you are: A spiritual Being having a human experience. Question and challenge all of your programmed belief systems. Cleanse yourself of old toxic energy, quiet the shadow, and honor your Higher self.

Close your eyes and expand your lungs by pulling in a deep cleansing breath. Know that you are breathing in a Life Force Energy that is coming from something much greater than yourself. Recognize that all of the Natural World is breathing in that same Life Force Energy.

Take that in… Marvel in it… Be Astonished by it.

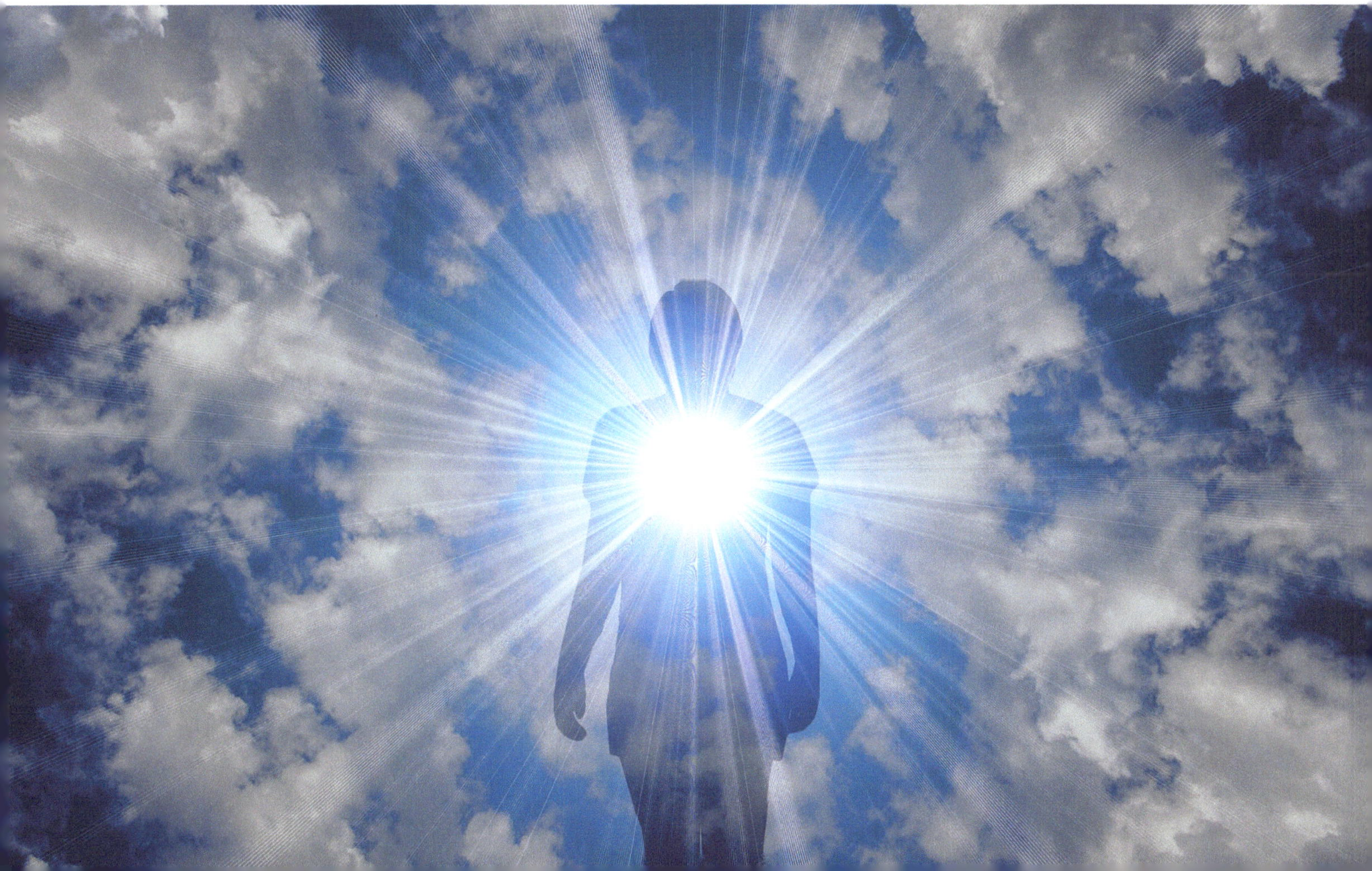

HOLISTIC WELLNESS

Practice Connecting to Source: Consciousness

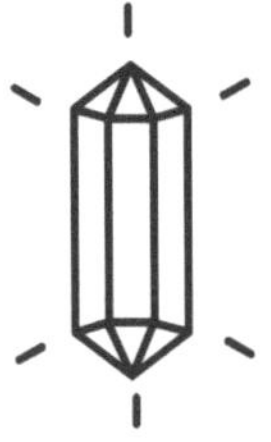

CRYSTALS

Rainbow Moonstone, Howlite, Selenite, Clear Quartz

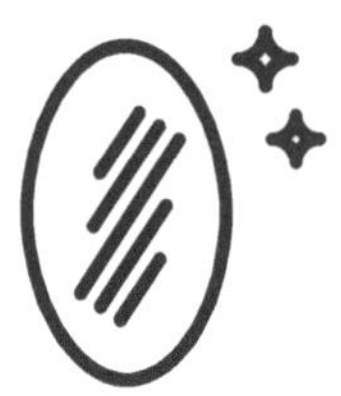

AFFIRMATION

I honor my Highest truth. I seek experiences that nourish my Spirit. I am infinite, one with the Universe. I pursue all paths that lead to the Light, in search of growth and transformation.

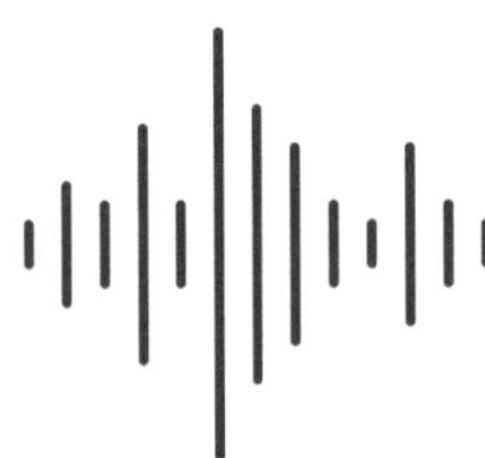

SOUND

Connect with Light and Spirit.

963 Hz

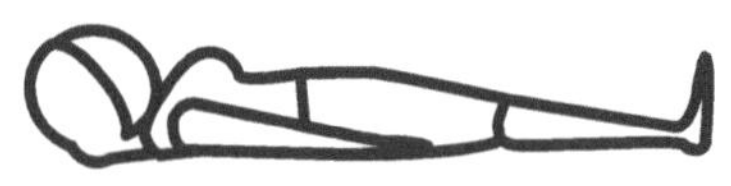

YOGA

Savasana

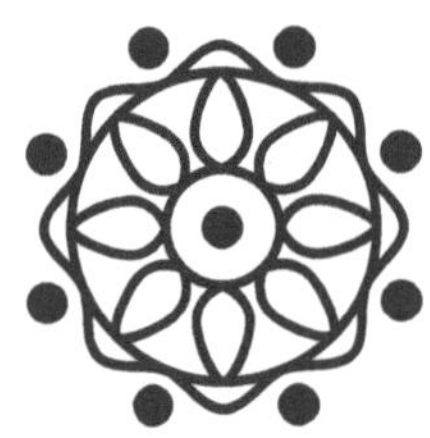

MEDITATION

Close your eyes and inhale a deep cleansing breath. Sit with the knowing that you are an expression of Source. You are the Universe experiencing itself.

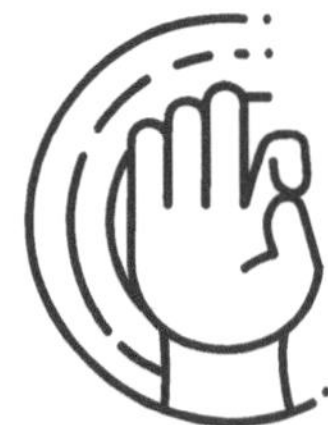

MUDRA

"Spiritual Connection"

Hands in front of your stomach, fingers interlaced, little fingers pointing upwards.

Long A-A-A-A-N-G

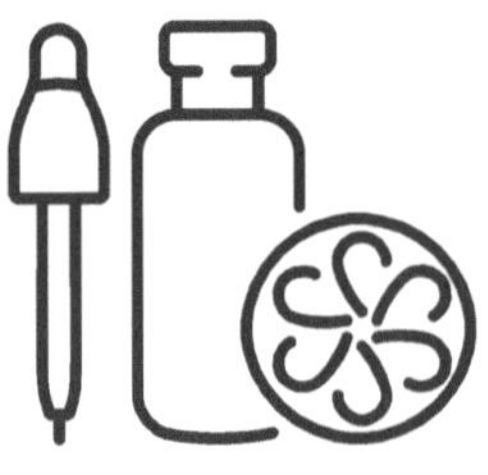

ESSENTIAL OILS

Jasmine, Lavender, Arborvitae, Roman Chamomile, Sandalwood

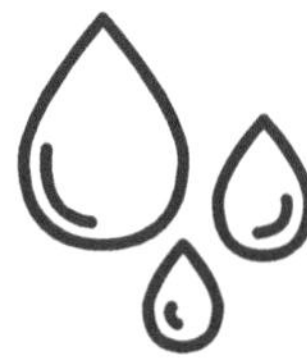

FOOD

Fasting (No Food), Water, Fresh Air, Sunlight, Barefeet in Nature

COLOR

Violet Stimulates: Intuition, Imagination, Self-Knowledge, Meditation, Artistic Qualitie

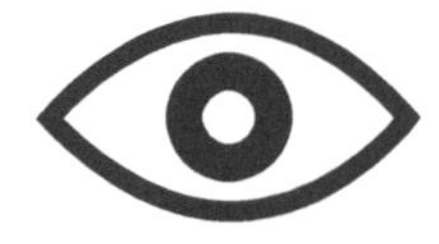

SPIRITUAL WELLNESS

Find meaning and purpose in your life related to your values, beliefs, and moral compass.

CONSCIOUSNESS

Breaking down the ego to allow more Light in.

SPIRITUALITY

Celebration, connection, and reverence for Life. Following all paths that lead to the Light.

CREATIVE FLOW
Artistic Expression

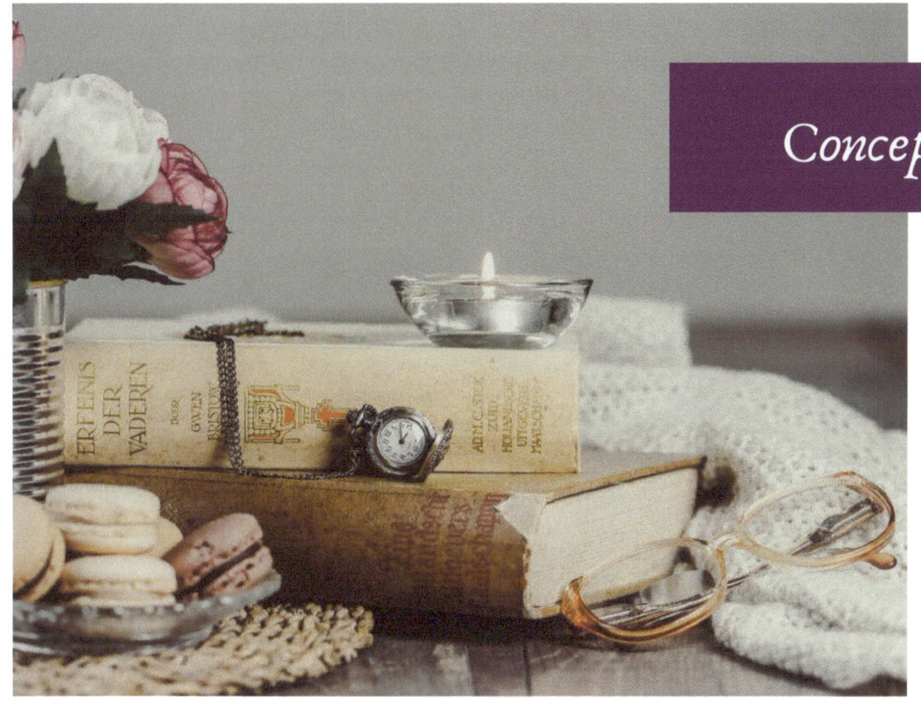

Conceptual Self Portrait

"Any activity done with love and presence is a spiritual practice."

—Unknown

Collect 'found objects' that represent the following 7 categories

1. Grounding - What makes you feel safe?

2. Happiness - What brings you joy?

3. Courage - What makes you feel confident?

4. Love - How do you pour love into yourself?

5. Peace - Where do you need grace?

6. Insight - What do you stand for?

7. Spirituality - What is your Highest truth?

"If you have good thoughts, they will shine out of your face like sunbeams and you will always look lovely."

—Roald Dahl

Intention: Connect to Source
Human experience: Self-knowledge (attachment and materialism)
Spiritual practice: Self-mastery (consciousness and spirituality)

CONCEPTUAL PORTRAIT
Instructions

*"Stop looking outside for scraps of pleasure or fulfillment, for validation, security or love—
you have a treasure within that is infinitely greater than anything the world can offer."*
—Eckhart Tolle

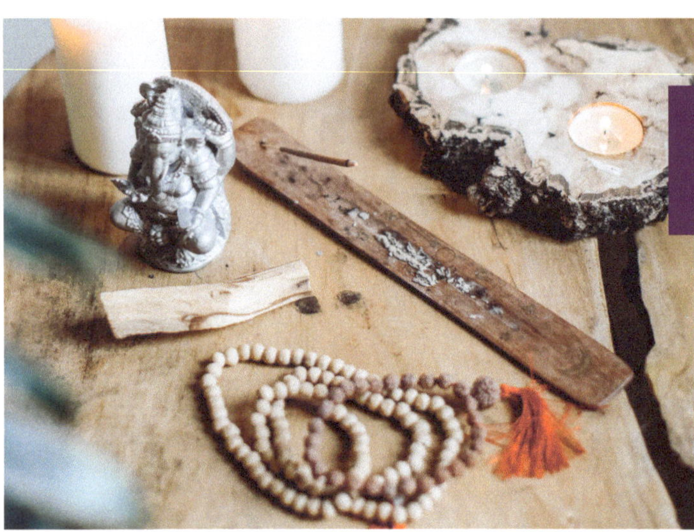

Step 1

Consider how you might represent each category using items that you own or use. Try to collect a variety of sizes, shapes, colors, and textures.

Step 2

Using your "found objects", create a still life arrangement that is reflective of your personality. Arrange and rearrange your items until you are happy with your design. Take a series of pictures using the camera on your phone. Shoot from different angles and perspectives. Print and frame your favorite shot!

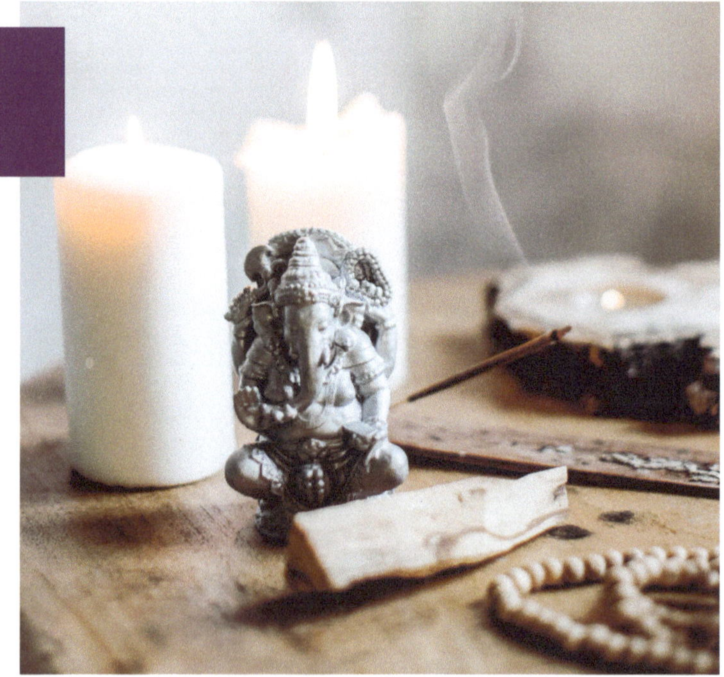

CROWN CHAKRA

CONSCIOUSNESS
CONNECT TO SOURCE

"There's something so naturally beautiful about the relationship a woman has with her Higher self. In trusting her inner voice, she is creating an unstoppable process of alchemy."
—Unknown

CONSCIOUS CONNECTIONS

Explore your Spiritual core

Lead with Love

Practice Meditation, Mindfulness, Presence

Offer Grace

Make daily affirmations

Identify your morals and values

Practice meditation

Look for the lessons

Practice total acceptance

DID YOU KNOW?
BENEFITS OF MEDITATION:

Increases gray matter

Boosts cognitive function

Physically changes the brain

Boosts the immune system

Lowers blood pressure

Reduces heart risk

Decreases pain and inflammation

Builds focus and concentration

Reduces depression

Improves sleep quality

Emotional resilience

Slows aging

Reduces stress and anxiety

Enhances concentration

Improves memory

Raises vibration

Purifies the environment around you

"Know, first, who you are, and then
adorn yourself accordingly."
—Epictetus

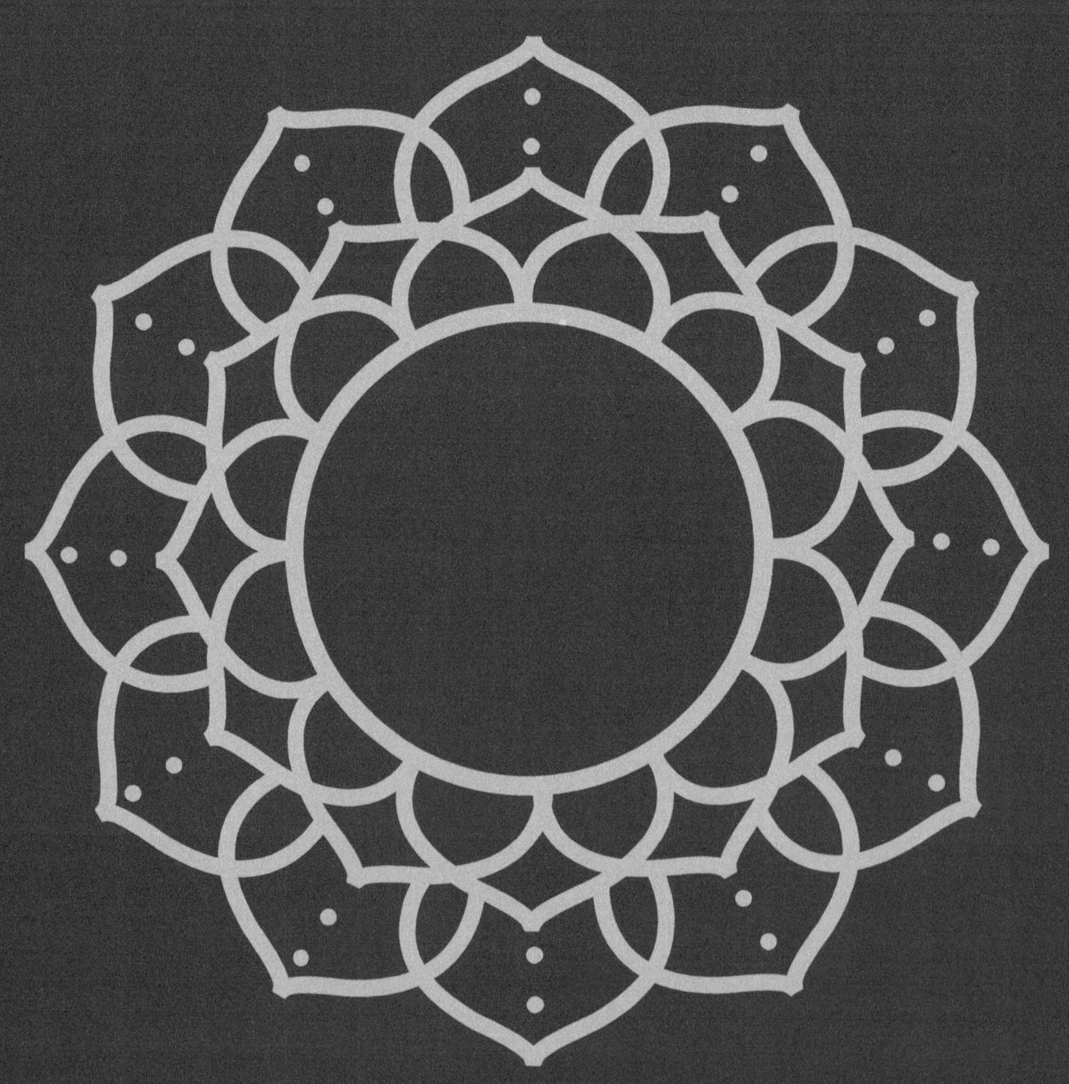

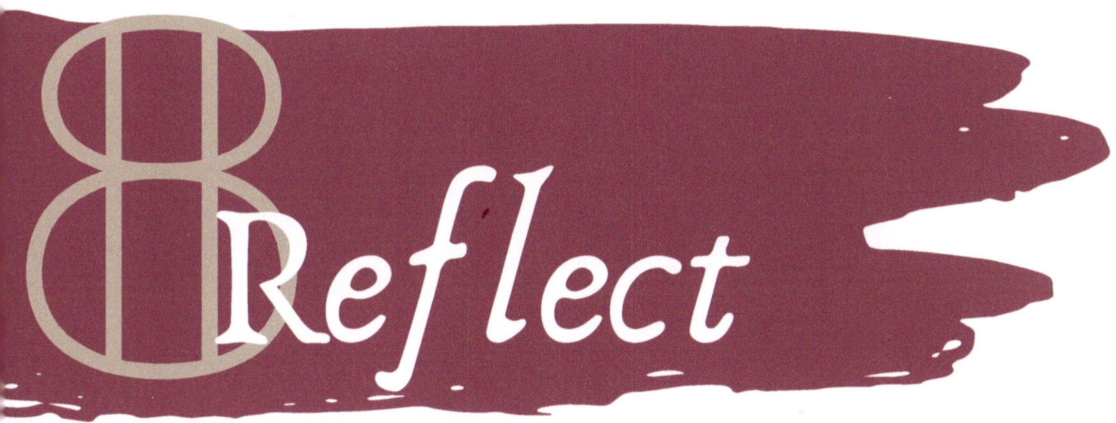

The Matrix is an agenda to keep us from the truth of who we really are. They want you to live in fear. They want to keep you in a state of unrest, uncertainty, on unfamiliar ground. They want you to be addicted to your tech, waiting for another news update, consuming the "bones of a dying world." The Matrix is a game; dialing the players down to a low-vibrational frequency. Your participation is what they need in order to control you, your thoughts, your emotions. When you are vibrating at a low frequency, you are much easier to manipulate. Creativity is the greatest rebellion in existence because creation is a reflection of Source. Creative expression is Divine Expression; a high-vibrational frequency, a deep breath, a long pause, magic unleashed, joy in our hearts, laughter in our soul. Creativity nourishes and restores the Spirit back to its original state. It reminds us of the power we have within our own hands.

Who is directing your attention, energy, and vibration?

Are you the creator of your own reality? Or is the Matrix your master?

What do you need to let go of, in order to Ascend?

"Each level up requires some sort of sacrifice. Ascension is a shedding process." —Unknown

ASCENSION:
Raise Your Vibration

IN ORDER TO ASCEND TO A HIGHER
FREQUENCY, YOU MUST BE WILLING TO LET
GO OF THE PEOPLE, PLACES, THOUGHTS,
AND BEHAVIORS THAT DO NOT MATCH
THE VIBRATION OF WHO YOU WANT TO BE.
ALLOW THE OLD TO FALL AWAY. IT'S TIME
TO MAKE ROOM FOR LIGHT.

*"Everything is energy and that's all there is to it.
Mach the frequency of the reality you want and you
cannot help but get that reality. It can be no other
way. This is not philosophy. This is physics."*
—Albert Einstein

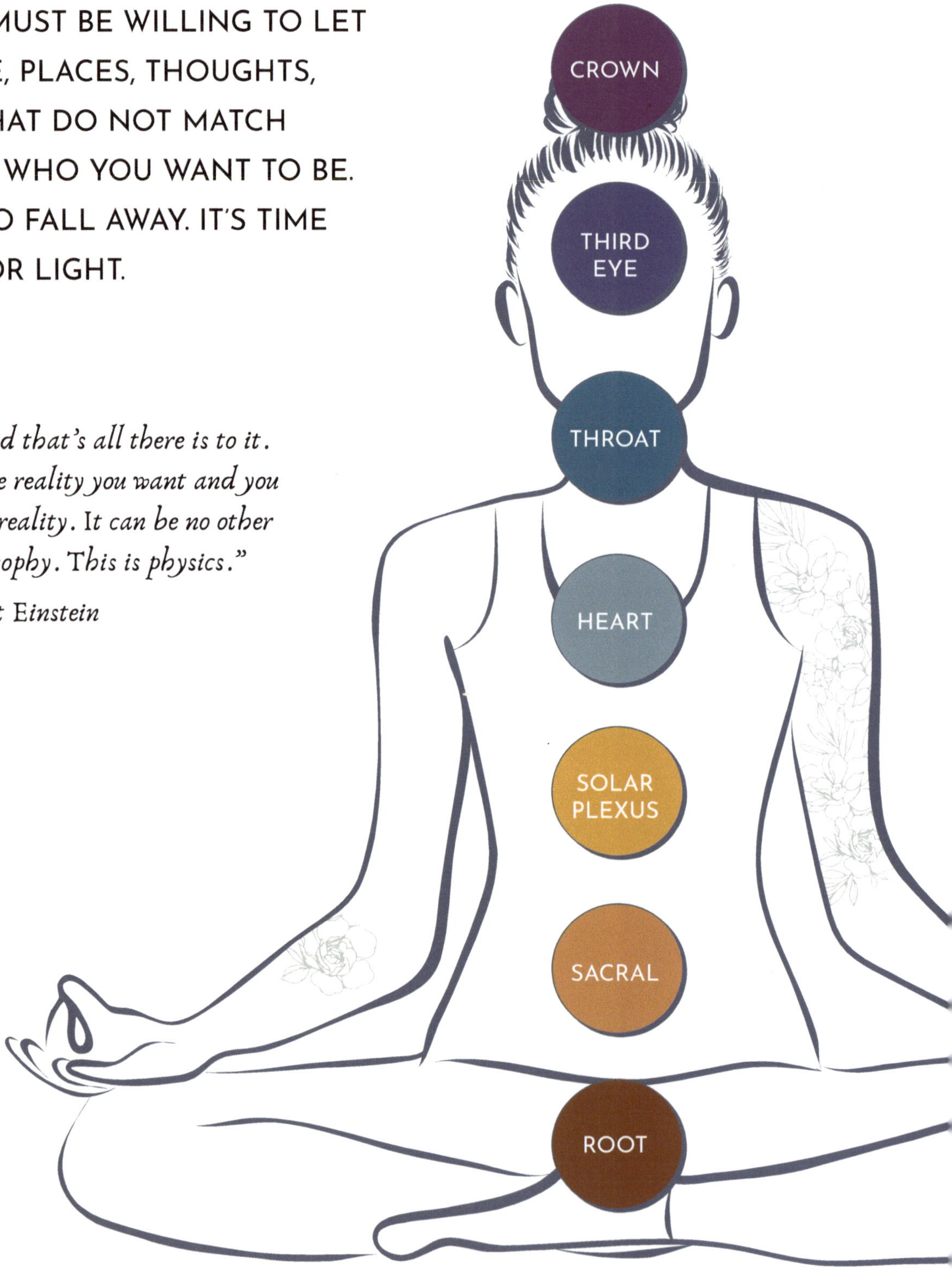

"Stay the fuck away from that tabloid bullshit, reality TV, the news channels feeding you fear and hatred, lulling your unique human consciousness into a materialistic slumber only useful for selfish gain and the aggrandization of the ego which is ultimately an illusion and which will never be satisfied no matter what you buy. This gratification is and will always be transient, so don't buy shit you don't need, don't hate people you don't know, and most importantly, don't spend your precious time on Earth consuming garbage styled as entertainment."

—Terence McKenna

ACKNOWLEDGEMENTS

I would like to acknowledge those who contributed their time and expertise to this project. A huge thank you to my editorial and production team for helping to bring this vision to life. You each made so many valuable contributions to the quality, coherence, layout, and design—I am forever grateful.

Natalie Mangrum
Own Your Story Movement, Baltimore, Maryland

Jordan Lacenski
Shewolf Collaborative, Greensboro, North Carolina

Megan McCarthy
Megan McCarthy Global Creative, Barcelona, Spain

Susana Morrison
SPM Editing, Los Angeles, California